Principles of
international biolaw

Seeking common ground at the intersection
of bioethics and human rights

COLLECTION
DROIT, BIOÉTHIQUE ET SOCIÉTÉ

7

Principles of international biolaw

Seeking common ground at the intersection of bioethics and human rights

Roberto Andorno

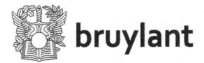

bruylant

Pour toute information sur nos fonds et nos nouveautés dans votre domaine de spécialisation, consultez nos sites web via www.larciergroup.com.

© Groupe Larcier s.a., 2013
Éditions Bruylant
Rue des Minimes, 39 • B-1000 Bruxelles

Imprimé en Belgique

Dépôt légal :
Bibliothèque nationale, Paris : septembre 2013   ISSN 2033 – 3498
Bibliothèque royale de Belgique, Bruxelles : 2013/0023/123   ISBN : 978-2-8027-4201-2

Collection
"DROIT, BIOÉTHIQUE ET SOCIÉTÉ"

Directed by Brigitte FEUILLET-LIGER
Professor of Law at the University of Rennes I,
Member of the Institut Universitaire de France,
President of the International Academic Bioethics Network
Director of CRJO (IODE, UMR, CNRS no. 6262)

The life sciences and in particular, biomedical science, have considerably progressed over the decades to offer a multitude of new treatments. Going beyond its initial therapeutic goal, medical practice offers the unique opportunity to respond to society's expectations related to individual personal desires. Men and women are now able to access techniques which allow them to have children; to assert their social identity; to decide about their end of life... in all, to respond to suffering instead of merely treating disease. Recourse to medical technologies has become, at least in part, a social and cultural phenomenon.

However, despite the unquestionable benefits of such progress, it also brings with it clear risks for fundamental human rights and can even impact upon the structure of families. Faced with increasing demands, we can observe the emergence of a market of 'well-being' medicine. The fundamental problem is to find a way to reconcile individual freedom, based on personal autonomy with the protection of the human being. Legal norms appear to be one of the best tools to address this goal, even if we rely increasingly on ethical norms to regulate the area of biomedicine. However, different cultures respond to the challenges of biomedicine in different ways. Biomedical practices deal with issues related to life, to the human body, to sexuality, reproduction and death. Yet, there is no single understanding of these concepts: it will depend on individuals, on culture or on religion. If we agree that the law of different countries translates the different social options it should however be analysed through the prism of other disciplines, such as anthropology, philosophy, sociology, psychoanalysis, psychology... in order to enable us to understand (and to respect) the cultural differences and to reflect upon a possible (universal?) harmonisation. The "Droit, Bioéthique et société" Collection strives to contribute to the diffusion and promotion of multi-disciplinary reflection on these critical questions.

Books published in the same collection :

- *Procréation médicalement assistée et Anonymat - Panorama international,* sous la direction de Brigitte Feuillet-Liger, 2008.

- *Who is my Genetic Parent? Donor Anonymity and Assisted Reproduction: a Cross-Cultural Perspective,* edited by Brigitte Feuillet-Liger, Kristina Orfali and Thérèse Callus, 2011.

- *Adolescent et Acte Médical, regards croisés,* sous la direction de Brigitte Feuillet-Liger et Ryuichi Ida, 2011.

- *Adolescents, Autonomy and Medical Treatment-Divergence and Convergence across the globe,* edited by Brigitte Feuillet-Liger, Ryuichi Ida et Thérèse Callus, 2012.

- *Les proches et la fin de vie médicalisée. Panorama international*, sous la direction de Brigitte Feuillet-Liger, 2013.

- *Families and End-of-Life Treatment Decisions. An International Perspective,* edited by Brigitte Feuillet, Kristina Orfali, Thérèse Callus, 2013.

FOREWORD

"The struggle for human rights is like an overflowing river that floods down across the valley making the fields ever more fertile".[1] This metaphor has been used to describe the expanding force of the human rights movement, which tends to cover all new areas in which human dignity and human rights are being challenged. The most recent field to be "fertilized" by the principles of human rights law is biomedicine, *i.e.* the application of biological and medical technologies to human beings. Because rapid advances in this area present new and complex ethical and policy issues for individuals, society, and humankind as a whole, it has become increasingly clear that specific legal responses are necessary to ensure that biomedical technologies are used in a way which is respectful of human dignity and human rights.

But the new challenges are so formidable and far-reaching that individual countries alone cannot satisfactorily address them. As science becomes increasingly globalized, a coherent and effective response to the new dilemmas raised by science should also be global. This is why coordinated intergovernmental action is required to harmonize legal standards and to establish appropriate mechanisms to ensure that such standards are effectively implemented.

This volume aims to present the recent global efforts to develop common biolegal norms, as well as some of the specific human rights issues that are at stake in this field. It brings together and updates a number of papers and contributions to edited volumes that I have written over the past decade in relation to this emerging discipline that can be called international biomedical law, or simply international biolaw.

Section I of this book sets forth the pivotal issues in this field, including the overarching principle of respect for human dignity

---

(1) A. Papisca, "L'internazionalizzazione dei diritti umani: Verso un diritto panumano", in C. Cardia (ed.), *Anno Duemila. Primordi della storia mondiale,* Milan, Giuffré, 1999, p. 139.

and a number of other principles that the international community has agreed should guide biomedical research and clinical activities.

Chapter 1 briefly sketches fourteen common principles that can be drawn from the international instruments relating to biomedicine. Among those principles are the requirement of informed consent, confidentiality of health data, non-discrimination on health grounds, beneficence and non-maleficence, special protection for vulnerable persons, and equitable access to health care. Certainly, most of these principles are not completely new, but are derived from previous international human rights instruments. Indeed, the greatest merit of biolegal instruments is not that they have "invented" new principles, but rather that they have adapted existing human rights standards to the specific field of biomedicine, and have drawn them together into coherent legal frameworks.

Chapter 2 examines the first and overarching principle of international biolaw –respect for human dignity– and its concretization by means of human rights. After some preliminary remarks about the relationship between bioethics and law, and about the status of soft law, this chapter explores the meaning and value of the notion of human dignity. Basically, it argues that the combined recourse to human dignity and human rights is the best, if not the only available ground for developing international legal standards in the field of biomedicine.

Chapter 3 is focused on the precautionary principle, which provides guidance to policy makers in deciding the action to be taken if there is good reason to believe that certain products or technologies may be seriously harmful to public health or the environment but when, at the same time, the risk is not currently fully understood. Strangely, while this principle has been formally enshrined in virtually every international treaty dealing with environmental protection, it is lacking in the international instruments relating to biomedicine. This is strange, not only because promoting public health is no less important than protecting the environment, but also because this principle already plays a central role in the domestic and regional (notably, European) policies in the public health area. This chapter aims to highlight the scope of the precautionary principle and to identify the conditions for its reasonable use.

Section II of this volume analyzes the work of two major intergovernmental bodies –UNESCO and the Council of Europe– in the development of biolegal principles. Chapter 4 examines the Universal Declaration on the Human Genome and Human Rights of 1997, which embodies the first concerted effort of the international community in setting up global standards on genetic issues. The Declaration aims to ensure the protection of the human genome against improper manipulation and all uses of genetic information that are incompatible with respect for human dignity and human rights. Taking this general purpose into account, this chapter explores, among other features of the document, the status of the human genome as the "heritage of humanity".

Chapter 5 argues that the Universal Declaration on Bioethics and Human Rights, adopted by UNESCO in 2005, represents an important step in the search for a comprehensive framework of principles in the field of biomedicine. Drawing on my experience as a member of the International Bioethics Committee between 1998 and 2005, and on my involvement in the drafting of the Declaration, I sketch the principal features of this document before responding to two general charges that have been leveled against both UNESCO's engagement in the field of bioethics and the Declaration itself.

The European Convention on Human Rights and Biomedicine (Oviedo Convention) is analyzed in Chapter 6. This instrument is unique in that it is the only comprehensive *binding* intergovernmental instrument addressing issues at the intersection of health law and human rights. In addition, despite the fact that it is a regional rather than a global instrument, it has an undeniable global significance, as its wide ranging approach has inspired the drafting of the Universal Declaration on Bioethics and Human Rights.

Section III elaborates upon certain human rights issues that are the subject of contemporary international standard-setting efforts in the field of biomedicine, including biomedical research, population biobanks, the right not to know one's genetic information, and advance directives. Chapter 7 examines the ethical and policy dilemmas raised by the establishment of large-scale biobanks from the perspective of the rights of participants. To this end, it focuses on the experiences of Iceland and Estonia during the 2000s, and analyzes the special laws passed by both countries to regulate this matter. The comparative study of the experiences of both countries, very different in many respects, provides a basis upon which to suggest possible solutions to specific issues raised by biobanks, in particular those regarding the modalities of the informed consent; the importance of confidentiality safeguards; the feedback to participants; and issues of property and benefit-sharing.

Dealing also with the field of genetics, Chapter 8 focuses on the right not to know one's genetic status. Despite having being formally recognized by several international instruments relating to bioethics, the basis and conditions for the exercise of this right still remain unclear. This chapter provides arguments in favor of such a right and tries to specify the conditions for its exercise. It argues, firstly, that individuals may have a legitimate interest in not knowing their genetic makeup to avoid serious psychological consequences; secondly, that this interest, far from being contrary to autonomy of patients and research subjects, may constitute an enhancement of their autonomy; thirdly, that the right not to know cannot be presumed, but must be "activated" by the individual's explicit choice; and fourthly, that this right is not absolute, in the sense that it may be restricted when disclosure is necessary in order to avoid a risk of serious harm to third parties, especially, family members.

Chapter 9 aims to highlight the human rights approach to biomedical research adopted by the Council of Europe's Biomedicine Convention, and to contrast it with the more market-oriented provisions of the EU's Clinical Trials Directive. While admitting that this difference of approach is understandable in the light of the dissimilar objectives of both European bodies, it stresses that this discrepancy has resulted in a number of unfortunate inconsistencies which might lead to less protection of research participants, in particular those who are most vulnerable.

The final chapter of this volume is devoted to an end of life issue which has generated much controversy in recent years, especially in Europe: the legal efficacy of advance health care directives. This chapter first outlines the strengths and shortcomings of Article 9 of the Biomedicine Convention, which specifically deals with this matter. Then, it analyzes the Council of Europe's Recommendation (2009)11 on continuing powers of attorney and advance directives for incapacity, which attempts to fill some of the gaps of the Convention in this regard.

ACKNOWLEDGEMENTS

Early versions of this book's chapters appeared as articles in various academic journals and as contributions to edited volumes. I would like to acknowledge the publishers for the permission to reprint them. The original sources of publication are the following:

Chapter 1: "First steps in the development of an international biolaw", in Ch. GASTMANS, K. DIERICKX, H. NYS, P. SCHOTMANS (eds.), *New Pathways for European Bioethics,* Antwerp, Intersentia, 2007, pp. 121-138.

Chapter 2: "Human Dignity and Human Rights as a Common Ground for a Global Bioethics", *Journal of Medicine and Philosophy,* 2009, vol. 34, issue 3, pp. 223-240. Publisher: Oxford University Press.

Chapter 3: "The Precautionary Principle: A New Legal Standard for a Technological Age", *Journal of International Biotechnology Law,* 2004, n° 1, pp. 11-19. Publisher: De Gruyter.

Chapter 4: "Seeking Common Grounds on Genetic Issues: the UNESCO Declaration on the Human Genome", in J. SANDOR (ed.), *Society and Genetic Information. Codes and Laws in the Genetic Era,* Budapest, Central European University Press, 2003, pp. 105-123.

Chapter 5: "Global bioethics at UNESCO: in defence of the Universal Declaration on Bioethics and Human Rights", *Journal of Medical Ethics,* 2007, vol. 33, pp. 150-154. Publisher: BMJ Group.

Chapter 6: "The Oviedo Convention: A European Legal Framework at the Intersection of Human Rights and Health Law", *Journal of International Biotechnology Law,* 2005, n° 2, pp. 133-143. Publisher: De Gruyter.

Chapter 7: "Population Genetic Databases: A New Challenge to Human Rights", in C. LENK, N. HOPPE, R. ANDORNO (eds.), *Ethics and Law of Intellectual Property. Current Problems in Politics, Science and Technology,* Aldershot, Ashgate, 2007, pp. 27-45.

Chapter 8: "The right not to know: an autonomy-based approach", *Journal of Medical Ethics*, 2004, vol. 30, issue 5, pp. 435-440. Publisher: BMJ Group.

Chapter 9: "Regulatory discrepancies between the Council of Europe and the EU regarding biomedical research", in A. DEN EXTER (ed.), *Human Rights and Biomedicine*, Antwerp, Maklu Press, 2010, pp. 117-133.

Chapter 10: "Regulating Advance Directives at the Council of Europe", in S. NEGRI (ed.), *Life, Death and Dignity. Regulating Advance Directives in National and International Law*, Series: Queen Mary Studies in International Law, Leiden, Brill Academic Publishers, 2012, pp. 73-85.

I am also indebted to Katherine Wade for her invaluable help with the editing of several chapters of this book.

Section I
PRINCIPLES OF INTERNATIONAL BIOLAW

CHAPTER 1

PRINCIPLES OF INTERNATIONAL BIOMEDICAL LAW

By the end of the 1990s, some intergovernmental organizations started to develop common standards relating to biomedicine.[1] Two organizations in particular have been at the forefront of this ambitious endeavour: the UNESCO (United Nations Educational, Scientific and Cultural Organization) and the Council of Europe. This chapter aims to show that a coherent set of principles already emerge from the instruments that have been adopted since 1997, and to argue that we are witnessing the emergence of the foundational core of an international biomedical law, which is an extension of international human rights law into the specific field of biomedicine.

I. – INTERGOVERNMENTAL INSTRUMENTS RELATING TO BIOMEDICINE

Rapid advances in the biomedical field present new and complex challenges for individuals and society. The current situation calls for the development of legal rules to ensure that technologies are used in a way which is consistent with full respect for human dignity and human rights. However, bioethical issues are so formidable and far-reaching that individual countries alone cannot satisfactorily address them. Concerted international efforts are required to establish a framework of common standards and to create appropriate mechanisms to promote their effective implementation at the domestic level. This need has been perceived by a number of intergovernmental bodies, in particular UNESCO and the Council of Europe, which have made significant efforts to

---

(1) The term "biomedicine" is used here with a broad meaning, which encompasses all applications of biological and medical knowledge and technologies to human beings. See B. FEUILLET-LE MINTIER, "La biomédecine, nouvelle branche du droit?", in B. FEUILLET-LE MINTIER (ed.), *Normativité et biomédecine,* Paris, Economica, 2003, pp. 1-11.

build an international consensus on a number of human rights principles relating to biomedical practice and research.

Since the end of the 1990s, UNESCO has adopted three international legal instruments on bioethics: the 1997 Universal Declaration on the Human Genome and Human Rights (UDHG); the 2003 International Declaration on Human Genetic Data (IDHGD), and the 2005 Universal Declaration on Bioethics and Human Rights (UDBHR). These three instruments have been approved by all Member States of UNESCO, that is, by virtually all countries in the world. Considering the sensitive nature of bioethical issues, which are closely related to socio-cultural and religious values of each society, this unanimity has great value in terms of granting legitimacy to the principles embedded in the declarations.

The main purpose of the UDHG is to preserve the human genome from improper manipulations that may endanger the identity and physical integrity of future generations. To this end, it recognizes the human genome as "the heritage of humanity" (Article 1), and declares "contrary to human dignity" practices such as "human reproductive cloning" (Article 11) and germ-line interventions (Article 24). In addition, the Declaration intends to prevent genetic reductionism and any use of genetic information that would be contrary to human rights and human dignity.

The IDHGD can be regarded as an extension of the 1997 Declaration. It sets out a number of rules for the collection, use and storage of human genetic data, which cover, among other issues, informed consent in genetic testing, confidentiality of genetic data, the ban on genetic discrimination, the anonymization of personal genetic information, population-based genetic studies, the right not to know one's genetic make-up, genetic counselling, international solidarity in genetic research, and benefit sharing.

The UDBHR has a much broader scope than the two previous documents as it aims to provide a comprehensive "framework of principles and procedures to guide States in the formulation of their legislation, policies and other instruments in the field of bioethics" (Article 2a). The overall objective of the document is to promote the development of biomedical practice and research in conformity with respect for "human dignity, human rights and fundamental freedoms" (Article 3.1).

Also the Council of Europe has made an important contribution to the establishment of transnational norms on this matter with the development of the Convention on Human Rights and Biomedicine (Biomedicine Convention), which is the only intergovernmental *binding* instrument that comprehensively addresses the linkage between human rights and biomedicine. It was opened for signature on 4 April 1997 in Oviedo, Spain. So far, it has been signed by 35 States and ratified by 29 of them. [2]

Although the Biomedicine Convention is a regional, not a global instrument, its global significance should not be overlooked. It is interesting to note that the Preamble of the UDBHR explicitly refers to the European Biomedicine Convention. This is worthy of note because it is unusual that UN declarations cite regional instruments. It shows that the comprehensive approach to bioethics of the Council of Europe has inspired the drafting of the UNESCO Declaration. [3] In this regard, it has been said that the global work being carried out by UNESCO with the drafting of the UDBHR has built on, and been informed by, the work done by the Council of Europe at the regional level. [4] In addition, it is noteworthy that the Biomedicine Convention has theoretically the potential to extend its applicability beyond European borders, as Article 34 leaves open the possibility of inviting non-member States of the Council of Europe to adhere to the document.

II. – THREE FEATURES OF INTERNATIONAL BIOMEDICAL LAW

A first comparative analysis between the three UNESCO declarations and the European Biomedicine Convention reveals that they share at least three important features: 1) The recognition of human dignity as an overarching principle; 2) The use of a human rights framework; 3) The adoption of a set of broad principles.

---

(2) For an updated list of ratifications see http://www.coe.int/bioethics

(3) H. NYS points out that "the European Convention on Human Rights and Biomedicine has clearly served as a source of inspiration to the UNESCO Declaration, especially its Articles 3, 6, 7 and 9" ("Towards an International Treaty on Human Rights and Biomedicine? Some Reflections Inspired by UNESCO's Universal Declaration on Bioethics and Human Rights", *European Journal of Health Law*, 2006, vol. 13, n° 1, pp. 5-8).

(4) E. GADD, "The global significance of the Convention on Human Rights and Biomedicine", in J.K.M. GEVERS, E. HONDIUS, and J.H. HUBBEN (eds.), *Health Law, Human Rights and the Biomedicine Convention. Essays in Honour of Henriette Roscam Abbing*, Leiden, Martinus Nijhoff, 2005, p. 35.

A. – *The recognition of human dignity*
as an overarching principle

The new intergovernmental instruments relating to bioethics assign a central and multifaceted role to the notion of human dignity. The UDBHR is paradigmatic in this regard, as respect for human dignity embodies not only the key purpose of the instrument (Article 2.c), but also the first principle governing the whole field of biomedicine (Article 3), the main reason why discrimination, including for instance, genetic discrimination, must be prohibited (Article 11), the framework within which cultural diversity is to be respected (Article 12), and the highest interpretive principle of all the provisions of the Declaration (Article 28).

Similarly, the purpose of the European Biomedicine Convention is defined by reference to the notion of human dignity.[5] The Explanatory Report to the Convention states that "the concept of human dignity (…) constitutes the essential value to be upheld. It is at the basis of most of the values emphasized in the Convention" (Paragraph 9). The Convention's Preamble refers three times to human dignity: the first, when it recognizes "the importance of ensuring the dignity of the human being;" the second, when it recalls that "the misuse of biology and medicine may lead to acts endangering human dignity;" and the third, when it underlines the need to take the necessary measures "to safeguard human dignity and the fundamental rights and freedoms of the individual with regard to the application of biology and medicine".

It is true that the recourse to human dignity is not new in international law. In this regard, the instruments relating to biomedicine follow a well-established tradition in international human rights law, which repeatedly appeals to the "inherent dignity of all members of the human family"[6] and refers to the concept as the *source* of all human rights.[7] Nevertheless, it is interesting to note that the instruments dealing with bioethics emphasize the notion of human dignity in a much powerful and pressing manner

---

(5) "Parties to this Convention shall protect the dignity and identity of all human beings and guarantee everyone, without discrimination, respect for their integrity and other rights and fundamental freedoms with regard to the application of biology and medicine" (Article 1).

(6)   Universal Declaration of Human Rights of 1948, Preamble.

(7)   "Recognizing that these rights derive from the inherent dignity of the human person…" (International Covenant on Civil and Political Rights and International Covenant on Economic, Social and Cultural Rights of 1966, Preambles).

than the founding human rights instruments. In this regard, we are not presented here with a mere shift in style, but a true shift in substance that deserves to be carefully considered.[8]

B. – *The use of a human rights framework*

The notion of human dignity alone is unable to provide a concrete response to most of the challenges raised by biomedical practice and research. To be operative, it needs other more specific and articulated notions, such as informed consent, bodily integrity, non-discrimination, confidentiality, etc., which are usually formulated using the terminology of *rights*. It is therefore not surprising that most international instruments relating to bioethics, including declarations, guidelines, recommendations, opinions and codes, are framed using a rights-based approach. This is particularly evident in the UNESCO declarations on bioethics and in the European Biomedicine Convention, which even include a reference to human rights in their titles. According to the chairman of the drafting group of the 2005 UNESCO Declaration, "the most significant achievement of the Declaration" is to have closely integrated "bioethical and human rights analysis".[9] Ultimately, it could be said that the emerging intergovernmental norms relating to bioethics are simply an extension of international human rights law into the field of biomedicine.[10]

C. – *The adoption of a set of broad guiding principles*

Legal philosophers make a distinction between *rules* and *principles*.[11] Both sets of standards point to particular decisions, but they differ in the *character* of the direction they give. Rules are applicable in an all-or-nothing fashion. Either a rule is valid, in which case the answer it supplies must be accepted, or it is not, in which case it contributes nothing to the decision. But this is not the way principles work. Principles have a dimension of weight or

---

(8) D. BEYLEVELD and R. BROWNSWORD, *Human dignity in bioethics and biolaw,* Oxford, Oxford University Press, 2002, p. 29.

(9) M. KIRBY, "UNESCO and Universal Principles on Bioethics: What's next?", in Twelfth session of the International Bioethics Committee (IBC), *Abstracts or Texts of the Presentations of Speakers,* Paris, UNESCO, 2005, pp. 121-136.

(10) See chapters 2 and 5.

(11) R. DWORKIN, *Taking Rights Seriously,* London, Duckworth, 1977, pp. 22-28.

importance. When there is a clash of principles, those who must resolve the conflict must take into account the relative weight of each one. Principles alone never completely determine the content of a particular decision. They are "optimization commands" (*Optimierungsgebote*), which can be carried out to different degrees depending on the circumstances. [12]

In this regard, the norms included in international biolegal instruments can fairly be characterized as *principles*. Initially, one may have the impression that they are merely rhetorical statements, either too obvious or too vague for having any practical impact. However, the importance of laying down broad principles in intergovernmental instruments should not be underestimated. General norms could be the starting point for further discussion and negotiation that could lead to more concrete regulations, especially at a national level. It should not be forgotten that *national governments,* not international organizations, are the primary agents for the realization of human rights. The international community has an important role to play in setting up widely accepted standards, but once these principles have been set up, the primary locus for their implementation is within nations. This is clear both in the European Convention and in the UNESCO declarations, which underline the State's responsibility in the implementation of the common standards adopted. [13] This is why in order to become operative in real life, the principles enunciated need, first, to be incorporated into the domestic legislation, and second, applied by their "natural intermediary": the judge. [14] Another reason explaining the recourse to a set of broad principles is the need to make them compatible with the necessary respect for cultural diversity. It would be indeed unfair, and in fact impossible, to impose a very detailed legal framework on societies with different socio-cultural and religious backgrounds. [15]

---

(12)   R. ALEXY, *Theorie der Grundrechte,* Frankfurt, Suhrkamp, 1994, pp. 71-77.

(13)   See Article 22 of the UDHG; Article 22(1) of the UDBHR; Articles 1 and 23 to 25 of the European Biomedicine Convention.

(14)   C. BYK, "Bioéthique, universalisme et mondialisation: la dynamique des contradictions", in C. BYK (ed.), *Bioéthique et droit international. Autour de la Déclaration universelle sur la bioéthique et les droits de l'homme,* Paris, LexisNexis, 2007, p. 44.

(15)   R. ANDORNO, "Comment concilier une bioéthique universelle et le respect de la diversité culturelle?", in C. BYK (ed.), *op. cit.,* pp. 55-60.

III. – CORE PRINCIPLES OF INTERNATIONAL BIOLAW

The three UNESCO declarations and the European Biomedicine Convention share not only general similarities but also specific substantive norms: at least 14 common principles can be drawn from these instruments. Certainly, most of these principles are not completely new, but are derived or developed from previous international human rights instruments. In fact, the greatest merit of the emerging international biomedical law is not to have "invented" entirely new principles, but to have developed them from previous international instruments, applied them to the specific field of biomedicine, and integrated them into a human rights framework. It is important to note that these principles are to be understood as "complementary and interrelated".[16] This means that there is no pre-established hierarchy between them.[17] However, it is clear that the principle of respect for human dignity, due to its non-negotiable character and overarching scope, will always play a crucial role in every decision concerning biomedical practice.

Principle 1. The recognition of human dignity as an overarching principle

See UDHG, Preamble, Articles 1, 2(a), 2(b), 6, 10, 11, 12, 15, 21 and 24; IDHGD, Preamble, Articles 1(a), 7(a), 26 and 27; UDBHR, Preamble, Articles 2(c), 2(d), 3(1), 10, 11, 12, and 28; European Biomedicine Convention, Preamble and Article 1; Charter of Fundamental Rights of the European Union, 7 December 2000, Article 1.[18]

The promotion of human dignity is the dominant principle of international biomedical law.[19] All the instruments relating to bioethics present respect for human dignity as their chief objective, and recognize it as the overarching norm governing this field. Apart from this general role, the principle of human dignity serves more specific functions: it puts limits to the use of human subjects

---

(16) UDBHR, Article 26.

(17) See E. GEFENAS, "Article 26. Interrelation and complementarity of the principles", in H. TEN HAVE and M. JEAN (eds.), *The UNESCO Universal Declaration on Bioethics and Human Rights. Background, principles and application,* Paris, UNESCO, 2009, pp. 327-333.

(18) "Human dignity is inviolable. It must be respected and protected". See C. DUPRÉ, "Human Dignity in Europe: A Foundational Constitutional Principle", *European Public Law,* 2013, vol. 19, n° 2, pp. 319-339.

(19) See chapter 2.

in research; it is an obstacle to genetic reductionism and to its consequence: genetic discrimination; it is invoked as a barrier to human cloning and to germ-line interventions; it is mentioned as a basis for a fair distribution of the benefits resulting from research; it is presented as a necessary condition for the respect of cultural diversity; and finally, it is the interpretative paradigm for the understanding of the more specific principles.

Principle 2. The primacy of the human individual over the sole interest of science and society

See UDHG, Article 10;[20] UDBHR, Article 3(2);[21] European Biomedicine Convention, Article 2.[22]

The primacy of the human being over science and society is a direct corollary of the principle of respect for human dignity and means that individuals should not simply become instruments for the benefit of science, because science is not an absolute end, but only a means by which to service the human person. This principle has its origins in the context of biomedical research and was formulated for the first time in the Declaration of Helsinki on medical research on human subjects adopted by the World Medical Association (1964/2008), which provides: "In medical research involving human subjects, the well-being of the individual research subject must take precedence over all other interests" (Article 6). Thereafter, it was incorporated into the Universal Declaration on the Human Genome and Human Rights (Article 10) and into the European Convention of Human Rights and Biomedicine (Article 2). The principle of primacy of the human being aims to emphasize two fundamental ideas. First, that science is not an end in itself but only a means for improving the welfare of individuals and society. Second, that people should not be reduced to mere instruments for the benefit of science. Certainly, the fact of living in society renders it indispensable that citizens should in some way contribute to the common good, according to their capacities and personal preferences. However, in democratic societies, people

---

(20) "No research or research applications concerning the human genome, in particular in the fields of biology, genetics and medicine, should prevail over respect for the human rights, fundamental freedoms and human dignity of individuals or, where applicable, of groups of people".

(21) "The interests and welfare of the individual should have priority over the sole interest of science or society".

(22) "The interests and welfare of the human being shall prevail over the sole interest of society or science".

do not live for the sake of society or science, but have their own purpose, which greatly transcends the boundaries of social or scientific interests.

Principle 3. Biomedical activities should first, do no harm to patients and research subjects and, if possible, in the case of clinical practice, contribute to the diagnosis, prevention or treatment of patients' condition

See UDHG, Article 5(a);[23] UDBHR, Article 4;[24] European Biomedicine Convention, Article 4.[25]

Both the promotion of the patient's good and the prevention of harm to him or her (*primum non nocere*) are the specific goals of clinical medicine.[26] This dual requirement dates back to the Hippocratic Oath, which commands: "Whatever houses I may visit, I will come for the benefit of the sick, remaining free of all intentional injustice". More specifically, the purpose of the doctor-patient encounter is to cure whenever possible, and to provide comfort and care when cure is not possible. The level of beneficence obliged by this principle is difficult to determine precisely because it depends on a variety of circumstances defining the human interaction in question. But clearly the lowest level of beneficence is non-maleficence, that is the obligation not to inflict harm.[27] In the case of medical research, which does not serve a therapeutic or preventive function for the individual subject, the prevention of harm becomes the dominant imperative.

---

(23) "Research, treatment or diagnosis affecting an individual's genome shall be undertaken only after rigorous and prior assessment of the potential risks and benefits pertaining thereto and in accordance with any other requirement of national law".

(24) "Benefit and harm: In applying and advancing scientific knowledge, medical practice and associated technologies, direct and indirect benefits to patients, research participants and other affected individuals should be maximized and any possible harm to such individuals should be minimized".

(25) Article 4 of the Biomedicine Convention vaguely mentions the need of carrying out biomedical interventions "in accordance with relevant professional obligations and standards". However, the Explanatory Report clarifies the meaning of this norm by providing that biomedical activities should be carried out for the patient's benefit (See Paragraph 32 of the Explanatory Report to the Convention: "It is the essential task of the doctor not only to heal patients but also to take the proper steps to promote health and relieve pain").

(26) E. PELLEGRINO and D. THOMASMA, *For the Patient's Good: The Restoration of Beneficence in Health Care*, New York, Oxford University Press, 1988.

(27) E. PELLEGRINO, "Article 4: Benefit and harm", in H. TEN HAVE and M. JEAN (eds.), *The UNESCO Universal Declaration on Bioethics and Human Rights. Background, principles and application*, Paris, UNESCO, 2009, pp. 99-109.

It is noteworthy that biolegal instruments tend to elaborate on these principles in terms of a *favorable risk-benefit balance*. This is probably not the best way of formulating them, because they have a deeper meaning that goes far beyond a mere calculation of risks and benefits, especially in the case of clinical practice. On the contrary, some guidelines issued by non-governmental organizations have adopted a more substantive definition of these principles. [28]

Principle 4. Respect for the autonomy of patients and research subjects and its direct corollary, the requirement of informed consent for any biomedical intervention

See UDHG, Article 5(b); [29] IDHGD, Article 8(a); [30] UDBHR, Articles 5 and 6; [31] European Biomedicine Convention, Article 5. [32] See also: International Covenant on Civil and Political Rights (ICCPR) of 1966, Article 7; [33] Charter of Fundamental Rights of the European Union, 7 December 2000, Article 3.2. [34]

---

(28) See WMA *Declaration of Geneva* (1948) ("Physician's Oath"): "The health of my patient will be my first consideration"; WMA *International Code of Medical Ethics* (1949-1983): "A physician shall act only in the patient's interest when providing medical care which might have the effect of weakening the physical and mental condition of the patient"; WMA *Declaration on the Rights of the Patient* (1981-2005): "The patient should always be treated in accordance with his/her best interests. The treatment applied shall be in accordance with generally approved medical principles" (Article 1c).

(29) "In all cases, the prior, free and informed consent of the person concerned shall be obtained".

(30) "Prior, free, informed and express consent, without inducement by financial or other personal gain, should be obtained for the collection of human genetic data, human proteomic data or biological samples, whether through invasive or non-invasive procedures, and for their subsequent processing, use and storage, whether carried out by public or private institutions. Limitations on this principle of consent should only be prescribed for compelling reasons by domestic law consistent with the international law of human rights".

(31) "The autonomy of persons to make decisions, while taking responsibility for those decisions and respecting the autonomy of others, is to be respected. For persons who are not capable of exercising autonomy, special measures are to be taken to protect their rights and interests".

(32) "1. Any preventive, diagnostic and therapeutic medical intervention is only to be carried out with the prior, free and informed consent of the person concerned, based on adequate information. The consent should, where appropriate, be express and may be withdrawn by the person concerned at any time and for any reason without disadvantage or prejudice. 2. Scientific research should only be carried out with the prior, free, express and informed consent of the person concerned. The information should be adequate, provided in a comprehensible form and should include modalities for withdrawal of consent (...)".

(33) "No one shall be subjected without his free consent to medical or scientific experimentation".

(34) "In the fields of medicine and biology, the following must be respected in particular: the free and informed consent of the person concerned, according to the procedures laid down by law".

This principle holds that patients and research subjects, insofar as they are legally competent, must be treated as autonomous agents and therefore have the right to make decisions for themselves about medical interventions without any kind of coercion or deception. At present, virtually all medical ethics guidelines and legal regulations relating to biomedicine hold that physicians and researchers must obtain the informed consent of patients and subjects prior to any substantial intervention. This presupposes the provision of sufficient and understandable information to them, so as to enable them to make a choice. It is important to stress that this requirement is already included in an international *binding* instrument (the International Covenant on Civil and Political Rights of 1966), although it only applies to biomedical research, not to clinical practice (see Article 7). The UDBHR is the first global legal (though not binding) instrument that makes explicit the need for informed consent for *any* biomedical intervention.

Principle 5. Equitable access to health care, in particular access to appropriate medical care and essential medicines

See UDHG, Article 12(a);[35] UDBHR, Articles 10 and 14;[36] European Biomedicine Convention, Article 3.[37] See also Universal Declaration of Human Rights of 1948, Article 25(1);[38] International Covenant on Economic, Social and Cultural Rights (ICESCR) of 1966, Article 12(1);[39] World Health Organization

---

(35) "Benefits from advances in biology, genetics and medicine, concerning the human genome, shall be made available to all, with due regard for the dignity and human rights of each individual".

(36) Article 10: "The fundamental equality of all human beings in dignity and rights is to be respected so that they are treated justly and equitably"; Article 14: "The promotion of health and social development for their people is a central purpose of governments that all sectors of society share (para 1); "progress in science and technology should advance: (a) access to quality health care and essential medicines, especially for the health of women and children, because health is essential to life itself and must be considered to be a social and human good (para. 2)".

(37) "Parties, taking into account health needs and available resources, shall take appropriate measures with a view to providing, within their jurisdiction, equitable access to health care of appropriate quality".

(38) "Everyone has the right to a standard of living adequate for the health and well-being of himself and of his family, including food, clothing, housing and medical care (...)".

(39) "The States Parties to the present Covenant recognize the right of everyone to the enjoyment of the highest attainable standard of physical and mental health".

(WHO) Constitution of 1946; [40] Convention on the Rights of the Child of 1989, Article 24. [41]

This requirement reflects what is usually called "principle of justice" in the bioethical literature. Justice implies, in general, a fair distribution of goods in society. In this context it refers to governments' responsibility to ensure that all individuals have access to at least a minimum standard of health care. Problems of distributive justice arise from the fact that some goods and services are in short supply and thus some fair means of allocating scarce resources must be determined. The principle of justice is basically implemented in the biomedical field through the recognition of the "right to health care", which is one of the most important economic, social and cultural rights, sometimes referred to as "second generation rights". The right to health care, as well as all rights of this kind, is considered a right of "progressive realization". This means that, by becoming party to the International Convention on Economic, Social and Cultural Rights, a state agrees "to take steps... to the maximum of its available resources" (Article 2.1 of the ICESCR) to achieve the full realization of this right. Although international instruments do not specify the kind of health care to be provided, the U.N. Committee on Economic, Social and Cultural Rights, the primary body responsible for interpreting the ICESCR, has enumerated the elements of health care services that are essential to this right: availability, accessibility (i.e. provided on a non-discriminatory basis), acceptability (i.e. respectful of ethical and cultural values), and quality. [42]

---

(40) "The enjoyment of the highest attainable standard of health is one of the fundamental rights of every human being".

(41) "States Parties recognize the right of the child to the enjoyment of the highest attainable standard of health and to facilities for the treatment of illness and rehabilitation of health. States Parties shall strive to ensure that no child is deprived of his or her right of access to such health care services. 2. States Parties shall pursue full implementation of this right and, in particular, shall take appropriate measures: (a) To diminish infant and child mortality; (b) To ensure the provision of necessary medical assistance and health care to all children with emphasis on the development of primary health care; (...)".

(42) UN Committee on Economic, Social and Cultural Rights (CESCR), General Comment 14. The right to the highest attainable standard of health, 2000, paragraph 12.

Principle 6. Freedom of scientific research, on the condition that it is carried out with due respect for human dignity and human rights

See UDHG, Article 12 (b);[43] UDBHR, Article 2(d);[44] European Biomedicine Convention, Article 15.[45]

Scientific research is one of the highest expressions of human capacities and makes a crucial contribution to the well-being and progress of humankind. This is why science deserves to enjoy the greatest freedom to advance in the different fields in which it is carried out and to be promoted at all levels. Freedom of research is regarded by international human rights instruments as a part of the right to freedom of thought and expression (Article 19 of the UDHR). However, scientific research, like any human activity, does not have absolute freedom to operate at the margin of respect for human dignity and human rights. Since the atomic bombings of the cities of Hiroshima and Nagasaki in 1945, modern societies are aware that science and technology are not ethically neutral, but may have a catastrophic impact on human beings and the environment. Taking into account the inevitable ambivalence of science and technology, which increases with every new development, this principle attempts to find a balance between these two potentially competing requirements.

---

(43) "Freedom of research, which is necessary for the progress of knowledge, is part of freedom of thought. The applications of research, including applications in biology, genetics and medicine, concerning the human genome, shall seek to offer relief from suffering and improve the health of individuals and humankind as a whole".

(44) "The aims of this Declaration are: (...) to recognize the importance of freedom of scientific research and the benefits derived from scientific and technological developments, while stressing the need for such research and developments to occur within the framework of ethical principles set out in this Declaration and to respect human dignity, human rights and fundamental freedoms".

(45) "Scientific research in the field of biology and medicine shall be carried out freely, subject to the provisions of this Convention and the other legal provisions ensuring the protection of the human being".

Principle 7. Protection of confidentiality of medical data associated with an identifiable person

See UDHG, Article 7;[46] IDHGD, Article 14;[47] UDBHR, Article 9;[48] European Biomedicine Convention, Article 10(1).[49]

According to a widely accepted principle of medical ethics and law, health care professionals have a duty of confidentiality towards their patients and research subjects and are not allowed to disclose their non-anonymized health data to third parties without their consent. This axiom, which is essential to preserve trust in the doctor-patient relationship, was already documented in the Hippocratic Oath, which states: "Whatever things I see or hear concerning the life of men, in my attendance on the sick or even apart there from, which ought not be noised abroad, I will keep silence thereon, counting such things to be as sacred secrets". In our time, with the arrival of the digital age and the relative ease with which electronically stored information can be exchanged, the risks to individual privacy have grown rapidly. This is why the performance of the duty of confidentiality requires today the use of special safeguards for the collection, storage and disclosure of personally identifiable health information. This means, in

---

(46) "Genetic data associated with an identifiable person and stored or processed for the purposes of research or any other purpose must be held confidential in the conditions set by law".

(47) "States should endeavour to protect the privacy of individuals and the confidentiality of human genetic data linked to an identifiable person, a family or, where appropriate, a group, in accordance with domestic law consistent with the international law of human rights" (para. a); Genetic data and biological samples linked to an identifiable person "should not be disclosed or made accessible to third parties, in particular, employers, insurance companies, educational institutions and the family, except for an important public interest reason in cases restrictively provided for by domestic law consistent with the international law of human rights or where the prior, free, informed and express consent of the person concerned has been obtained provided that such consent is in accordance with domestic law and the international law of human rights" (para b); the privacy of an individual participating in a genetic study "should be protected and the data should be treated as confidential" (*Ibid.*); Genetic data and biological samples collected for the purposes of scientific research "should not normally be linked to an identifiable person. Even when such data or biological samples are unlinked to an identifiable person, the necessary precautions should be taken to ensure the security of the data or biological samples" (para c); such data "can remain linked to an identifiable person, only if necessary to carry out the research and provided that the privacy of the individual and the confidentiality of the data or biological samples concerned are protected in accordance with domestic law" (para. d).

(48) "The privacy of the persons concerned and the confidentiality of their personal information should be respected. To the greatest extent possible, such information should not be used or disclosed for purposes other than those for which it was collected or consented to, consistent with international law, in particular international human rights law".

(49) "Everyone has the right to respect for private life in relation to information about his or her health".

particular, that such information should be collected and used only for specific, clearly defined, and limited purposes and disclosed only to those for whom it is intended. Nevertheless, this principle does not preclude the possibility that physicians may be allowed or required by law, in certain circumstances, to disclose personal health information without the patient's consent (for instance, to track highly contagious diseases or to fulfill other legally-mandated public health responsibilities).

Principle 8. Right to know and right not to know one's health (especially genetic) information

See UDHG, Article 5(c);[50] IDHGD, Article 10;[51] European Biomedicine Convention, Article 10(2).[52] See also WHO Guidelines on Ethical Issues in Medical Genetics and the Provision of Genetic Services (1997);[53] World Medical Association's Declaration of the Rights of the Patient (1981-2005).[54]

Over the last decades it has been strongly emphasized, in contrast to the old paternalistic model of the doctor-patient relationship, that competent patients, as autonomous agents, have the right to be adequately informed about their medical status and to be involved in the decisions concerning possible treatments. This means that patients are entitled to have access to their medical records and to be free from any mistaken beliefs concerning their condition ("right to know"). This is linked to the importance of informed consent, since it is only through adequate information that patients are able to make decisions regarding medical treatment. Exceptionally, information may be withheld from patients when there is good reason to believe that its release

---

(50) "The right of each individual to decide whether or not to be informed of the results of genetic examination and the resulting consequences should be respected".

(51) At the time of the collection of biological samples and data, "the information provided at the time of consent should indicate that the person concerned has the right to decide whether or not to be informed of the results. This does not apply to research on data irretrievably unlinked to identifiable persons or to data that do not lead to individual findings concerning the persons who have participated in such a research. Where appropriate, the right not to be informed should be extended to identified relatives who may be affected by the results".

(52) "Everyone is entitled to know any information collected about his or her health. However, the wishes of individuals not to be so informed shall be observed".

(53) "The wish of individuals and families not to know genetic information, including test results, should be respected, except in testing of newborn babies or children for treatable conditions" (Table 7).

(54) "The patient has the right not to be informed on his/her explicit request, unless required for the protection of another person's life" (Article 7d).

may seriously affect their physical or mental health ("therapeutic privilege"). In addition to the "right to know", international instruments also recognize a "right not to know" one's health data (in particular, genetic data). This right is usually justified as a way to prevent a psychological harm which may result from the knowledge that one has or is likely to develop a certain genetic condition, especially when no treatment or preventive measure is available. Like the right to know, the right not to know is not absolute, because disclosure may be allowed if necessary to prevent serious harm to third persons.[55]

Principle 9. Special protection for vulnerable persons

See UDHG, Article 5(e);[56] IDHGD, Article 8(b,c,d);[57] UDBHR, Articles 7 and 8;[58] European Biomedicine Convention, Articles 6, 7 and 17.[59] See also Council for International Organizations of Medical Sciences (CIOMS), International Ethical Guidelines for Biomedical Research Involving Human Subjects, 2002, Guideline 13.

Society bears specific responsibilities towards those who are more vulnerable to exploitation or harm. Although vulnerability

---

(55) See chapter 8.

(56) Article 5 (e) provides that genetic research on persons unable to consent can only be carried out for their "direct health benefit". Exceptionally, research without direct benefit can be carried out "with the utmost restraint" if it exposes the person only to a "minimal risk and minimal burden" and if the research "is intended to contribute to the health benefit of other persons in the same age category or with the same genetic condition".

(57) In the case of persons unable to consent, Article 8 requires to obtain the consent of the legal representative, who should have regard to the best interest of the person concerned (para b). As far as possible, the individual should take part in the authorization procedure (para. c). Genetic screening and testing of persons unable to consent should have "important implications for the health of the person" and take into account their best interest (para. d).

(58) According to Article 7, persons unable to consent should be given "special protection," which includes the need for the relevant authorization, which should be "obtained in accordance with the best interest of the person concerned" and giving the individual the possibility to be involved, to the greatest extent possible, in the decision-making process and in the withdrawal of consent (para. a). In principle, research should only be carried out for their direct health benefit and if there is no research alternative of comparable effectiveness with research participants able to consent. However, research without potential direct health benefit can be exceptionally carried out, "with the utmost restraint, exposing the person only to a minimal risk and minimal burden and if the research is expected to contribute to the health benefit of other persons in the same category" (para. b). As a general principle, vulnerability of individuals and groups "should be taken into account" in medical practice and research (Article 8).

(59) Biomedical interventions on persons unable to consent may only be carried out for their direct benefit (Art. 6, para. 1) and with the authorization of their legal representatives (*id.*, para. 2). Nevertheless, research without direct therapeutic benefit on persons unable to consent is permitted if it only entails "minimal risk and minimal burden" for the individual (Article 17, para. 2).

is a common feature of many human relationships, it becomes especially important in the doctor-patient relationship, which is inherently characterized by an imbalance in power and knowledge. This inescapable inequality imposes a special obligation on the physician to protect the patient's vulnerability against exploitation.[60] However, beyond the doctor-patient relationship, the issue of vulnerability emerges with particular force in the field of biomedical research. In this domain, "vulnerable persons" are those who, due to their age, physical or mental condition or socioeconomic status are particularly exposed to exploitation as research subjects. This category includes, among others, neonates, children, prisoners, people with physical or mental disabilities, or those who are economically disadvantaged. Special justification is needed for involving these individuals in biomedical research and extra protection should be provided to them (for instance, the requirement that the research must entail no more than minimal risk and minimal burden for the individual).

Principle 10. Non-discrimination and non-stigmatization on the basis of health (including genetic) information

See UDHG, Article 6;[61] IDHGD, Article 7(a);[62] UDBHR, Article 11;[63] European Biomedicine Convention, Article 11.[64]

This principle is an extension of the more general right to freedom from discrimination included in international human rights instruments, in particular in the International Covenant on Civil and Political Rights (ICCPR, Article 2) and in the International Covenant on Economic, Social and Cultural Rights (ICECSR, Article 2). The term "discrimination" was defined by the UN Committee on Civil and Political Rights as: "any distinction, exclusion, restriction or preference which is based on

---

(60) E. PELLEGRINO and D. THOMASMA, *The Virtues in Medical Practice*, New York, Oxford University Press, 1993.

(61) "No one shall be subjected to discrimination based on genetic characteristics that is intended to infringe or has the effect of infringing human rights, fundamental freedoms and human dignity".

(62) Genetic data should not be used "for purposes that discriminate in a way that is intended to infringe, or has the effect of infringing human rights, fundamental freedoms or human dignity of an individual or for purposes that lead to the stigmatization of an individual, a family, a group or communities".

(63) "No individual or group should be discriminated against or stigmatized on any grounds, in violation of human dignity, human rights and fundamental freedoms".

(64) "Any form of discrimination against a person on grounds of his or her genetic heritage is prohibited".

any ground such as race, colour, sex, language, religion, political or other opinion, national or social origin, property, birth, or other status, and which has the purpose or effect of nullifying or impairing the recognition, enjoyment or exercise by all persons, on an equal footing, of all rights and freedoms".[65] Although discrimination on grounds of health status is internationally proscribed,[66] instruments relating to bioethics have considered it necessary to specifically refer to it. In particular, they prohibit genetic discrimination, that is, the use of genetic information to discriminate against people, especially in the workplace and in health insurance.

Principle 11. Non commercialization of the human body and its parts

See UDHG, Article 4;[67] European Biomedicine Convention, Article 21;[68] Charter of Fundamental Rights of the European Union, 7 December 2000, Article 3.2;[69] Biomedicine Convention's Additional Protocol on the Transplantation of Organs and Tissues of Human Origin, 2002, Articles 21 and 22;[70] WHO Guiding principles on human organ transplantation, 1991, Principle 5.[71]

This principle reflects an ethical and legal axiom according to which human organs and tissues should be regarded as *gifts*, not

---

(65) UN Committee on Civil and Political Rights (CCPR), General Comment 18 (Non-discrimination), 1989, paragraph 7.

(66) See UN Committee on Economic, Social and Cultural Rights (CESCR), General Comment 14 (The right to the highest attainable standard of health), 2000, paragraph 18.

(67) "The human genome in its natural state shall not give rise to financial gains".

(68) "The human body and its parts shall not, as such, give rise to financial gain".

(69) "In the fields of medicine and biology, the following must be respected in particular: (...) the prohibition on making the human body and its parts as such a source of financial gain".

(70) Article 21: "1. The human body and its parts shall not, as such, give rise to financial gain or comparable advantage. The aforementioned provision shall not prevent payments which do not constitute a financial gain or a comparable advantage, in particular: compensation of living donors for loss of earnings and any other justifiable expenses caused by the removal or by the related medical examinations; payment of a justifiable fee for legitimate medical or related technical services rendered in connection with transplantation; compensation in case of undue damage resulting from the removal of organs or tissues from living persons. 2. Advertising the need for, or availability of, organs or tissues, with a view to offering or seeking financial gain or comparable advantage, shall be prohibited." Article 22: "Organ and tissue trafficking shall be prohibited".

(71) "The human body and its parts cannot be the subject of commercial transactions. Accordingly, giving or receiving payment (including any other compensation or reward) for organs should be prohibited". See also the World Medical Association's Statement on Human Organ and Tissue Donation and Transplantation (2000): "In the case of living donors, special efforts should be made to ensure that the choice about donation is free of coercion. Financial incentives for providing or obtaining organs and tissues for transplantation can be coercive and should be prohibited" (Paragraph 26).

as mere *commodities*. The prohibition of the sale of human body parts, no matter how voluntary or well informed, is grounded in the conviction that such practice would diminish human dignity and our sense of solidarity. [72] But the legal ban on the sale of live organs does not merely respond to a philosophical or symbolic concern. Rather, it has very practical connotations: it aims to prevent the exploitation of potential donors, especially, of poor people from developing societies. If money is offered, there is no doubt that the most desperate, such as the extreme poor, would be the most easily attracted to selling their organs. In such circumstances, it is hard to believe that their consent would be truly "autonomous". Furthermore, markets for organs can also be unfair to would-be recipients who are unable to pay. Another objection to organ sales is that they would undermine voluntary organ donation by destroying the present willingness of members of the public to donate their organs out of altruism.

Principle 12. The protection of the integrity and identity of humankind, in particular, the prohibition of reproductive human cloning and human germ-line interventions

See (on the protection of future generations): UDHG, Article 1; [73] UDBHR, Article 16; [74] European Biomedicine Convention, Preamble; [75] UNESCO Declaration on the Responsibilities of the Present Generations Towards Future Generations of 1997. See (on human cloning and germ-line interventions): UDHG, Articles 11 and 24; [76] European Biomedicine Convention, Article 13. [77] See also Biomedicine Convention's Additional Protocol on the

---

(72) C.B. COHEN, "Public Policy and the Sale of Human Organs", *Kennedy Institute of Ethics Journal*, 2002, vol. 12, n° 1, pp. 47-64.

(73) "The human genome underlies the fundamental unity of all members of the human family, as well as the recognition of their inherent dignity and diversity. In a symbolic sense, it is the heritage of humanity".

(74) "Protecting future generations: The impact of life sciences on future generations, including on their genetic constitution, should be given due regard".

(75) "Affirming that progress in biology and medicine should be used for the benefit of present and future generations".

(76) "Practices which are contrary to human dignity, such as reproductive cloning of human beings, shall not be permitted" (Article 11); "The International Bioethics Committee of UNESCO should (...) give advice concerning the follow-up of this Declaration, in particular regarding the identification of practices that could be contrary to human dignity, such as germ-line interventions" (Article 24).

(77) "An intervention seeking to modify the human genome may only be undertaken for preventive, diagnostic or therapeutic purposes and only if its aim is not to introduce any modification in the genome of any descendants".

Prohibition of Human Cloning, 1998; UN Declaration on Human Cloning, 2005; Charter of Fundamental Rights of the European Union, 7 December 2000, Article 3.2.[78]

There is growing awareness that the present generation has a responsibility towards meeting the likely needs of future generations. This responsibility entails not only the preservation of the world's environment, but also of the integrity of human species itself, which could be harmed by practices such as germ-line interventions and reproductive cloning.[79] Intergenerational justice requires us indeed to abstain from deliberately predetermining the features of our descendants, because that would amount to instrumentalizing them in a way which would be contrary to human dignity. This is especially clear in the case of cloning, because it entails that some individuals would be deliberately created as genetically identical to an existing person or even a dead one just to satisfy the desires of others.

It must be noted that germ-line interventions for supposedly therapeutic purposes (i.e. for preventing the transmission of diseases) are also ethically problematic because of the risks of serious and irreversible harm to future generations they pose. Given the extraordinary complexity of the relationship between genes and environment, and the notion that some genes associated with disease may be beneficial in another context, the most basic prudence requires us to abstain from introducing irreversible changes in germ cells or in early embryos.[80]

---

(78) "In the fields of medicine and biology, the following must be respected in particular: (...) the prohibition of the reproductive cloning of human beings".

(79) J. HABERMAS, *The Future of Human Nature,* Cambridge, Polity, 2003; H. JONAS, *Technik, Medizin und Ethik. Zur Praxis des Prinzips Verantwortung,*Frankfurt, Suhrkamp, 1987. G.J. ANNAS, L.B. ANDREWS, and R.M. ISASI, "Protecting the Endangered Human: Toward an International Treaty Prohibiting Cloning and Inheritable Alterations", *American Journal of Law and Medicine,* 2002, vol. 28, pp. 151-178.

(80) UNESCO International Bioethics Committee. Report of the IBC on Pre-implantation Genetic Diagnosis and Germ-line Intervention, 24 April 2003; British Medical Association. *Human genetics. Choice and responsibility,* Oxford, Oxford University Press, 1998.

Principle 13. The requirement to establish independent, multidisciplinary and pluralist ethics committees at the appropriate level to assess the ethical, legal and social issues raised by biomedical activities

See: UDHG, Article 16;[81] IDHGD, Article 6(b);[82] UDBHR, Article 19;[83] European Biomedicine Convention, Article 16(iii).[84]

The complexity of the dilemmas posed by biomedical advances has lead modern societies to promote the creation of ethics committees to contribute to the search for adequate answers. At present, such committees are being established at different levels and with various purposes. For example, they provide clinical case consultation in hospitals, guarantee that biomedical research is conducted according to ethical and legal standards, and assist lawmakers in evaluating and formulating policy choices. Taking into account this salutary trend, international biomedical law intends, first, to encourage the establishment of ethics committees at various levels, and second, to provide some criteria to ensure that they operate adequately and are truly representative of the various interests involved and of the population or community they are intended to serve.

---

(81) "States should recognize the value of promoting, at various levels as appropriate, the establishment of independent, multidisciplinary and pluralist ethics committees to assess the ethical, legal and social issues raised by research on the human genome and its applications".

(82) "Independent, multidisciplinary and pluralist ethics committees should be promoted and established at national, regional, local or institutional levels (...). Where appropriate, ethics committees at national level should be consulted with regard to the establishment of standards, regulations and guidelines for the collection, processing, use and storage of human genetic data, human proteomic data and biological samples. They should also be consulted concerning matters where there is no domestic law. Ethics committees at institutional or local levels should be consulted with regard to their application to specific research projects".

(83) "Independent, multidisciplinary and pluralist ethics committees should be established, promoted and supported at the appropriate level in order to: (a) assess the relevant ethical, legal, scientific and social issues related to research projects involving human beings; (b) provide advice on ethical problems in clinical settings; (c) assess scientific and technological developments, formulate recommendations and contribute to the preparation of guidelines on issues within the scope of this Declaration; (d) foster debate, education and public awareness of, and engagement in, bioethics".

(84) Among other conditions for conducting research on human subjects, Article 16 requires the research project "to be approved by the competent body after independent examination of its scientific merit, including assessment of the importance of the aim of the research, and multidisciplinary review of its ethical acceptability".

Principle 14. The need for justice in transnational research, in particular between developed and developing countries

See UDHG, Articles 17, 18 and 19;[85] IDHGD, Articles 18 and 19;[86] UDBHR, Articles 13 and 14.[87]

This principle relates to a requirement of global justice in biomedical research. As scientific research becomes increasingly globalized, the benefits resulting from it should also be global and contribute to the wellbeing of all countries, also of those countries which do not have the financial resources to conduct research themselves. This issue needs to be addressed because, without solidarity, scientific advances threaten to widen rather than narrow the gap between rich and poor and between developed and developing countries. In the field of genetic research, for instance, there has been criticism that data collected in developing countries are used to promote profit for the sponsors and bring no benefit to the community from which the samples and data are obtained. This is why solidarity and some form of benefit-sharing with developing countries are being increasingly required by international instruments relating to biomedicine.

CONCLUSION

The intergovernmental efforts made since the end of the 1990s to develop common norms relating to bioethics can be regarded as the first steps towards the development of an international biomedical law. This new domain is characterized by the recourse to human dignity as an overarching principle, the use of a human

---

(85)   The Section E, entitled "solidarity and international cooperation," includes three articles. Article 17 provides that "states should respect and promote the practice of solidarity towards individuals, families and population groups who are particularly vulnerable to or affected by disease or disability of a genetic character. They should foster, inter alia, research on the identification, prevention and treatment of genetically-based and genetically-influenced diseases, in particular rare as well as endemic diseases which affect large numbers of the world's population". Article 18 is focused on "fostering the international dissemination of scientific knowledge" in the field of genetics". Article 19 enumerates the measures that states may adopt to promote international cooperation.

(86)   States should foster international medical and scientific cooperation and ensure fair access to human genetic data and biological samples obtained for research purposes (Article 18). Benefits resulting from such research should be shared with the society as a whole and the international community (Article 19).

(87)   Article 13 provides that "solidarity among human beings and international cooperation towards that end are to be encouraged". Article 14 indicates a number of specific areas where governments should be actively engaged in promoting health.

rights framework, and the development of broad guiding principles. From the analysis of the instruments relating to bioethics adopted by intergovernmental organizations it is possible to draw at least 14 principles that constitute the foundational core of international biomedical law.

Despite the inherent difficulties of developing universal norms in this sensitive field, the instruments that have been adopted show that this ambitious objective is feasible. The use of a human rights framework has been decisive in this regard, because international law presupposes that human rights transcend cultural diversity. In fact, the new discipline can be regarded as an extension of international human rights law into the field of biomedicine.

CHAPTER 2

HUMAN DIGNITY AND HUMAN RIGHTS AS A FRAMEWORK FOR INTERNATIONAL BIOLAW

Recent intergovernmental instruments dealing with biomedicine assign a very central role to the notion of human dignity, which is presented as the ultimate rationale behind the new common standards. At the same time, they appeal to a human rights framework as a way to reinforce their provisions and to articulate specific rules to govern this field. The aim of this chapter is to examine the recourse to human dignity and human rights in the domain of global bioethics, with particular reference to the Universal Declaration on Bioethics and Human Rights (UDBHR) adopted by UNESCO in 2005. To this end, after some preliminary remarks about the relationship between bioethics and law, this chapter will first briefly examine the meaning and value of the notion of human dignity in the international norms relating to bioethics; second, it will argue that human dignity and human rights are the best, if not the only available ground for the development of international legal standards for biomedicine.

I. – Bioethics, law and soft law

A. – *Bioethics and law: what relationship?*

Before focusing on the role played by human dignity and human rights in global bioethics, two preliminary remarks ought to be made. The first relates to the meaning of the word "bioethics," which is terribly ambiguous and may lead to some misunderstandings. Depending on the context, it can be used with a narrow meaning or with a broad meaning. The narrow meaning refers to the purely *ethical* dimension of life sciences. From this perspective, bioethics is just *a part of ethics*. When the term "bioethics" is so understood, it is a contradiction in terms to speak of "laws on bioethics", because what is ethical or unethical is not, and indeed cannot, be prescribed by law.[1] Certainly, ethics and law are two forms of practical reasoning, i.e. of reason concerning action. Moreover, it can be argued that there is a "necessary connection" between law and morality.[2] It is therefore not surprising that these two forms of practical reason interact in various ways and may overlap with one another. However, they remain as two different normative systems for the simple reason that they pursue different goals: the goal of ethics is to promote human flourishing, i.e. the fulfilment of our tendencies towards the good. In contrast, law has a less ambitious scope than ethics, because it does not seek to make men moral, even if legal norms certainly have an indirect positive impact on the moral fulfilment of persons. The basic purpose of law is just to ensure that human relationships are governed by the principle of justice, or in other words, that the rights of each individual, as well as the common interests of society as a whole, are guaranteed. While the fundamental question of ethics is "What should I do to become a good, a better person?", the key question of law is: "What rules do we need to promote a peaceful and fair society?"

In an attempt to illustrate the intricate relationship between ethics and law, the German legal philosopher Georg Jellinek characterized law as "the minimum ethics" (das ethische Minimum).[3] By this expression he meant that law only embodies those moral requirements that have to do with "the indispensable conditions of social life". An understanding of the different objectives that ethics and law try to achieve is fundamental to grasp why ethics inevitably covers and will always cover a much broader spectrum than law; it also shows why what is unethical is not (and should not be) necessarily illegal. Only a totalitarian regime could attempt, with any chance of success, to make them overlapping. The distinction between these two realms is extremely important and in a field like bioethics, in which one may have the impression that they fuse, it should be carefully maintained. In this regard, it is noteworthy that, precisely in order to prevent any confusion between ethics and law, the Council of Europe has preferred to

---

(1) See B. FEUILLET-LE MINTIER, "La biomédecine, nouvelle branche du droit?", in B. FEUILLET-LE MINTIER (ed.), Normativité et biomédecine, Paris, Economica, 2003, p 7.

(2) R. DWORKIN, Taking Rights Seriously, London, Duckworth, 1977; R. ALEXY, Begriff und Geltung des Rechts, Freiburg, Alber, 1992.

(3) G. JELLINEK, Die sozialethische Bedeutung von Recht, Unrecht und Strafe, Berlin, Häring, 1908, p. 45.

avoid the use of the word "bioethics" in the Convention on Human Rights and Biomedicine (1997). This is the reason why even the title of this instrument, which included the term "bioethics" in its draft version, was changed from "Convention on human rights and bioethics" to "Convention on human rights and biomedicine".

But this risk of confusion can be eliminated by explaining that the term "bioethics" can also be used with a broad meaning, which in addition to biomedical *ethics*, also includes the *legal* aspects of biomedical issues ("biomedical law" or simply "biolaw"). In this respect, "regulatory and policy bioethics" has been sometimes mentioned as one of the four main varieties of "bioethics".[4] The possibility of such a broad understanding of the term "bioethics," which may include rules and issues of a legal nature, explains why this word can be used without any embarrassment by the UNESCO declarations, which far from attempting to "subsume medical ethics",[5] are conceived as an extension of the human rights framework to encompass biomedical issues.

B. – *Why is soft law really law*

The second preliminary remark is closely connected with the first one and relates to the status of the UNESCO declarations. There is a widely diffused idea that these documents are purely ethical or political recommendations deprived of any legal effect. This view probably stems from the fact that, unlike treaties, the UNESCO declarations, as any soft law agreements, are usually characterized as "nonbinding instruments". Although this depiction is not entirely wrong, it may be misleading because while soft law does not have a binding effect *per se*, it is *conceived to have such effect in the long term*. This means that although treaties are *actually* binding (after ratification by States), soft law instruments are only *potentially* binding. Soft law is indeed envisaged as the *beginning of a gradual process* in which further steps are needed to make of such agreements binding rules for States.

---

(4) D. CALLAHAN, "Bioethics", in S. POST (ed.), *Encyclopedia of Bioethics,* 3rd. ed., New York, Macmillan, 2004, p. 281.

(5) T. FAUNCE, "Will international human rights subsume medical ethics? Intersections in the UNESCO Universal Bioethics Declaration", *Journal of Medical Ethics,* 2005, vol. 31, issue 3, p. 177. See also: R. ASHCROFT, "Could Human Rights Supersede Bioethics?", *Human Rights Law Review,* 2010, vol. 10, n° 4, pp. 639-660.

It is noteworthy that the use of soft law has rapidly developed in recent decades as a new source of international law for dealing with particularly sensitive matters such as human rights, the protection of the environment and bioethical issues. Soft law presents the great advantage of allowing countries to gradually become familiar with the commonly agreed standards before they are confronted with the adoption of enforceable rules at the national or international level. This gradual procedure leaves more room for discussion and achieving consensus on issues that are especially complex or sensitive, or more exposed to change, like those related to scientific developments.[6]

The most notable example of the significant role that soft law can play in the development of binding norms is provided by the Universal Declaration of Human Rights (UDHR) of 1948. This document, which took the form of a soft law instrument, is today recognized as the cornerstone of the entire international human rights system that emerged in the aftermath of the Second World War. The UDHR did not only pave the way for the adoption of more than seventy treaties, which are applied today on a permanent basis at global and regional levels. It also served as a model for many constitutions and laws throughout the world, and helped to ground uncountable decisions of national and international courts.

Regarding the UNESCO declarations, it is important to note that if the binding effect were totally absent from them, they would not be "law" at all, because one of the classical distinctions between "ethics" and "law" is precisely that law is made up of *enforceable* norms while ethics is *not enforceable*. Thus, it is misleading to affirm that soft law only creates *moral or political* commitment for States. This is only true if we consider the *immediate* effect of soft law instruments. But the fact is that, in a more indirect and persuasive way, they have an influence on States which is not very different from that of treaties. Indeed, some studies show that, surprisingly, declarations and treaties are complied with to largely the same extent.[7] We should not forget that, after all, soft law instruments are formal intergovernmental agreements, and

---

(6)   N. LENOIR and B. MATHIEU, *Les normes internationales de la bioéthique*, 2nd ed., Paris, Presses Universitaires de France, 2004, p. 17.

(7)   H. HILLGENBERG, "A Fresh Look at Soft Law", *European Journal of International Law*, 1999, vol. 10, n° 3, pp. 499-515, at p. 502.

in this respect they do not differ essentially from the traditional international binding instruments.

Furthermore, there is no doubt that the UNESCO declarations have been adopted with the *intention* that in the long run, in one way or another, they will become binding rules for States. This "hardening" of soft law may happen in two different ways. One is when declarations are the first step towards a *treaty-making process,* in which reference will be made to the principles already stated in the declarations. Another possibility is that nontreaty agreements are intended to have a direct influence on the practice of States, and to the extent that they are successful in doing so, they may lead to the creation of *customary law.* As some experts explain, declarations may "catalyse the creation of customary law by expressing in normative terms certain principles whose general acceptance is already in the air (...) and thereby making it easier and more likely for States to conform their conduct to them".[8] Thus, if the same nonbinding standards are reaffirmed in successive international treaties, or invoked by international courts to support their decisions, in the course of time they may become binding rules in the form of customary law, as it happened with the Universal Declaration of Human Rights of 1948.[9]

II. – HUMAN DIGNITY: THE OVERARCHING PRINCIPLE
OF GLOBAL BIOETHICS

Respect for human dignity is at the very heart of the intergovernmental instruments dealing with bioethics that have been adopted since the end of the 1990s. The emphasis on this notion is impressive enough to lead scholars to characterize human dignity as "the shaping principle" of international bioethics.[10] Far from representing a shift merely in style, the higher profile accorded to this notion in bioethics is seen as a true shift in substance that needs to be carefully considered.[11] The UDBHR, which formulates

---

(8)   P. Szasz, "International norm-making", in E. Brown Weiss (ed.), *Environmental change and International law. New challenges and dimensions,* Tokyo, United Nations University Press, 1992, p. 60.

(9)   V. Dimitrijevic, "Customary Law as an Instrument for the Protection of Human Rights", ISPI (Istituto per gli Studi di Politica Internazionale) Working Papers, 2006, n° 7, pp. 1-28. Available at: http://www.ispionline.it/it/documents/wp_7_2006.pdf

(10)   N. Lenoir and B. Mathieu, *op. cit.,* p. 16.

(11)   D. Beyleveld and R. Brownsword, *Human Dignity in Bioethics and Biolaw,* Oxford, Oxford University Press, 2002, p. 29.

a set of norms to guide biomedical practice, assigns the first place to the principle of respect for "human dignity, human rights and fundamental freedoms" (Article 3.1). The Declaration emphasizes the same idea when it stipulates that "the interests and welfare of the individual should have priority over the sole interest of science or society" (Article 3.2).

Certainly, the recourse to human dignity is neither new in international law, nor specific to policy documents relating to bioethics. The UDHR of 1948 states in its Preamble that "the inherent dignity" of all members of the human family is "the foundation of freedom, justice and peace in the world". Thereafter, the idea of human dignity has been at the heart of the major human rights instruments, beginning with the two international covenants on human rights adopted in 1966: the International Covenant on Civil and Political Rights (ICCPR) and the International Covenant on Economic, Social and Cultural Rights (ICECSR), as well as in most treaties banning torture, slavery, inhuman and degrading treatments, and discriminations of all sorts.

Nevertheless, although the notion of human dignity has always held an important position in international law, the key role it plays in the emerging international biomedical law is really impressive. It is therefore not exaggerated to characterize it as the "overarching principle" of international biolaw. Regarding the UDBHR, respect for human dignity not only is placed first in the list of principles governing the biomedical field (Article 3), but it also embodies the central aim of the whole instrument (Article 2.c). In addition, it is mentioned as the main ground on which discrimination is prohibited (Article 11), as the framework within which cultural diversity is to be respected (Article 12), and as the highest interpretive principle of all the provisions of the Declaration (Article 28). It is also interesting to note that that the need to include the principle of respect for human dignity was one of the points most often mentioned by Member States during the worldwide consultations that took place between January and March 2004.[12]

---

(12) UNESCO International Bioethics Committee, *Towards a Declaration on Universal Norms on Bioethics*. Report of the Extraordinary Session of the International Bioethics Committee, rapporteur L. DE CASTRO, Paris, UNESCO, 2004, p. 2.

This emphasis on human dignity in international biolaw is due to several reasons. The first one is that biomedical practice is closely related to the most basic human rights, namely the rights to life, to physical integrity, to privacy, to access to basic health care, among others. If human dignity is generally recognized as the foundation on which human rights are based, then it is understandable that it is invoked as the ultimate rationale of the legal norms governing biomedical practice. But there is another reason explaining this phenomenon. The notion of human dignity is beginning to be seen as the last barrier against the alteration of some basic features of the human species that might result from practices such as reproductive cloning or germ-line interventions. It should be noted that resorting to human rights is insufficient to cope with these new challenges because human rights only belong to existing individuals, not to humanity as such. In fact, an act like reproductive cloning which is done prior to the existence of an individual cannot, by definition, infringe the rights and dignity of that individual. This is so because the so-called "future persons", who are contingent in the sense that they may or not come into existence, are not persons at all, neither from a legal, nor from a philosophical perspective. Thus, reproductive cloning, as well as germ-line interventions may be seen as a threat, not to individuals, but to the integrity of the human species as such. [13] This is the reason why the Universal Declaration on the Human Genome and Human Rights directly appeals to the notion of human dignity, not to human rights, to reject both practices (Articles 11 and 24).

III. – CAN 'HUMAN DIGNITY' BE DEFINED BY LAW?

Although the notion of human dignity is at the heart of the major international human rights instruments, it is never explicitly defined by them. They provide however a valuable guidance for the understanding of this concept when they state: first, that dignity is "inherent... to all members of the human family" (UDHR, Preamble); second, that all human beings are "free and equal in dignity and rights" (UDHR, Article 1); third, that "these rights

---

(13) G.J. ANNAS, L. ANDREWS, R. ISASI, "Protecting the Endangered Human: Toward an International Treaty Prohibiting Cloning and Inheritable Alterations", *American Journal of Law and Medicine*, 2002, vol. 28, n°s 2-3, pp. 151-78.

derive from the inherent dignity of the human person" (ICCPR and ICESCR, Preambles).

These three ideas, even though they may appear to be extremely vague, offer a precious guidance for clarifying the meaning with which the notion of human dignity is used by international law:

a. The term "inherent" means "involved in the constitution or essential character of something",[14] "intrinsic", "permanent or characteristic attribute" of something.[15] The idea expressed in this term, when it is accompanied by the adjective "human", is that dignity is *inseparable from the human condition;* it is "the value of humans as humans".[16] Thus, dignity is not an accidental quality of some human beings, or a value derived from some personal features such as the fact of being young or old, man or woman, healthy or sick, but rather an unconditional worth that everyone has simply by virtue of being human. The same idea can be expressed by saying that all human beings are "persons". Indeed, the term "person" is not merely descriptive or generic (like for instance "mammal" or "omnivore"), but prescriptive, a *nomen dignitatis*.[17]

b. The second important consequence of the meaning that "human dignity" bears in international law is that basic rights are *equal* for all: if human dignity is the same for all and the ground of human rights, then all human beings possess equal basic rights. This is the reason why discrimination, i.e. the unjust distinction in the treatment of different categories of people, is directly contrary to human dignity.

c. The third statement of international law, which stresses that rights *derive* from human dignity, has also an important practical consequence: if basic rights are not given by authority, but are preexisting values which are inherent in

---

(14) *Merriam-Webster's Collegiate Dictionary,* 11th ed., 2004, p. 643.

(15) *Oxford Dictionaries Online.* Available at: http://oxforddictionaries.com/

(16) M. MAHLMANN, "Human Dignity and Autonomy in Modern Constitutional Orders", in M. ROSENFELD and A.SAJÓ (eds.), *The Oxford Handbook of Comparative Constitutional Law,* Oxford, Oxford University Press, 2012, pp. 370-396.

(17) R. SPAEMANN, *Personen. Versuche über den Unterschied zwischen 'etwas' und 'jemand',* Stuttgart, Klett-Cotta, 1996, p. 13.

every human being, then they cannot be legitimately taken away by the government. [18]

Considering these three basic features of human dignity, it is not surprising that this notion is at the center of human rights instruments prohibiting practices such as torture, inhuman or degrading treatments, slavery, exploitative working conditions, discrimination, arbitrary arrests, etc. But even in these cases, the term is not explicitly defined by international law. Rather, its meaning is "left to intuitive understanding, conditioned in large measure by cultural factors". [19] The UDBHR is not an exception in this regard, as it does not attempt to provide any definition of this concept.

However, this lack of definition does not mean that dignity is a merely formal or rhetorical concept that means no more than "respect for autonomy". [20] It is not because it is too poor but because it is too rich that it cannot be encapsulated into a very precise definition. In reality, its core meaning is quite clear and simple and embodies a very basic requirement of *justice* towards people. Such requirement conveys the idea that "each person possesses an inviolability founded on justice that even the welfare of society as a whole cannot override". [21] This latter statement is very revealing of the inescapable need for the idea of human worthiness as the precondition of any society seeking to realize justice among its members. Even a contractualist account of equal respect, like the Rawlsian one, which intends to ground society's norms on a hypothetical agreement between individuals (and not on any substantive moral reason) can ultimately not avoid referring to human dignity. The truth is that social agreement alone is not enough to *justify* the moral norms governing a human community. The principles guiding every just society are not right just because its members have agreed on them, but it is the other way round: they have agreed on them because such principles are right. Torture, slavery, or any other practice that seriously disregard human dignity are not wrong because they are prohibited, but they are prohibited because they are wrong.

---

(18) O. SCHACHTER, "Human Dignity as a Normative Concept," *The American Journal of International Law,* 1983, vol. 77, p. 853.

(19) *Ibid.*, p. 849.

(20) R. MACKLIN, "Dignity is a useless concept", *British Medical Journal,* 2003, vol. 327, pp. 1419-1420.

(21) J. RAWLS, *A Theory of Justice,* Oxford, Oxford University Press, 1973, p. 3.

Obviously, the concept of human dignity is open to abuse and misinterpretation. But the same happens with all basic moral and legal principles (justice, freedom, common good, solidarity, etc.), which are not defined by law, not only because of the impossibility of finding a precise definition of such fundamental concepts that satisfies everyone, especially in a transcultural context, but also because lawmakers are well aware that rigid definitions may in some cases lead to unsolvable difficulties in the implementation of legal norms. In this regard, they prefer to follow the old Roman dictum: *omnis definitio in iure periculosa est* (every definition in law is perilous).

It is also true that bioethical debates often show an inflationary use of the term "dignity" that should be avoided, especially when no additional explanation is given to make it clear why a particular practice is regarded as being in conformity (or not) with this basic principle. In such cases, dignity appears to be used as "mere rhetorical dressing, adding little more to the policy debate than the weight or cachet of the concept".[22]

However, beyond all the abusive rhetoric that may surround this notion, a careful analysis of intergovernmental policy documents relating to bioethics, and of the discussion that led to their adoption, shows that the recourse to human dignity reflects a real concern about the need to ensure respect for the inherent worth of every human being. This concern is far broader than simply ensuring "respect for autonomy" for the simple reason that it also includes the protection of those who are not yet, or are no more, morally autonomous (newborn infants, senile elderly, people with serious mental disorders, comatose patients, etc.). As noted above, this broad view of the concept of human dignity is explicitly enshrined in international human rights law, which assumes that the worth of human beings does not rest on their actual intellectual or moral abilities, but merely on their *human condition*.

IV. – IS DIGNITY A SYNONYM FOR RESPECT?

There is no doubt that the concept of "dignity" is very close to that of "respect". However, this does not mean that these two

---

(22) T. CAULFIELD and A. CHAPMAN, "Human Dignity as a Criterion for Science Policy," *Plos Medicine,* 2005, vol. 2, n° 8, p. 737. Available at: www.plosmedicine.org

concepts are synonymous with each other, or that we can simply avoid the difficulties posed by the abstract notion of "dignity" just by replacing it with the more practical idea of "respect". This would be a false solution because respect for persons is just the *consequence* of human dignity, not dignity itself, in a similar way that the bell's sound is an effect produced by the bell, not the bell itself. Moreover, this explanation would inevitably beg the question and lead to circular reasoning: "we are obliged to respect persons because... they deserve respect". In fact, the idea of dignity is not a synonym for respect for the simple reason that dignity is what provides the rationale to the requirement of respect for persons.

Why do people deserve respect? Why are there "some things that cannot be done to anyone, anywhere"?[23] Why is this unconditional moral requirement previous to any domestic law or international agreement? The reason for this is that every human individual is a *person,* not an *object;* everyone is an end in him- or herself, and never a mere means to another's end, according to the famous Kantian imperative. While things have a price, i.e. the kind of value for which there can be equivalent, dignity makes a person irreplaceable.[24]

The widely shared conviction that human beings deserve to be treated with unconditional respect is not merely subjective and arbitrary, but is grounded on an indisputable fact: human beings are entities capable, *as a kind,* of understanding, self-understanding, loving, self-determining by judging and choosing, expressing themselves by means of art, etc. These extraordinary abilities that characterize human beings as a kind and qualitatively distinguish them from all other known living beings (even if those capacities are not currently present in all human individuals, or not in all to the same degree) make of every human being something absolutely unique, precious and irreplaceable. In other words, those typically human features make of every human individual a *self* (i.e. a person), an entity with a certain absoluteness of being.[25]

---

(23)   M. MIDGLEY, "Towards an ethic of global responsibility", in T. DUNNE and N. J. WHEELER (eds), *Human Rights in Global Politics,* Cambridge, Cambridge University Press, 1999, p. 160.

(24)   I. KANT, "Groundwork of the Metaphysics of Morals", in *Practical Philosophy* (The Cambridge Edition of the Works of Immanuel Kant), transl. M. GREGOR, Cambridge, Cambridge University Press, 1996, p. 79.

(25)   R. ANDORNO, "International Policy and a Universal Conception of Human Dignity", in S. DILLEY and N. PALPANT (eds.), *Human Dignity in Bioethics. From Worldviews to the*

Contrary to what is sometimes maintained in bioethical circles, the idea of human dignity does not rely on a "speciesist" claim, i.e. on the merely *biological* fact of belonging to the species *Homo sapiens*. It is not just because it is *our* species that we attach a very special value to the individuals belonging to it, but because human beings are endowed, as a kind, with the extraordinary faculties mentioned above. If there were other entities in the universe besides human beings having, as a kind, those capacities, they would also have intrinsic dignity.[26]

The Kantian requirement of non-instrumentalization (or non-commodification) of persons is extremely helpful in bioethics. It means, for instance, that no one should be subjected to biomedical research without his or her informed consent, even when very valuable knowledge could result from that research; it also means that law must prevent poor people from being induced to sell their organs as a means to support themselves or their families.[27] These two examples illustrate that the idea of dignity as a requirement of non-instrumentalization of persons, far from being purely rhetorical, has some immediate applications. But beyond such extreme examples, the view that people have inherent worth plays a major role in everyday medical practice and can greatly contribute to enhance the quality of the doctor-patient relationship. More concretely, this vision helps to keep alive in the minds of health care professionals the conviction that each patient, no matter what his or her diagnosis, is not a "case", a "disease", or a "room number", but a *person* that deserves to be treated with the greatest respect and care.

V. – THE VARIOUS FUNCTIONS OF HUMAN DIGNITY IN BIOETHICS

To understand how the notion of human dignity operates in bioethics, it is essential to make some conceptual distinctions, particularly between the above described *inherent dignity* of the human person and the *moral dignity,* which is a synonym of "honor". Whereas the former plays a central role in legal instruments relating to bioethics, the latter has less relevance in this field.

Public Square, New York, Routledge, 2013, p. 131. See also P. BECCHI, *Il principio dignità umana,* 2nd ed., Brescia, Morcelliana, 2013.

(26) D. SULMASY, "Human Dignity and Human Worth", in J. MALPAS and N. LICKISS (eds.), *Perspectives on Human Dignity: A Conversation,* Dordrecht, Springer, 2007, pp. 9-18.

(27) C. B. COHEN, "Public Policy and the Sale of Human Organs", *Kennedy Institute of Ethics Journal,* 2002, vol. 12, n° 1, pp. 47-64.

On the one hand, the *inherent dignity,* as it is inseparable from the human condition, is the same for all, cannot be gained or lost and does not allow for any degree. [28] Even the worst criminal cannot be stripped of his or her human dignity and should consequently not be subjected to inhuman treatments or punishments. Ronald Dworkin employs the expression human dignity with this meaning when he points out that it refers to "the intrinsic importance of human life" and requires that "people *never* be treated in a way that denies the distinct importance of their own lives". [29]

On the other hand, *moral dignity,* does not relate to the *existence* itself of persons, but to their *behavior* and stems from their ability to freely choose good and to contribute beneficially to their own lives and the lives of others. It can be said that we give to ourselves this second kind of dignity by making good moral choices. This is why, unlike inherent dignity, which is the same for all, moral dignity is not possessed by all individuals to the same degree. Indeed, we can say, for instance, that an honest man has "more dignity" than a thief.

Alan Gewirth makes this same distinction when he writes that

"[t]he sense of 'dignity' in which all humans are said to have equal dignity is not the same as that in which it may be said of some person that he lacks dignity or that he behaves without dignity (...). This kind of dignity is one that humans may occurrently exhibit, lack, or lose, whereas the dignity in which all humans are said to be equal is a characteristic that belongs permanently and inherently to every human as such". [30]

Another distinction that has been suggested as being relevant to bioethics is between "human dignity as empowerment" and "human dignity as constraint". [31] Whereas the former emphasizes freedom to pursue one's autonomously chosen goals, the latter is more concerned with *duties* than with human rights, and acts as a constraint on freedom in the interest of the common good.

---

(28) H. Spiegelberg, "Human Dignity: A Challenge to Contemporary Philosophy", in R. Gotesky and E. Laszlo (eds.), *Human Dignity. This Century and the Next,* New York, Gordon and Breach, 1970, p. 55.

(29) R. Dworkin, *Life's Dominion. An Argument About Abortion, Euthanasia and Individual Freedom,* New York, Vintage, 1994, p. 236.

(30) A. Gewirth, *Human Rights. Essays on Justification and Applications,* Chicago, University of Chicago Press, 1982, pp. 27-28.

(31) D. Beyleveld and R. Brownsword, *op. cit.,* pp. 1-47.

Beyleveld and Brownsword characterize both notions as "opposed" or "competing" and argue that whereas the founding international instruments of human rights appeal to the first conception of human dignity, dignity as constraint would be typical of the recent instruments dealing with biomedicine and much more controversial.

In my view, this distinction is somehow misleading. These two facets of human dignity do not really constitute rival notions; they are not mutually exclusive but complementary, in the same way that "rights" and "duties", or "freedom" and "responsibility" are complementary concepts. Indeed, the same principle stating that human beings have intrinsic worth results in two consequences. First, that each individual is entitled to fundamental rights and freedoms. Second, that people deserve to be protected from serious threats to their dignity, even if they might appear to be consenting to such acts. The reason for the complementary nature of these two facets of human dignity is that most rights are not absolute but subject to such reasonable limits as are generally accepted in a free and democratic society, as it is explicitly recognized by all major international human rights instruments. In this regard, for instance, Article 12.3 of the ICCPR stipulates that

"[t]he above-mentioned rights shall not be subject to any restrictions except those which are provided by law, are necessary to protect national security, public order (*ordre public*), public health or morals or the rights and freedoms of others, and are consistent with the other rights recognized in the present Covenant".

As a matter of fact, the notion that individual freedoms can be restricted to ensure respect for human dignity is neither new, nor specific to the instruments dealing with biomedicine. Rather on the contrary, such restrictions are quite common in legal documents, both at the domestic and international level. Just to give two examples: labor laws do not allow workers to waive their basic rights and benefits or to accept working conditions close to slavery; contract laws do not recognize the validity of contracts containing terms that are unfairly burdensome to one party and unfairly beneficial to the other. Thus, from this perspective, there is nothing new in the recent instruments relating to biomedicine, except that they cover novel issues. This is why, rather than presenting "dignity as constraint" as a new concept and opposed to "dignity as empowerment", it would be perhaps more accurate to describe both perspectives as being two facets of the same need to ensure respect for people. In this line of thinking, some scholars suggest distinguishing between the "subjective" and the "objective" dimensions of dignity, which are complementary and correspond to freedom and to restrictions of freedom respectively. [32]

Another distinction that needs to be made is between the "individual" and the "collective" dimensions of dignity. The former is the primary expression of dignity and the ground of all basic rights and freedoms, whereas the latter is another, more recently developed category of dignity that goes far beyond the mere individual sphere and refers to the value of humanity *as such*, including future generations. [33] Whereas individual dignity refers to the idea that every human being has inherent worth, collective dignity is a derivative notion, which embodies the idea that the existence and integrity of humanity as such also has intrinsic worth and therefore also deserves to be protected. This extended notion of dignity lies in the background of the ban on certain biotechnological developments that may affect basic features of the human species, like reproductive cloning and germ-line interventions. It amounts to a sort of "species solidarity" and inevitably leads to prescribe some limits on potential developments that could be harmful for the identity and integrity of humanity. [34]

It is important to stress, however, that collective dignity is only a *derivative* notion, because dignity belongs primarily to the individual. As Teresa Iglesias points out while commenting on the Universal Declaration of Human Rights

"Upholding 'human dignity' or the 'dignity of the species' without upholding the dignity of each one and of all, is not to uphold dignity in its universal significance. In the name of the 'dignity of the whole' (of a 'whole' group) others have come to suffer the atrocities to which the Declaration refers". [35]

It is also noteworthy here that an analysis of international human rights instruments and of the decisions of national and

---

(32) D. MANAÏ, *Les droits du patient face à la biomedicine,* Berne, Stämpfli, 2006, pp. 20-24.

(33) This distinction has been suggested, among others, by Birnbacher. See D. BIRNBACHER, "Ambiguities in the concept of Menschenwürde", in K. BAYERTZ (ed.), *Sanctity of Life and Human Dignity,* Dordrecht, Kluwer, 1996, p. 114.

(34) D. MANAÏ, *op. cit.,* pp. 20-22

(35) T. IGLESIAS, *The Dignity of the Individual. Issues of Bioethics and Law,* Dublin, Pleroma, 2001, p. 13.

international courts shows indeed that human dignity does not play just one, but *several* roles. Although this notion has a primary *meaning,* which refers to the intrinsic value of human beings, it has multiple *functions,* which operate at different levels. First of all, dignity provides the deepest justification for human rights. But it is also often mentioned, for instance, as the ultimate reason behind the prohibition of discriminatory practices, as well as an argument against torture, inhuman and degrading treatment and punishment, and various forms of instrumentalization of people (slavery, organ trafficking, etc.). In this regard, the Universal Declaration on Bioethics and Human Rights is a good example of the various roles that human dignity can play. As noted above, the promotion of respect for human dignity constitutes not only the main purpose of the document (Article 2.c), but also the first principle that should govern biomedical issues (Article 3), the rationale for the prohibition of discrimination and stigmatization of individuals or groups of individuals (Article 11), the framework within which cultural diversity is to be respected (Article 12), and the interpretative principle for a correct understanding of all the Declaration's provisions (Article 28).

VI. – THE NECESSARY RECOURSE TO HUMAN RIGHTS

The central role attached to human dignity in global bioethics is necessary, but not sufficient for providing an effective response to the complex challenges posed by biomedical clinical and research practice. "Dignity" alone cannot directly solve most bioethical dilemmas, because it is not a magic word that provides immediate response to them. Some further explanations are usually required to indicate *why* some practices are considered to be in conformity (or not) with what is required by the intrinsic worth of human beings. Thus, to become *functional,* dignity needs other more concrete notions that are normally formulated using the terminology of "rights" (e.g., informed consent, physical integrity, confidentiality, nondiscrimination, etc.). Human dignity and human rights are therefore mutually dependent, but in different ways. The relationship between them is that of a principle and the concrete legal norms that are needed to flesh out that principle in real life. In other words, although we need to recur to human dignity as the ultimate justification of legal norms, "the practical business of pressing one's interests against others" is conducted in terms of claimed human rights.[36]

The need to appeal to human rights for governing biomedicine is even greater at the global level. As our world becomes increasingly interconnected and threats to global public health continue to proliferate, it is hard to see how the global governance of health could be managed without assigning an integral role to human rights.[37] It is therefore not by chance that the UDBHR constantly adds a reference to "human rights" every time that it mentions human dignity. The importance of this document lies precisely in the fact that it is the first intergovernmental global instrument that addresses the linkage between human rights and bioethics. According to the chairperson of the drafting group of the Declaration, the most important achievement of the text consists precisely in having integrated the bioethical analysis into a human rights framework.[38]

As noted by the Explanatory Memorandum to the Preliminary Draft Declaration, "the drafting group also stressed the importance of taking international human rights legislation as the essential framework and starting point for the development of bioethical principles".[39] This document also points out that there are two broad streams at the origin of the norms dealing with bioethics. The first one can be traced to antiquity, in particular to Hippocrates, and is derived from reflections on the practice of medicine. The second one, conceptualized in more recent times, has drawn upon the developing international human rights law. Furthermore, it states: "One of the important achievements of the declaration is that it seeks to unite these two streams. It clearly aims to establish the conformity of bioethics with international human rights law".[40] After all, as Kirby points out, no UN agency may afford the

---

(36) D. BEYLEVELD and R. BROWNSWORD, op. cit., p. 13.

(37) L. GABLE, "The Proliferation of Human Rights in Global Health Governance", *Journal of Law, Medicine & Ethics*, 2007, vol. 35, n° 4, pp. 534-544.

(38) M. KIRBY, "UNESCO and Universal Principles on Bioethics: What's next?", in UNESCO International Bioethics Committee, *Twelfth Session of the International Bioethics Committee (IBC). December 2005. Proceedings*, Paris, UNESCO, 2006, p. 126.

(39) UNESCO, *Explanatory Memorandum on the Elaboration of the Preliminary Draft Declaration on Universal Norms on Bioethics*, Paris, UNESCO, 2005, para. 11. See also J. SANDOR, "Bioethics and Basic Rights: Persons, Humans, and Boundaries of Life", in M. ROSENFELD and A. SAJÓ (eds.), *The Oxford Handbook of Comparative Constitutional Law*, Oxford, Oxford University Press, 2012, pp. 1142-1165.

(40) *Ibid.*, para. 12.

luxury of ignoring the binding force of international human rights law. The initiatives taken by UNESCO in this field have therefore "an element of the inevitable about them: paying due regard to relevant provisions of international human rights law as it affects bioethical decisions".[41]

Several other reasons explain the recourse to human rights in this field. As mentioned above, there is a very close relationship between biomedical activities and the most basic human rights such as the right to life and to physical integrity. Therefore it is not surprising that both modern bioethics and international human rights were born from the same historical events: the Second World War, the Holocaust, and the Nuremberg tribunals that condemned the Nazi doctors.[42] The common origin of both systems makes even more understandable the recourse to the existing human rights framework to protect individuals from harm in the biomedical field.

Moreover, the human rights approach facilitates the formulation of universal standards, because international human rights law is grounded on the assumption that basic rights transcend cultural diversity. Human rights are indeed conceived as entitlements that people have simply by virtue of their human condition, and regardless of their ethnic origin, sex, age, socio-economic status, health condition, or religious or political ideas. Human rights are held to be universal in the sense that "all people have and should enjoy them, and to be independent in the sense that they exist and are available as standards of justification and criticism whether or not they are recognized and implemented by the legal system or officials of a country".[43] In such a sensitive field as bioethics, where diverse sociocultural, philosophical and religious traditions come into play, the importance of having principles of universal validity should not be underemphasized.

A more practical reason for the use of a human rights framework in this field is that there are few, if any, mechanisms available

---

(41) M. KIRBY, "Human Rights and Bioethics: The Universal Declaration of Human Rights and the Universal Declaration of Bioethics and Human Rights", *The Journal of Contemporary Health Law and Policy*, 2009, vol. 25, issue 2, p. 324.

(42) G.J. ANNAS, *American Bioethics. Crossing Human Rights and Health Law Boundaries*, New York, Oxford University Press, 2005, p. 160.

(43) J. NICKEL, *Making Sense of Human Rights: Philosophical Reflections on the Universal Declaration of Human Rights*, Berkeley, University of California Press, 1987, p. 561.

other than human rights to function as a "global normative foundation" in biomedicine, [44] or as a "lingua franca of international relations". [45] As a well-known expert on public health issues has pointed out, "the human rights framework provides a more useful approach for analyzing and responding to modern public health challenges than any framework thus far available within the biomedical tradition". [46] Similarly, it has been argued that the recourse to human rights is fully justified on the ground that bioethics suffers from the plurality and range of actors involved and the overproduction of divergent norms, whereas human rights offers "a strong framework and a common language, which may constitute a starting point for the development of universal bioethical principles". [47]

VII. – OBJECTIONS TO THE USE OF A HUMAN RIGHTS FRAMEWORK

The use of a human rights framework to set up global norms on bioethics must often face the objection that human rights are a Western ideological construct of little relevance in non-Western (mainly African and Asian) societies. A corollary of this view is the argument that attempts to impose human rights values on non-Western countries amount to cultural imperialism. [48] This objection is often linked to a moral relativistic position according to which moral principles are thought of as socially and historically contingent, valid only for those cultures and societies in which they originate. Consequently, there is no such thing as universally valid moral principles, not even the idea that people have inherent dignity and rights.

Although the philosophical debate between universalists and relativists is far too complex to be adequately covered in this chapter, some responses to the first of the above-mentioned

---

(44)   D. THOMASMA, "Proposing a New Agenda: Bioethics and International Human Rights", *Cambridge Quarterly of Healthcare Ethics,* 2001, vol. 10, p. 300.

(45)   L. KNOWLES, "The lingua franca of human rights and the rise of a global bioethic", *Cambridge Quarterly of Healthcare Ethics,* 2001, vol. 10, p. 253.

(46)   J. MANN, "Health and human rights. Protecting human rights is essential for promoting health", *British Medical Journal,* 1996, vol. 312, p. 924.

(47)   H. BOUSSARD, "The 'Normative Spectrum' of an Ethically-inspired Legal Instrument: The 2005 Universal Declaration on Bioethics and Human Rights", in F. FRANCIONI (ed.), *Biotechnologies and International Human Rights,* Oxford, Hart Publishing, 2007, p. 114.

(48)   D. SCHROEDER, "Human Rights and Their Role in Global Bioethics", *Cambridge Quarterly of Healthcare Ethics,* 2005, vol. 14, pp. 221-223.

criticisms are immediately available. First, it is true that the notion of human rights has recent origins in the European Enlightenment philosophers and in the political revolutions of the end of the eighteenth century, notably, the American and French Revolutions. However, this historical circumstance does not necessarily invalidate the widely accepted claim that people should be entitled to basic rights by the mere fact of being humans. This is the relevant question, no matter where the idea of such inherent rights comes from. Merely pointing to moral diversity and the presumed integrity of individual cultures does not, by itself, provide a philosophical justification for relativism, nor a sufficient critique of universalism.

As a matter of fact, international human rights law has been elaborated by representatives of the most diverse countries and cultures, and is not intended to impose one cultural standard, but rather to promote a legal standard of minimum protection necessary for human dignity. As such, universal human rights can be reasonably seen as the "hard-won consensus of the international community", and not as the cultural imperialism of any particular region or set of traditions. [49] Even though the modern conceptualization of human rights is an historical product of Western civilization, the idea, which is at the heart of this notion (that every human being deserves to be respected) is present, though in different conceptual terms, in every human society.

In addition to the criticism of "cultural imperialism", it is also argued that human rights are conceived as excessively individualist for non-Western mentalities and lack a significant concern for personal duties and for the common interest of society. It is true that human rights have been originally conceived having in mind the *individual* person as the principal bearer of such rights. However, it would be equally fair to say that international law has made substantial efforts over the last decades to be more attuned to the communal and collective basis of many non-Western societies. This was done, in particular, trough the development of the "second generation of rights" that are included in the above-mentioned ICCPR 1966, such as the right to education, the right to social security, the right to a fair remuneration, the right to healthy

---

(49) D. AYTON-SHENKER, "The Challenge of Human Rights and Cultural Diversity", United Nations Background Note, New York, United Nations Department of Public Information, 1995, p. 2. Available at: http://www.un.org/rights/dpi1627e.htm

working conditions, the right to health care, the protection of the family and children, the right to adequate housing, etc. This trend towards a broader understanding of human rights has been even further developed with the "third generation of human rights", the so-called "rights of solidarity", or "rights of groups", which include the right to development, to peace, to self-determination and to a healthy environment. In sum, although human rights remain philosophically grounded within an individualist moral doctrine, there can be no doubt that serious attempts are being made by the international community to adequately apply them to more communally oriented societies.

In any case, the truth is that today these *theoretical* controversies have lost much of their *practical* significance. The first reason for this is that, at present, virtually all States accept the authority of international human rights law. The six core international human rights treaties (on civil and political rights, economic, social, and cultural rights, racial discrimination, women, torture, and children) have an average 166 ratifying States, which represents a truly impressive 85% ratification rate.[50] The second reason is that human rights emerge from international law instruments with sufficient flexibility to be compatible with respect for cultural diversity. The universality of human rights norms is not incompatible with some local variations in the *form* in which particular rights are implemented.[51]

CONCLUSION

One of the most impressive features of the international instruments relating to biomedicine is the very central role they assign to the principle of respect for human dignity. The UDBHR is a good example of this trend. Although the Declaration does not provide a definition of human dignity, this notion is to be understood as referring, first, to the intrinsic worth of human beings, and second, in a derivative way, to the value of humanity as such. But the emerging international biolaw also appeals to human rights to set up global norms in this field. Several reasons

---

(50) UNESCO. Division of Human Rights, Philosophy and Democracy, *Human Rights. Major International Instruments. Status as at 30 June 2011,* Paris, UNESCO, 2011.

(51) J. DONNELLY, *Universal Human Rights in Theory and Practice*, Ithaca, NY, Cornell University Press, pp. 109-42.

justify this strategy: the obvious link between health issues and basic human rights; the universalistic claim of human rights, which facilitates the formulation of transcultural standards; the fact that the key notions employed at the domestic level to protect people from misuse in the biomedical field are already formulated using the terminology of rights; and the lack of any conceptual and institutional instrument other than human rights to produce an international framework of norms relating to biomedicine.

CHAPTER 3

THE PRECAUTIONARY PRINCIPLE: A NEW LEGAL STANDARD FOR THE TECHNOLOGICAL AGE

The classical virtue of prudence, especially when it deals with policy matters, offers a good conceptual framework for understanding the nature and scope of the precautionary principle. This is because ultimately this new legal standard is an appeal to caution (or prudence) when we are dealing with technologies that may be potentially harmful to public health and the environment.

Prudence is not to be understood here as meaning unwillingness to take action or lack of courage to face new challenges. Rather on the contrary, this term is employed in this context with its classical meaning of "ability to discern the most suitable course of action". [1] Prudence constitutes what Aristotle called "practical wisdom" (*phronesis*), as opposed to the "theoretical wisdom" (*sophia*): whereas the latter aims at universal truths and is concerned with knowledge of things that cannot be otherwise, practical wisdom is always concerned with the particular, with contingent matters, with things that can be other than they are. [2] The role of prudence is therefore much more modest than that of theoretical wisdom, but not less important for everyday life. As prudence, "wisdom in the service of action", [3] deals with contingent matters, it cannot be codified in advance in a very detailed fashion. Each new situation is different and may require a different response. Accordingly, a prudent person can only be defined in formal terms as one who, having to choose some actions rather than others, is able to deliberate well about the things that have to be done for a good end.

---

(1) *The Oxford English Dictionary*, 2nd ed., vol. XII, Oxford, Clarendon Press, 1989, p. 728.
(2) ARISTOTLE, *Nicomachean Ethics*, VI, 8. See also P. AUBENQUE, *La prudence chez Aristote*, Paris, PUF, 1997.
(3) D. ARNAUD and T. LE BON, "Practical and Theoretical Wisdom", *Practical Philosophy*, 2000, vol. 3, n° 1, pp. 6-9.

In Aristotle's view, prudence is one of the most important virtues for policymakers, to such an extent that politics was regarded by him as the highest form of prudence, as it is directed to the common good of society and not to purely individual interests. Political prudence is the virtue that enables authorities to assess the pros and cons of alternative courses of actions and to take the most appropriate decision in every case.

Political prudence is closely related to the precautionary principle because the latter presupposes situations where policymakers must take decisions about specific products or activities when there is a serious suspicion that they may be potentially dangerous for the public but when, at the same time, the hazard is not well understood yet.[4] Faced with uncertain risks, the wisdom of political authorities consists in finding an adequate balance between two extreme positions: on the one hand, an irrational fear of new technologies for the solely reason that they are new and, on the other hand, an irresponsible, passive attitude towards products or activities that could really be harmful.

The challenge of dealing with uncertain risks is becoming increasingly urgent today due to the accelerated technological developments of the last decades, which create unprecedented potential risks to public health and the environment. Furthermore, some of the new hazards, far from having a merely local impact, present a global dimension as many of the new products are distributed worldwide by multinational companies and therefore may harm the health and physical integrity of entire populations and the planet's environment. Among the examples where the precautionary principle has been used along the last decade (successfully or not) are the consumption of genetically modified foods; the use of growth hormones in cattle raising; the possible link between eating beef infected with BSE (bovine spongiform encephalopathy, or "mad cow disease") and the Creutzfeldt-Jakob disease in humans; AIDS transmitted through blood transmission; health claims linked to phthalates in PVC toys; the use of nanoparticles in various products, including medical devices; and the exposure to chemicals that behave as endocrine disruptors and may have serious adverse effects on the hormone system.

---

(4) The word precaution (from Latin *prae-* "before" and *cautio,* "caution") means literally "caution practiced in advance".

In the years to come, the number of products or activities posing uncertain risks is likely to grow due to the accelerating pace of technological change. In the biomedical field, we can think of the potential risk of increased birth defects with the use of certain assisted reproductive technologies such as ICSI (intracytoplasmic sperm injection);[5] xenotransplantation (i.e. the use of animal organs for transplantation purposes in humans), which may transmit infectious agents to organ recipients and create new and uncontrollable diseases in humans;[6] and the possible irreversible harm to future generations caused by germ-line interventions.[7]

The logic behind the precautionary principle is that when facing the possibility of serious harmful effects, it is not acceptable to say: "we do not have definitive evidence that serious harm will happen, so we can do nothing to prevent it". If there are good reasons, based on empirical evidence or plausible causal hypothesis, to believe that damage might occur, and given the crucial importance of what is at stake (the life and health of people and the preservation of ecosystems), adequate measure should be taken to prevent such disastrous outcomes. In other words, it is better to err on the side of caution. What I intend to argue is that the precautionary principle does not rest on a complicated theory, but just on common sense. As one of its proponents says, all this principle actually amounts to is this: "if one is embarking on something new, one should think very carefully about whether it is safe or not, and should not go ahead until *reasonably* convinced it is".[8]

Perhaps the main originality of the precautionary principle is that measures need to be taken *before* definitive scientific evidence of the harmful effects becomes available. Another revolutionary

---

(5) Practice Committee of American Society for Reproductive Medicine; Practice Committee of Society for Assisted Reproductive Technology, "Genetic considerations related to intracytoplasmic sperm injection (ICSI)," *Fertility and Sterility,* 2006, vol. 86, issue 5, pp. S103-S105; French National Advisory Committee on Ethics, "Ethical issues raised by the development of ICSI", Opinion N° 75, 12 December 2002. Available at: http://www.ccne-ethique.fr

(6) In 2004, the World Health Assembly urged Member States to ensure effective national regulatory control and surveillance mechanisms before allowing xenotransplantations (Resolution WHA57.18 of 22 May 2004).

(7) The precautionary principle is explicitly invoked to prevent germ-line interventions in humans. See UNESCO International Bioethics Committee (IBC), "Report on Pre-implantation Genetic Diagnosis and Germ-line Intervention", 24 April 2003, Paragraph 81.

(8) P.T. SAUNDERS, "Use and Abuse of the Precautionary Principle", Institute of Science in Society (ISIS) submission to US Advisory Committee on International Economic Policy (ACIEP) Biotech. Working Group, 13 July 2000. Available at: http://www.i-sis.org.uk/prec.php

feature of it is the requirement of *transparency* of the political decisions related to public health and environment, and even a direct participation of the public in the choice between the different available technological options. It also presupposes a more *global view* of our responsibilities towards humanity as a whole, including future generations. From this perspective, it constitutes a kind of "planetary wisdom".[9]

The new "imperative of responsibility" that is emerging in modern societies is a logic consequence of our increasing technological powers. Whereas in the past our actions could only affect the people who surrounded us and within the short-term, the new technological developments give us the ability to harm not only existing individuals but also future generations and humanity as a whole.[10] It is precisely in this context of global responsibility that over the last decades there has been an increasing trend to promote a *sustainable development*, which means development that "meets the needs of the present without compromising the ability of future generations to meet their own needs".[11] The notion of sustainable development is at the core of the precautionary principle, because this latter is in the end an instrument to ensure a good quality of life for present and future generations.

This chapter aims to show the spectacular rise of the precautionary principle in international law (I), and to specify the conditions that must be met for the adoption of precautionary measures (II).

I. – THE PRECAUTIONARY PRINCIPLE IN INTERNATIONAL LAW

It would not be surprising if in a few decades the theorists of law refer to the precautionary principle as a paradigmatic example of the development of a legal principle in modern societies. Actually, it is remarkable how few years took to the precautionary principle to pass from the German environmental law to other European

---

(9) F. EWALD, "Philosophies du principe de précaution", in F. EWALD, C. GOLLIER, and N. DE SADELEER, *Le principe de précaution*, Paris, Presses Universitaires de France, 2001, p. 33.

(10) H. JONAS, *Das Prinzip Verantwortung. Versuch einer Ethik für die technologische Zivilisation*, Frankfurt, Suhrkamp, 1984.

(11) World Commission on Environment and Development, *Our Common Future* (Bruntland Report), Oxford, Oxford University Press, 1987, p. 43.

legal systems, and then to be enshrined as one of the pillars of international environmental law.

The introduction of a precautionary approach to risk regulation in Europe dates from 1971, when the concept of *Vorsorgeprinzip* was incorporated into the German program of environmental protection.[12] Thereafter it was included in various German laws relating to environmental issues.[13] From the German law, the precautionary principle spread to the legal systems of other European countries, such as Denmark, Sweden and France, not only for dealing with environmental matters, but also with food safety and public health issues.[14] The principle was officially enshrined as one of the four pillars of the EU environmental policy by the Treaty on the European Union signed in Maastricht in 1992. The Treaty of Maastricht was subject of amendments by subsequent treaties, the latest being the Treaty of Lisbon which came into force in 2009. Article 191.2 (former Article 174.2) of the consolidated version of the Treaty provides that:

"Union policy on the environment shall aim at a high level of protection taking into account the diversity of situations in the various regions of the Union. It shall be based on the precautionary principle and on the principles that preventive action should be taken, that environmental damage should as a priority be rectified at source and that the polluter should pay".[15]

---

(12) M. KLOEPFER, *Umweltrecht,* Munich, Beck, 1998, p. 166.

(13) See Law on protection from contamination (*Immissionsschutzgesetz*) of 1974 (Arts. 1 and 5, par. I.2); Law on chemical products (*Chemikaliengesetz*) of 1980 (Art. 1); Law on the use of atomic energy (*Atomgesetz*) of 1985 (Art. 7, par. II.3); Law on environmental tolerance tests (*Umweltverträglichkeitsprüfung*) of 1990 (Art. 1). The precautionary principle is implicit in other legal provisions, like the Law on genetic techniques (*Gentechnikgesetz*) of 1990 (Arts. 1 and 13, par. 4) and the Law on water conservation (*Wasserhaushaltsgesetz*) of 1996 (Art. 4). According to the German Constitution, "the State is responsible for ensuring the natural life conditions of future generations" (Art. 20a).

(14) Denmark has introduced the precautionary principle into the Law n° 583 on chemical substances of 1993. Sweden recognizes it as a general principle in the Environmental Code of 1999 (See Chapter 2 of Part I). In France, the precautionary principle can be found in the Environmental Code of 2000, which defines it as: "the principle according to which the absence of certainty, taking account of current scientific and technical knowledge, ought not to delay the adoption of effective and proportionate measures aimed at preventing a risk of serious and irreversible damage to the environment, at an economically acceptable cost." (Article L110-1).

(15) Paragraph 3 of Article 191 provides that the environmental policy of the Community "shall take account of available scientific and technical data" as well as of "the potential benefits and costs of action or lack of action".

This spectacular evolution leads legal scholars to affirm that "today, there is no doubt that the precautionary principle has obtained in communitarian law the status of a legal principle of direct application".[16] In order to clarify the scope of this principle and the conditions under which it would be applied, the European Commission issued on 2 February 2000 an important policy guideline entitled "Communication on the Precautionary Principle". The document makes it clear that, although the Treaty on the European Union only refers to the precautionary principle in relation to environmental protection, the scope of the principle is much wider as it responds to the concern that "potentially dangerous effects on the environment, human, animal or plant health may be inconsistent with the high level of protection chosen for the Community".[17] Basically, this guideline adopts a middle ground position between industry groups who wanted preventive measures to be taken only after having clearly and scientifically identified the extent of the risks, and environmental groups who claimed that the precautionary principle should be applied not only in the case of uncertainty, but also in the case of ignorance.[18]

Another important document in this regard is the Resolution on the Precautionary Principle endorsed by the Heads of Governments in December 2000 on the occasion of the European Council Meeting that adopted the Treaty of Nice on the European Union. The Resolution reaffirms the broad lines of the Commission's Communication and recognizes that "the precautionary principle is gradually asserting itself as a principle of international law in the fields of environmental and health protection" (Paragraph 3). The document states that the precautionary principle should be used "where the possibility of harmful effects on health or the environment has been identified and preliminary scientific evaluation, based on the available data, proves inconclusive for assessing the level or risk" (Paragraph 7). Among the conditions that must be met for the adoption of precautionary measures are the involvement of scientific committees in the decision

---

(16) P. KOURILSKY and G. VINEY, *Le principe de précaution. Rapport au Premier ministre,* Paris, La Documentation française, 2000, p. 132.

(17) European Commission, *Communication on the Precautionary Principle,* 2 February 2000, Paragraph 3.

(18) D. VOGEL, *The Politics of Precaution. Regulating Health, Safety, and Environmental Risks in Europe and the United States,* Princeton NJ, Princeton University Press, 2012, p. 267.

making process (Paragraph 9), the transparency of the procedure (Paragraph 14), the participation of the civil society (Paragraph 15), and the proportionality of the measures (Paragraph 17). Although it recognizes that the precautionary measures "presuppose examination of the benefits and costs of action and inaction", it is also stressed that "requirements linked to the protection of public health (...) must be given priority" (Paragraph 20).

At a global level, the precautionary principle has been included in virtually every recently adopted international treaty and policy document related to the protection of the environment. Despite the different formulations of the principle in these documents, its main features are virtually the same. Probably the first international instrument to endorse a precautionary approach was the Ministerial Declaration of the Second International Conference on the Protection of the North Sea, issued in London in November 1987.[19] Paragraph VII of the Declaration provides that:

" ...in order to protect the North Sea from possibly damaging effects of the most dangerous substances, a precautionary approach is necessary which may require action to control inputs of such substances even before a causal link has been established by absolutely clear scientific evidence".

In March 1990 the principle was reaffirmed by the Third International Conference on the Protection of the North Sea. Signatories to the Baltic Sea Declaration state their "firm intention" to:

"Apply the precautionary principle, i.e. to take effective action to avoid potentially damaging impacts of substances that are persistent, toxic and liable to bioaccumulate even where there is a lack of full scientific certainty to prove a causal link between emissions and effects" (Article 12).

The 1990 Bergen Declaration on Sustainable Development, adopted by the European Commission for Europe (ECE) of the United Nations, was the first international act to state the principle

---

(19) Although the UN "World Charter for Nature" of 1982 includes notions that could be associated with the precautionary principle, it is usually not considered as an antecedent because it is seen as too radical. According to Article 11: "Activities which are likely to pose a significant risk to nature shall be preceded by an exhaustive examination (...); and where potential adverse effects are not fully understood, the activities *should not proceed"*.

as one of general application which was linked to sustainable development. The Declaration states that:

"In order to achieve sustainable development, policies must be based on the precautionary principle. Environmental measures must anticipate, attack and prevent the causes of environmental degradation. Where there are threats of serious or irreversible damage, lack of full scientific certainty should not be used as a reason for postponing measures to prevent environmental degradation".

The UN Conference on Environment and Development (UNCES), also known as Earth Summit, held in Rio de Janeiro in June 1992, marks the first recognition of the precautionary principle as a universal standard. This Conference represents also a shift in global regulatory leadership from the United States to the EU.[20] Indeed, for approximately three decades, between roughly 1960 and 1990, the United States had taken the initiative in identifying new health, safety and environmental risks and in enacting a wide range of stringent and often precautionary standards. But around 1990, mainly due to a complex of political and commercial factors, the United States started to weaken its risks regulations, and to abstain from ratifying a number of major international environmental agreements. At the same time, European policymakers began to be very active in the identification of new risks and in the adoption of more stringent health, safety and environmental regulations. Clearly, the EU has taken over the role of world leader in risks regulations that was previously played by the US.[21]

The 1992 Rio Declaration is a landmark in the development of the precautionary principle at a global level. Contrary to many of the previously mentioned documents, the Rio Declaration firmly establishes that at least some form of minimum precautionary approach is globally accepted. Principle 15 provides one of the most often quoted definitions of the precautionary principle:

"Where there are threats of serious or irreversible damage, lack of full scientific certainty shall not be used as a reason for postponing cost-effective measures to prevent environmental degradation".

---

(20) D. VOGEL, *op. cit.*, pp. 3-6.
(21) *Ibid.*

The 1992 Rio Conference marked also the signature of the Convention on Biological Diversity (also known as Biodiversity Convention), which is considered the key international instrument regarding sustainable development. Basically the convention aims to promote strategies for the conservation of biological diversity and a sustainable use of its resources. The precautionary principle, which appears as one of the tools for achieving those goals, is defined in the Preamble as follows:

"Where there is threat of significant reduction or loss of biological diversity, lack of full scientific certainty should not be used as a reason for postponing measures to avoid or minimize such a threat".

Another important document that resulted from the Rio Conference was the UN Framework Convention on Climate Change, which also encourages the adoption of precautionary measures in this area. Similarly to the Rio declaration, this document stresses that such measures should be cost-effective. Article 3(3) provides that

"The Parties should take precautionary measures to anticipate, prevent or minimize the causes of climate change and mitigate its adverse effects. Where there are threats of serious or irreversible damage, lack of full scientific certainty should not be used as a reason for postponing such measures, taking into account that policies and measures to deal with climate change should be cost effective so as to ensure global benefits at the lowest possible cost".

The Cartagena Protocol on Biosafety, signed in Montreal in January 2000, which is a supplementary agreement to the Convention on Biological Diversity, stipulates in Article 1 that the objective of the Protocol is "in accordance with the precautionary approach contained in Principle 15 of the Rio Declaration on Environment and Development." As a specific application of the precautionary principle to measures regarding the import of genetically modified organisms, Article 10.6 stipulates that:

"Lack of scientific certainty due to insufficient relevant scientific information and knowledge regarding the extent of the potential adverse effects of LMO [Living Modified Organisms] on biodiversity, taking into account risks to human health, shall not prevent a Party of import from taking a decision, as appropriate, with regard to the import of the LMO in question, in order to avoid or minimize such potential adverse effects".[22]

International courts of law have also had the opportunity to deal with the precautionary principle. The best example in this regard is the Court of Justice of the European Union (CJEU), which has adopted a clear position in support of this principle. For instance, in 1998 the Court confirmed the validity of the decision of the European Commission that had prohibited the United Kingdom from exporting to other Member States and third countries live bovine animals, bovine meat and products obtained from bovine meat. The decision was adopted after the discovery of a probable link between the Creutzfeldt-Jakob disease, a degenerative brain disease, and bovine spongiform encephalopathy (BSE, or "mad cow disease"), which was widespread in the United Kingdom at the time.[23] Although the Court's judgment does not explicitly mention the precautionary principle, it is clearly inspired on it, especially when it states that:

"Where there is uncertainty as to the existence or extent of the risks to human health, the institutions may take protective measures without having to wait until the reality and seriousness of those risks become fully apparent" (Paragraph 99)

It is interesting to note that this judgment made an extensive application of the precautionary principle to the field of public health on the basis of Article 130r (now Article 191.2) of the Treaty on the European Union, which in fact only refers to the protection of the environment.

On 21 March 2000, the CJEU reaffirmed the validity of the precautionary principle in a controversy regarding the release into the French market of genetically modified varieties of maize produced by the company Novartis. The Court decided that even if an authorization to place a GMO on the market was initially given, national authorities may revise their decision if, in the

---

(22)   Accordingly, Annex III on risk assessment to the Cartagena Protocol states: "Lack of scientific knowledge or scientific consensus should not necessarily be interpreted as indicating a particular level of risk, an absence of risk, or an acceptable risk."

(23)   CJEU, Case C-180/96, *United Kingdom v. Commission of the European Communities*, 5 May 1998, *ECR* 1998, I-2265.

light of new information, they have good reasons to fear that the product is harmful.[24]

Two years later, on 11 September 2002, the Court rejected an application by Pfizer Animal Health against the Regulation 2821/98 that had banned the use of the antibiotic virginiamycin as an additive in animal feeding. The company, which produced and marketed this antibiotic, brought proceedings before the Court seeking annulment of that regulation. The Court concluded that despite uncertainty as to whether there is a link between the use of virginiamycin as an additive in feedingstuffs and increased resistance to antibiotics in humans, the ban on the products is not a disproportionate measure given the need to protect public health.[25] The Pfizer case is regarded as a landmark case, as the Court discussed extensively the interpretation and correct application of the precautionary principle for the first time.[26]

Whereas the CJEU has strongly supported the use of the precautionary principle, other international courts are reluctant to take a clear stance on this issue. The International Court of Justice (ICJ) was confronted with at least two cases relating to the precautionary principle, and in both cases has cautiously avoided taking a position on this matter. The first case was *New Zealand v. France* of 1995, which had to do with underground nuclear tests that France intended to conduct in the territory of French Polynesia in the South Pacific. New Zealand argued that France was bound by customary international law to respect the precautionary principle and therefore to prove the innocuousness of such nuclear tests and to assess their environmental impact before conducting them. The order of the ICJ of 22 September 1995, which dismissed New Zealand's claim on procedural grounds, did not rule upon the nature of the precautionary principle. Nevertheless, it is interesting to note that dissenting Judge Weeramantry, having reviewed all the international treaties applying the precautionary principle, arrived at the conclusion that it had developed sufficiently to be

---

(24) CJEU, Case C-6/99, *Association Greenpeace France and Others v. Ministère de l'Agriculture et de la Pêche and Others,* 21 March 2000, *ECR* 2000, I-1651.

(25) CJEU, Case T-13/99, *Pfizer Animal Health SA v. Council of the European Union,* 11 September 2002, *ECR* 2002, II-03305.

(26) The Court's decision in the Pfizer case has been criticized for giving too much discretionary power to EU decision-makers in the adoption of precautionary measures, even against the opinion of expert committees. See J. Zander, *The Application of the Precautionary Principle in Practice: Comparative Dimensions,* Cambridge, Cambridge University Press, 2010, pp. 122ff.

considered a principle of customary international law relating to the environment.[27]

In the second case, *Hungary v. Slovakia,* decided in 1997, Hungary invoked the precautionary principle and the notion of sustainable development to repudiate the Treaty with Slovakia aimed at the construction of the Gabcikovo-Nagymaros system of locks on the Danube River. Hungary argued on that basis that Slovakia should provide the proof of no harm to the environment derived from the diversion of the Danube River. The Court, without denying the importance of the precautionary principle, decided that Hungary was not entitled the abandon the common project. Interestingly, in this case both parties agreed on the need for precautionary measures for the protection of the environment, but they fundamentally disagree on the consequences of this common concern for the joint Project.[28]

The European Court of Human Rights (ECtHR) made use of the precautionary principle in one case decided on 27 January 2009.[29] The applicants lived near a gold mine in Romania where sodium cyanide was used in the extraction process. In spite of an accident in 2000, when large quantities of cyanide were spilled into the environment, the authorities continued to allow the mining company to use the same extraction process. According to the Court's decision, Romania was obliged under Article 8 of the Convention (right to private and family life) to adopt precautionary measures to protect the complainants against health problems that might be caused by the gold mine. In summary, the absence of definitive scientific evidence about the existence of a causal link between exposure to sodium cyanide and asthma cannot justify any delay in adopting effective and proportionate measures aimed at preventing serious and irreversible harm.

The World Trade Organization (WTO) too was the scenario of a dispute on the precautionary principle. The controversy was about the use of growth hormones in beef cattle, as growth promoters are widely used in the United States and Canada, while they are

---

(27) Request for an Examination of the Situation in Accordance with Paragraph 63 of the Court's Judgment of 20 December 1974 in the nuclear tests (*New Zealand v. France*) case, Order of 22 September 1995, *ICJ Reports* 1995, p. 288.

(28) ICJ, *Hungary v. Slovakia*, Judgment of 25 September 1997, *ICJ Reports* 1997, p. 7.

(29) ECtHR, *Tatar v. Romania* (Appl. n° 67021/01), Judgment (Third Section), 27 January 2009.

forbidden in Europe because of the concerns that eating such beef could be carcinogenic. In January 1998 the WTO Appellate Body held that the EU was not entitled under the WTO SPS Agreement (Agreement on the Application of Sanitary and Phytosanitary Measures) to maintain its ban on the importation of meat from cattle treated with growth hormones. [30] The European Union argued that the precautionary principle had become "a general customary rule of international law", or at least "a general principle", whereas the United States and Canada maintained that it is just an "approach". Concerning the substantial issue, the US/Canada position was that the EU ban was not based on scientific principles, because there were no evidence that hormones pose a risk to human health. The WTO Appellate Body noted that the precautionary principle has been incorporated into Article 5.7 of the SPS Agreement, [31] but that it did not apply to the case because it cannot override the specific obligations resulting from Articles 5.1 and 5.2 of the SPS Agreement, which provide that SPS measures must be based on risk assessment and scientific evidence.

To sum up, what is the status of the precautionary principle in international law? Can it be regarded as a principle of customary international law? It should be remembered that the formation of customary international law requires the presence of two elements: the "quantitative" element of a stable and uniform international practice (*usus*), and the "qualitative" element of *opinio juris*. This latter element holds that States must act with the belief that the practice is undertaken to fulfill a legal duty. Some consider the precautionary principle to be already part of customary international law, because the mere fact of having been included in virtually every recently adopted treaty and policy document related to the protection of the environment is an evidence of *opinio juris*. [32] For

---

(30) WTO Appellate Body Report, *EC Measures Affecting Meat and Meat Products (Hormones), Complaint by the United States and Canada,* 13 February 1998.

(31) SPS Agreement, Article 5.7: "In cases where relevant scientific evidence is insufficient, a Member may provisionally adopt sanitary or phytosanitary measures on the basis of available pertinent information, including that from the relevant international organizations as well as from sanitary or phytosanitary measures applied by other Members. In such circumstances, Member shall seek to obtain the additional information necessary for a more objective assessment of the risk and review the sanitary or phytosanitary measures accordingly within a reasonable period of time".

(32) N. DE SADELEER, *Environmental Principles. From Political Slogans to Legal Rules,* Oxford, Oxford University Press, 2002, p. 319; J. CAMERON, "The Precautionary Principle", in G. SAMPSON and W. BRADNEE CHAMBERS (eds.), *Trade, Environment and the Millennium,* Hong Kong, United Nations University Press, 1999, p. 246; *id.,* "The

others, while the "quantitative" condition was already fulfilled, it is still doubtful that such a stable and uniform practice is followed by States with the conviction that it entails a legal duty.[33]

It is hard to answer this question, because it largely depends on a very subjective assessment, i.e. the *value* we attach to an international practice. In order to settle this issue we would need an explicit and formal recognition of the principle by an international court of justice. What is clear at present is that "the precautionary principle is *gradually asserting* itself as a principle of international law in the fields of environmental and health protection".[34] Even maintaining that is not yet born as a general principle of international law, it can be said that it is, at least, *in statu nascendi*.[35] The reference to the precautionary principle by a number of national and international courts and by international organizations shows that there is an international consensus on at least some of the basic elements characterizing the precautionary principle. In this sense it has been said that it is "a principle of international law on which decision makers and courts may rely in the same way that they may be influenced by the principle of sustainable development".[36]

II. – Conditions for the recourse
to the precautionary principle

The greatest merit of the precautionary principle is that it has succeeded to reflect the current public concern about the need to favor the protection of the public health and the environment over short term commercial interests at the time of choosing among different technological alternatives. From this perspective, this

---

precautionary principle: Core meaning, constitutional framework and procedures for implementation", in R. Harding and E. Fisher (eds.), *Perspectives on the Precautionary Principle,* Sidney, The Federation Press, 1999, p. 29-58; Dissenting opinion of Judge Weeramantry in the Second Nuclear Tests Case (*New Zealand v. France*), *ICJ Reports* 1995, p. 342.

(33) P.-M. Dupuy, "Le principe de précaution, règle émergente du droit international général", in C. Leben and J. Verhoeven (eds.), *Le principe de précaution. Aspects de droit international et communautaire,* Paris, Editions Panthéon-Assas, 2002, pp. 95-111; P. Martin-Bidou, "Le principe de précaution en droit international de l'environnement", *Revue Générale de Droit International Public,* 1999, n° 3, p. 663.

(34) EU Resolution on the Precautionary Principle of December 2000, Paragraph 3.

(35) P.-M. Dupuy, *op. cit.,* p. 95.

(36) P. Birnie and A. Boyle, *International Law and the Environment,* 2nd. ed., Oxford, Oxford University Press, 2002, p. 120.

principle challenges the hegemony of cost-benefit analysis to give place to a broader view in time and space in the interest of present and future generations.

Despite the criticism that the precautionary principle is in conflict with science or with technological innovations, the truth is that this new standard requires *more* and *different* science than traditionally used, because it encourages the exploration of *alternative modes of development* that are compatible with a good quality of life for present and future generations. In this respect, the precautionary principle calls for a greater imaginative effort in the development of safer and cleaner technologies. This principle does not offer however a catalogue of pre-determined solutions to the new dilemmas raised by scientific uncertainty, because it "is not an algorithm for making decisions".[37] As it is basically *prudence*, it is not able to provide a uniform answer to the difficult questions arising from the use of potentially harmful technologies.

In fact, the precautionary principle offers no more than a *broad guidance* to policy-makers to anticipate problems before they occur.[38] This is why some scholars include this principle among the so-called "rules of indeterminate content", which are flexible rules that cannot constrain those to whom they are addressed to adopt or to avoid one or another type of behavior in the same way as rules of determinate content.[39] In other words, we have to do with a new legal standard that only provides general guidance to policy decision-makers, who retain a wide margin of interpretation of what is the most adequate response to a particular problem.

Nevertheless, and precisely because of its *flexible* nature, it is important to specify the conditions that must be met for the adoption of precautionary measures. From the analysis of the above mentioned international legal instruments and policy documents, it is possible to draw the following conditions:

---

(37) P. SAUNDERS and M.W. HO, "The Precautionary Principle is Coherent," ISIS Paper 31 October 2000. Available at: http://www.i-sis.org.uk/precautionary-pr.php

(38) A. JORDAN and T. O'RIORDAN, "The Precautionary Principle in Contemporary Environmental Policy and Politics", in C. RAFFENSPERGER and J. TICKNER (eds.), *Protecting Public Health and the Environment. Implementing the Precautionary Principle,* Washington, Island Press, 1999, p. 18.

(39) N. DE SADELEER, *op. cit.,* p. 306-308; *Id.,* "Le statut juridique du principe de précaution", in F. EWALD, C. GOLLIER, and N. DE SADELEER, *op. cit.,* p. 77.

1. Uncertainty of risk
2. Scientific assessment of risk
3. Serious or irreversible damage
4. Proportionality of measures
5. A shifting burden of proof

A. – *Uncertainty of risk*

Much of the misunderstanding regarding the precautionary principle stems from a confusion between *precautionary* and *preventive* measures. Precaution goes beyond prevention in the sense that it urges policy makers to anticipate problems before they arise or before definitive scientific proof of risk is established. In the case of *prevention,* the harmfulness of the product or activity is well-known (for instance, the health risks associated with smoking, or the higher risks of having an accident when driving under the influence of alcohol) and the only thing that remains unknown is whether the damage will factually occur in a particular situation. In the case of *precaution,* even if there are reasons to believe that a particular product or activity may endanger human health or the environment, the *existence* itself of the risk cannot be fully demonstrated due to insufficient or inconclusive scientific data. Thus, precautionary measures are adopted *before* a clear causal link between a technology and a specific harm has been established. In other words, preventive measures face situations of *actual risk*, while precautionary measures respond to situations of *potential risk.*

B. – *Scientific assessment of risk*

Although the precautionary principle operates in the context of scientific uncertainty, it should be applied only when, on the basis of the best scientific advice available, there is *good reason* to believe that harmful effects might occur to public health or to the environment. Therefore, a purely hypothetical or imaginary risk, which is not based on any scientific indication for its possible occurrence, cannot justify the adoption of precautionary measures. The implementation of the precautionary principle "should start with a scientific evaluation, as complete as possible, and where possible, identifying at each stage the degree of scientific uncertainty".[40]

Certainly, the line between a reasonable precaution and an excessive one is thin and allows a wide margin of appreciation to decision-makers. But precisely for that reason and in order to prevent the recourse to this standard as a pretext for the adoption of protectionist measures, the potential risks must be defined and their likelihood evaluated to the greatest extent possible by independent experts in accordance with sound scientific principles. Thus, the implementation of the precautionary principle demands a clear functional separation between those responsible for the scientific evaluation of the risk (*risk assessment*) and those responsible for taking the final decision (*risk management*), who are the policy decision-makers, with the necessary involvement of all those having a direct interest in the issue, such as consumer groups and representatives of the industry.[41]

C. – *Serious or irreversible damage*

According to the international documents mentioned above, the recourse to the precautionary principle is justified in order to avert "threats of serious or irreversible damage". Therefore, the suspected damage should be *significant enough* to justify measures that might in some cases lead to restrictions on free trade and manufacture. In other words, the application of the precautionary principle requires the determination of a *threshold of non-negligible damage*. In general terms, it can be argued that damage is "serious" when it affects the life and health of individuals, vital natural resources (such as soil, water, and air), the preservation of species, the climate, and the balance of the ecosystem. But, leaving aside the damages that are unquestionably serious, it must be recognized that the determination of a more precise threshold of damage ultimately depends on the cultural context in which the measure is to be implemented. What is precautionary in one society may not appear as precautionary in another. The extinction of a

---

(40) European Commission, *Communication on the Precautionary Principle*, 2 February 2000, Paragraph 6.1.

(41) See EU Resolution on the Precautionary Principle of December 2000, Paragraph 11. In this regard, the precautionary principle creates a new model of relationship between scientists and decision-makers (see N. DE SADELEER, *op. cit*, p. 175-185).

rare and almost unknown species of butterfly may be perceived as a serious damage in a society and as insignificant in another, especially when the benefits expected from a technological project are considerable (e.g. a dam that will provide electricity and water for irrigation and for domestic water supply).

The *irreversible* nature of the damage may also justify the adoption of precautionary measures. Irreversibility is usually defined as involving environmental resources that cannot be replaced, or which could be restored but only in the long term or at a great expense.[42] It seems clear that an irreversible damage affecting the environment or the public health is also serious. Nevertheless, a serious damage is not necessarily irreversible: the often spectacular marine pollution caused by oil spills is largely reversible, but nobody doubts of its seriousness.[43] This is why the reference to both criteria as alternative ("or") rather than additive ("and") seems justified.[44] It should also be noted that in some cases the precautionary principle may also be applied when the harm is not serious or irreversible in the short term, but may become serious or irreversible in the long term, as a result of the cumulative effects of apparently innocuous activities or products.

D. – *Proportionality of measures*

Precautionary measures should be proportionate to seriousness of the threat. Not every situation of potential risk justifies any kind of precautionary measure. This requirement goes far beyond the classic cost-benefit analysis based on purely economic criteria and includes, more broadly, the socio-economic sacrifices required by the measure (e.g. the elimination of job positions), the efficacy of different possible options and their acceptability to the public.[45] These heterogeneous elements can certainly not be estimated alone by experts on risk assessment. They also must be considered from

---

(42) S. R. DOVERS and J. W. HANDMER, "Ignorance, sustainability, and the precautionary principle: Towards an analytical framework", in R. HARDING and E. FISHER (eds.), *op. cit.*, p. 172.

(43) N. DE SADELEER, *op. cit.*, p. 165.

(44) According to the French Environmental Code, the two conditions (seriousness *and* irreversibility) must be met for the adoption of precautionary measures. See footnote 14.

(45) See European Commission, *Communication on the Precautionary Principle*, 2 February 2000, Paragraph 6.3.4. See also Article 191.3 of the Treaty on European Union, which provides that "in preparing its policy on the environment, the Community shall take into account (...) the potential benefits and costs of action or lack of action".

a political perspective. It is true that precaution supposes giving priority to the protection of the public health and the environment over commercial and industrial interests. However, this approach does not pretend to exclude the examination of the overall cost to the community of action and lack of action, especially when there are different alternative responses to the potential risk. Let us recall that there is a wide range of precautionary measures available to the decision maker, such as reduction of exposure, monitoring, labeling, pre-market testing and research to reduce uncertainty. An outright ban on an activity or a product should be a last resort, when the potential damage is particularly serious and when it is more likely to happen. Another element of the proportionality is that precautionary measures should always be *provisional*, which means that they should be kept under active review and eventually modified when more precise information about the potential risks is available.

E. – *A shifting burden of proof*

According to traditional legal standards, public authorities have to demonstrate reasonable grounds, based on scientific evidence, to restrict the sale of certain products or the use of certain technologies. Thus, until proven wrong, proponents of technology can continue the activity in question. The precautionary principle challenges this traditional policy by proposing to shift the burden of proof towards those whose actions may seriously threaten the public health or the environment. This change is justified for various reasons. First, because hazard creators are those who will benefit economically from the products or activities in question, and therefore society has the right to expect them to assume, at least in part, the costs of the risk assessment. Second, because producers are in the best position to address issues about the potential risks of their activities. Moreover, this gives them a stronger reason than they ordinarily would have without that burden of proof to minimize any potential damage. [46]

Nevertheless, the reversal of the burden of proof should not be understood as requiring proponents of technology to provide

---

(46) C.F. CRANOR, "Asymmetric Information, the Precautionary Principle, and Burdens of Proofs", in C. RAFFENSPERGER and J. TICKNER (eds.), *Protecting Public Health and the Environment. Implementing the Precautionary Principle, op. cit.*, p. 86.

definitive evidence that their products or activities are harmless. The precautionary principle is not based on a "zero risk" approach but aims to achieve lower or more acceptable levels of risk.[47] Precisely in an area characterized by scientific uncertainty, it would be contradictory to require one of the parties involved in the issue to prove a total absence of risk. Moreover, since proving a negative is often impossible (this is why it is called *probatio diabolica*), this would in fact prevent any technological innovation.

Thus, the shift in the onus of proof should be understood in the sense that hazard creators must show that they have undertaken the necessary research to establish the nature and extent of any potential risk, having come to the conclusion that their products or activities offer an acceptable level of safety. Thereafter, it will be the responsibility of the political authorities to decide what course of action is the most appropriate, taking into account the conclusions of their own experts or specialized agencies. In sum, this shift in the *onus probandi* basically means that proponents of new technologies or products should play a more *active role* in the efforts aimed at improving the risk assessment.

Conclusion

The precautionary principle is essentially an appeal to caution addressed to policy makers who must take decisions about products or activities that could be seriously harmful to public health and the environment. The main originality of the precautionary principle is that measures are to be taken *before* definitive scientific evidence of the harmful effects becomes available. Another revolutionary feature of this principle is the requirement of *transparency* of the political decisions related to public health and environment, and even a direct participation of the public in the choice between the different available options. It also presupposes a more *global view* of our responsibilities towards humanity as a whole, including future generations

This emerging principle of international law does not offer a predetermined solution to every new problem raised by scientific uncertainty. On the contrary, it is just a *guiding principle* that

---

(47) UNESCO's World Commission on the Ethics of Scientific Knowledge and Technology (COMEST), *The Precautionary Principle*, Paris, UNESCO, 2005, p. 16.

provides certain criteria for determining the most reasonable course of action in confronting situations of potential risk. Far from being antithetical to science or to technological innovation, it aims to promote alternative modes of development (safer and cleaner technologies) in order to ensure a good quality of life for present and future generations.

Section II

THE DEVELOPMENT OF PRINCIPLES BY INTERNATIONAL ORGANIZATIONS

CHAPTER 4

THE UNESCO DECLARATION ON THE HUMAN GENOME AND HUMAN RIGHTS: AN INNOVATIVE INSTRUMENT

While genetic advances hold great promise for the diagnosis, prevention and treatment of diseases, they also raise significant ethical and legal questions, such as: How should genetic information be obtained, stored, and disclosed? How can the use of personal genetic data for discriminatory purposes be prevented? Do people have a right not to know their predisposition to genetically-related diseases? Can human genetic sequences be "owned" and commercialized? Can genetic technologies be used to "design" the humans of the future? The urgency to address the emerging questions relating to genetics became especially evident in the beginnings of the 1990s, after the launch of the Human Genome Project.[1]

In 1997, the United Nations Educational, Scientific and Culture Organization (UNESCO) made a first step towards addressing these questions with the adoption of the Universal Declaration on the Human Genome and Human Rights (UDHG). This instrument represents indeed a significant advance in international law. In fact, the Declaration is currently the most complete global initiative aimed at protecting human rights and human dignity with regard to genetic technologies.[2]

The involvement of UNESCO in this area can be explained by the fact that it is the only UN agency whose goal is directly

---

(1) The Human Genome Project (HGP) was an international project launched in 1990 by the US Department of Energy and the National Institutes of Health with the primary goals of identifying the approximately 20,000-25,000 genes in human DNA, and of determining the sequences of the chemical base pairs that make up human DNA. In addition to the United States, the international consortium comprised geneticists in the United Kingdom, France, China, Australia, and Japan. The project was declared completed in April 2003. See F. S. COLLINS et al., "A vision for the future of genomics research", Nature, 2003, vol. 422, pp. 835-847.

(2) A.L. TAYLOR, "Globalization and Biotechnology: UNESCO and an International Strategy to Advance Human Rights and Public Health", American Journal of Law and Medicine, 1999, vol. 25, n° 4, pp. 479-541.

related to both scientific and human rights issues. Indeed, UNESCO is the only global intergovernmental organization which has been involved in standard-setting activity at the intersection of sciences, ethics and human rights for decades.[3] As Harmon notes, "few international organizations could claim the same level of experience and knowledge regarding science, its cross-cultural impact, and its significance for human rights".[4] In addition, none of UNESCO's competitors in the human rights field "represent any measurable improvement in representation or structure, nor do the instruments they have drafted represent any significant improvement in form or content".[5]

It should be remembered that, according to Article 1 of its Constitution, the main purpose of UNESCO is "to contribute to peace and security by promoting collaboration among nations through education, science and culture in order to further universal respect for justice, the rule of law and human rights and fundamental freedoms". Bearing in mind that the enterprise of laying down common standards in this sensitive area requires an open dialogue between cultures, UNESCO is the ideal body for the development of such common criteria, since it is an organization where different cultural traditions are represented.

A circumstantial factor that also contributed to the involvement of the organization in the field of bioethics, and particularly in genetics, was the personal concern about these issues of the then UNESCO's Director General Federico Mayor Zaragoza, who had been himself a professor of biochemistry. In 1993 Dr. Mayor Zaragoza took the initiative of establishing the UNESCO International Bioethics Committee (IBC), whose first task was to consider the opportunity of elaborating an international instrument on the ethical and legal implications of genetic developments. After four years of consultation and discussion between representatives of a large number of countries, the Legal Commission, which was charged with the task of developing proposals, concluded that UNESCO should gradually develop global political consensus for international norms relating to the human genome. As an initial

---

(3) For a more detailed discussion about the involvement of UNESCO in bioethics, see chapter 5.

(4) S. HARMON, "The Significance of UNESCO's Universal Declaration on the Human Genome and Human Rights", *SCRIPT-ed. A Journal of Law, Technology, and Society*, 2005, vol. 2, n° 1, pp. 18-47. Available at http://www.law.ed.ac.uk/ahrb/script-ed/

(5) S. Harmon, *Ibid.*

step, they proposed the development of a non-binding document. The draft, finalized by a committee of governmental experts from 81 Member States, was adopted by the UNESCO General Conference on 11 November 1997 and endorsed by the UN General Assembly in 1998.

The UDHG, like all declaration, is a soft law (i.e. nonbinding) instrument. The drafters of the document were aware of the fact that if they had decided to prepare a binding instrument (i.e. a convention or treaty), it would never have been approved because of the sensitive nature of bioethical issues. The nonbinding nature of the Declaration does not mean that it is legally irrelevant. Its immediate purpose is not to not to *oblige* States to adopt a number of minimum standards relating to genetics, but to *encourage* them to do so. The UDHG intends to model the evolution of customary law and eventually to develop into more detailed standards.

The mere fact that the Declaration has been unanimously approved by the community of States shows the broad acceptance of its principles. As Francioni points out:

> "It is difficult to deny that the Declaration has already affected the *opinio iuris* of the international community. Its text emanates from the UNESCO General Conference, a body of universal character, where states can express their opinion and cast their vote. Its adoption by acclamation was preceded by extensive consultations and technical preparatory work, with the participation of civil society and the epistemic community with all its scientific, legal, ethical components. No objections or reservations were put on the record at the time of its adoption. After its adoption, the UN General Assembly endorsed its text by Resolution of 9 December 1998".[6]

I. – THE HUMAN GENOME AS A COMMON HERITAGE OF HUMANKIND

The general objective of the UDHG is to ensure that the new possibilities which have emerged due to genetic developments will not be used in a way that would be contrary to human rights

---

(6)   F. FRANCIONI, "Genetic Resources, Biotechnology and Human Rights: the International Legal Framework", in F. FRANCIONI (ed.), *Biotechnologies and International Human Rights,* Oxford, Hart Publishing, 2007, p. 12.

and human dignity. Within this context, the central concern of the drafters of the Declaration was to protect the human genome from improper manipulations that may endanger the identity and physical integrity of future generations. To respond to this concern, the Declaration labels the human genome as "the heritage of humanity" (Article 1). This notion is inspired by the international law concept of "common heritage of humanity," which holds that the world's natural and cultural resources should be held in trust for future generations and be protected from exploitation by nation States or corporations.

According to international law theorists, the notion of common heritage of humankind is composed by five elements: first, the common heritage cannot be appropriated; second, it requires a system of management in which all users have a right to share; third, it implies an active sharing of benefits; fourth, it supposes reservation for peaceful purposes; and fifth, it implies reservation for future generations. [7]

The inclusion of the human genome into this category has a "revolutionary character" in international law. [8] However, UNESCO is not alone in this approach, as other organizations have also approved similar statements, such as the Human Genome Organization (HUGO), [9] and the Council of Europe. [10]

The UDHG marks the first time that humanity as such is regarded by the international community of States as a common heritage to be protected. [11] Certainly the notion of "crimes against humanity", the clearest example being genocide, has been part of international law since the end of the Second World War. However, the category of crimes against humanity aims to prevent particularly odious offenses committed against specific

---

(7) See K. BASLAR, *The Concept of the Common Heritage of Mankind in International Law,* The Hague, Nijhoff, 1998, p. 81.

(8) See statement by M. BEDJAOUI, in UNESCO, *Proceedings of the Fourth Session of the IBC* (3-4 October 1996), vol. I, Paris, UNESCO, 1997, p. 47.

(9) The Human Genome Organization (HUGO), "Statement on the Principled Conduct of Genetics Research", March 21, 1996, in *Eubios Journal of Asian and International Bioethics,* 1996, n° 6, pp. 59-60. Available at: http://www.eubios.info/HUGO.htm; idem, "Statement on Benefit Sharing", April 9, 2000, in *Eubios Journal of Asian and International Bioethics,* 2000, n° 10, pp. 70-72. Available at: http://www.eubios.info/BENSHARE.htm

(10) Council of Europe (Parliamentary Assembly), Recommendation 1512(2001). Protection of the Human Genome by the Council of Europe, April 25, 2001.

(11) Ch. BYK, "A Map to a New Treasure Island: The Human Genome and the Concept of Common Heritage", *Journal of Medicine and Philosophy,* 1998, vol. 23, n° 3, p. 235.

ethnic, social or religious groups. It does not cover the integrity of humanity as such (i.e. its genetic structure), which is precisely the main purpose of the Declaration. [12]

It is true that the final version of the UDHG did not adopt the complete expression "common heritage of humankind" which was included in the previous drafts of the document. Instead, Article 1 provides that "in a symbolic sense, it [the genome] is the heritage of humanity". This change was not intended to weaken the purpose of Article 1, but to respond to the concern of some Member States that the notion of "common heritage of humankind" could be interpreted in the sense of a "common property", and facilitate the appropriation of human genetic sequences by multinational companies. [13] There was also the fear that the category of "common heritage of humankind" could pose a threat to individual rights and be used as an entitlement for enhancing the human gene pool for eugenic purposes. [14] Therefore, the use of the qualifying phrase "in a symbolic sense" intends to stress the radical difference between the genetic structure of humankind and other "external" goods that have been included in this category in the past (sea beds, the outer space, the moon, etc.). In sum, the label of "heritage of humanity", when applied to the human genome, aims first, to emphasize that genetic research engages the responsibility of the whole of humanity and that its results should benefit present and future generations, [15] and second, that the human genome is not suitable for appropriation by any state or corporation. [16]

However, contrary to how it might seem, the description of the human genome as the "heritage of humanity" does not rule out the patenting of human genetic sequences. The drafters of the Declaration were explicit on this point. [17] In fact, the Declaration

---

(12) B. MATHIEU, *Génome humain et droits fondamentaux*, Paris, Economica, 2000, p. 92.

(13) B.M. KNOPPERS, *Le génome humain: patrimoine commun de l'Humanité ?*, Montreal, Fides, 1999, p. 35; F. FRANCIONI, *op. cit.*, p. 11.

(14) L. HONNEFELDER, "Stellungnahme aus ethischer Perspektive zur 'Allgemeinen Erklärung über das menschliche Genom und die Menschenrechte' der UNESCO", *Jahrbuch für Wissenschaft und Ethik*, 1998, n° 3, p. 226.

(15) H. GROS ESPIELL, "Introduction", in UNESCO, *Genèse de la Déclaration universelle sur le génome humain et les droits de l'homme*, Paris, UNESCO, 1999, p. 3.

(16) R. IDA, "Human Genome as Common Heritage of Humankind", in N. FUJIKI and D. MACER (eds.), *Bioethics in Asia*, Tsukuba, Eubios Ethics Institute, 1998, pp. 59-63.

(17) H. GROS ESPIELL, *op. cit.*, p. 1. See also P. OSSORIO, "The human genome as a common heritage: common sense or legal nonsense?", *Journal of Law, Medicine and Ethics*, 2007, vol. 35, n° 3, pp. 425-439.

did not seek to take a stand on the patenting debate because of the complexity of the issue and the many interests at stake. In addition, whereas UNESCO has competence in the area of copyright, it is the World Intellectual Property Organization (WIPO) and the World Trade Organization (WTO) that are responsible for establishing regulations concerning patents.[18]

The only UDHG provision that relates to the patenting issue merely stipulates that "the human genome in *its natural state* shall not give rise to financial gains" (Article 4). Given that the ethical and legal problems are raised precisely by the patenting of human genetic sequences in something other than their natural form, and that this kind of patent is currently permitted in the United States and Europe, it is obvious that the authors of the Declaration have preferred not to address this controversial issue. Nevertheless, in an attempt to clarify the situation, the UNESCO International Bioethics Committee approved in 2001 an "Advice on the patentability of the human genome" emphasizing that "there are strong ethical grounds for excluding the human genome from patentability". The Advice also recommends "that the World Trade Organization (WTO), in its review of the TRIPS Agreement,[19] clarify that, in accordance with the provision of Article 27(2), the human genome is not patentable on the basis of the public interest considerations set out therein, in particular, public order, morality and the protection of human life and health".

II. – HUMAN DIGNITY AND GENETIC DATA

The most impressive feature of the UDHG is the central role it gives to the notion of human dignity, which is referred to 15 times in the document.[20] No other international instrument had ever before focused so much on this notion. Dignity may indeed be considered as a "central and self-standing value" of the Declaration.[21]

---

(18) N. LENOIR, "UNESCO, Genetics and Human Rights", *Kennedy Institute of Ethics Journal,* 1997, vol. 7, issue 1, p. 34

(19) TRIPS Agreement means "Agreement on Trade Related Aspects of Intellectual Property Rights".

(20) See Preamble, Articles 1, 2, 6, 10, 11, 12, 15, 21, and 24.

(21) S. HARMON, "Ethical rhetoric: genomics and the moral content of UNESCO's 'universal' declarations", *Journal of Medical Ethics,* 2008, vol. 28, n° 11, p. e24.

Articles 1 and 2 of the Declaration adopt the notion of human dignity as a basis for their provisions, the former, with regard to humanity as such, and the latter, with regard to individuals. According to Article 1, "the human genome underlies the fundamental unity of all members of the human family, as well as the recognition of their inherent dignity and diversity." The wording of this Article is ambiguous, because it could be interpreted in a crude materialistic way, as if the incommensurable value we attach to every human person were solely based on the DNA that characterizes the human species. However, this interpretation would be contrary to the intent of the drafters, as it results from other provisions of the Declaration, in particular from Article 2(b), which provides that "dignity makes it imperative not to reduce individuals to their genetic characteristics and to respect their uniqueness and diversity". In other words, the unity of the human family and the dignity of the human person are expressions of philosophical ideals that transcend biology. Human dignity is not the result of a particular combination of DNA, even of a very complex one. For the same reason, the theories of genetic determinism, which intend to explain every aspect of the human personality and behavior on the basis of specific genes, are rejected by Article 2.

What is then the purpose of Article 1? This provision aims to stress that, from a genetic perspective, there is a deep interrelatedness between all members of the human species. Human genes are common to all past, present and future generations because the same genetic structure is inherited from one generation to the next. [22] Therefore, and independently of any changes that might naturally occur in the very long term —which are recognized by Article 3—, each individual inherits the same basic genetic structure of those that preceded him or her. Thus, it is fully appropriate to consider the human genome as a "common heritage of humanity" and therefore to protect it from irresponsible manipulations.

In addition to this, the "genetic unity" of the human species contributes to reaffirm the principle of equality between individuals. In this respect, Article 2(a) states that "everyone has a right to respect for their dignity and for their rights regardless

---

(22) E. AGIUS, "Patenting Life: Our Responsibilities to Present and Future Generations", in E. AGIUS and S. BUSUTTIL (eds.), *Germ-Line Intervention and our Responsibilities to Future Generations*, Dordrecht, Kluwer, 1998, p. 76.

of their genetic characteristics". This provision reminds us that the principle of equal value of all human beings does not admit any exception due to predisposition to genetic diseases that might be discovered among individuals. In other words, each human being, as a holder of intrinsic dignity, is entitled to inalienable rights, which are the same for all, regardless of their genetic make-up.

The scope of Article 2(a) is however larger than the prohibition of discriminative practices for genetic reasons, which are explicitly forbidden by Article 6. Its purpose is to reaffirm a vision of a society founded on the principle of equality, which is one of the pillars of democratic societies. More precisely, it attempts to prevent the division of society into haves and have-nots, as this would constitute a disastrous consequence of genetic knowledge. [23]

The conditions for genetic testing, in particular, the informed consent of the individual and a prior assessment of potential risks and benefits, are addressed by Article 5 of the Declaration. This provision embodies a fundamental principle of medical ethics according to which a biomedical intervention may only be carried out after the patient has been informed of its purpose, nature, risks and consequences, and has freely consented to it.

For an informed consent to be valid, the patient must be considered competent to make the decision. If the individual is unable to consent, the intervention may only be carried out if it offers him or her a direct health benefit and subject to the authorization prescribed by law. An exception is set out in Article 5(d), which states that an intervention without direct benefit may only be carried out on a person unable to consent so long as the individual is exposed to a minimal risk and a minimal burden. Interestingly, the Declaration adopts in this regard exactly the same wording used by Article 17.2 of the European Convention on Human Rights and Biomedicine.

Article 5(c) recognizes both the right to know and the right not to know the results of genetic tests. In this regard, the UDHG is in conformity with other international instruments which recognize both rights. [24] Concerning the right not to know, it must be pointed out that it is not an absolute but a relative right, in the sense that

---

(23) M.J. MEHLMAN and J.R. BOTKIN, *Access to the Genome. The Challenge to Equality*, Washington DC, Georgetown University Press, 1998.

(24) See Principle 8 in chapter 1 of this book.

it may be restricted when disclosure to the individual is necessary to prevent a serious harm to family members, for instance, because preventive or therapeutic measures are available. In this regard, Article 9 of the Declaration makes it clear that the principles governing informed consent and confidentiality, far from being absolute, can be limited by law "for compelling reasons within the bounds of public international law and the international law of human rights".

Article 7 aims to emphasize that the general duty of confidentiality that doctors have towards their patients also includes genetic information. As a result of the widespread access to genetic tests, an increasing volume of genetic information about individuals becomes more and more available. While this information has the potential to provide health benefits, it may also be a source of harm to people. One of the major concerns is the potential misuse of genetic information resulting in any kind of discrimination or stigmatization.

Regulation of the duty of confidentiality in this specific area is needed because of the uniqueness of genetic information. First, genetic tests have implications not only for the individuals who have been tested, but also for their blood relatives. Secondly, this information has an almost uniquely identifying nature, including its capacity to confirm, deny or reveal family relationships. Thirdly, genetic tests not only concern the past, but also the future of people and therefore, may have a significant predictive value. Fourthly, genetic information could be obtained from a very small amount of material, possibly secured without the donor's consent. [25]

From the patient's point of view, there is a corresponding "right to genetic privacy". This right may be regarded as deriving from the more general "right to privacy", recognized by the Universal Declaration of Human Rights (Article 12) and the International Covenant on Civil and Political Rights (Article 17). The difficult question is to determine what practice may constitute a violation of the right to genetic privacy. Article 7 of the UDHG does not provide any guidance in this respect. However, the International Declaration on Human Genetic Data approved by UNESCO in 2003, which may be regarded as an extension of the UDHG, sets out specific rules

---

(25) J. K. MASON, A. McCALL SMITH, and G. LAURIE, *Law and Medical Ethics*, 8th ed., New York, Oxford University Press, 2011, p. 209.

for the collection, use and storage of human biological samples and genetic data. It covers various issues relating to informed consent in genetics; confidentiality of personal genetic information; genetic discrimination; anonymization of genetic data; population-based genetic studies; the right not to know one's genetic make-up; genetic counseling; international solidarity in genetic research, and benefit sharing.

III. – HUMAN CLONING AND GERM-LINE INTERVENTIONS

The UDHG was initially conceived to only include general guiding principles. However, the text that was finally adopted has two provisions that are exceptionally precise as they declare two concretes practices (human reproductive cloning and germ-line interventions) as "contrary to human dignity" (Articles 11 and 24). The preliminary draft presented by the IBC in December 1996 did not include these two provisions, which were incorporated during the last round of discussions held by governmental experts. The last-minute ban on cloning can be explained by the circumstance that the announcement of the successful cloning of the sheep Dolly was made in February 1997. This announcement raised worldwide political concern over the possibility that this technique could be used to produce genetically identical human beings. Consequently, governmental representatives of a number of countries insisted on including a formal condemnation of human cloning in the UNESCO Declaration. [26]

The term "cloning" is used in the UDHG to indicate the conception of an entire individual (i.e. an embryo) by "nuclear transfer". This technology involves transferring the nucleus from a cell of an adult person into an oocyte of another whose own nucleus has been removed. If successful, this procedure leads to the formation of an embryo, genetically identical to the cell's donor. Depending on the destination of the embryo, a distinction is made between "reproductive cloning" and "therapeutic cloning". In the first case, the embryo is transferred to a woman's uterus, beginning a process that may lead eventually to the birth of a baby. In the second case, the embryo's inner mass is harvested

---

(26) See the preliminary draft declaration in: UNESCO, *Proceedings of the Fourth Session of the IBC* (3-4 October 1996), vol. I, Paris, UNESCO, 1997, pp. 67-71.

and grown in culture for subsequent derivation of embryonic stem cells, which may have therapeutic applications in the treatment of serious degenerative disorders, like Alzheimer or Parkinson's diseases. Although the ethical and legal debate has predominantly focused on reproductive cloning, the acceptability of therapeutic cloning is also controversial, because it relates to the debate on the use of human embryos for research purposes.

Article 11 appears to be focused on reproductive cloning. Several objections have been leveled against this procedure. First, it gives those who create the clone unjustifiable powers over that individual, who would be deliberately produced (i.e. instrumentalized) to resemble another (alive or dead) individual just to satisfy the desires of the potential parents.[27] A second objection is that, although human beings are not reducible to their genes, the fact is that, given their physical similarity to the "original" and between themselves, clones would seem like replacements. This situation would undermine their quest for individual identity as the procedure make them appear, to themselves and to society, as replaceable "copies", rather than irreplaceable originals. A third objection is that the cloned child would be produced without genetic parents and would therefore be irreversibly deprived of the possibility to relate his or her existence to a "father" and a "mother" in the normal sense of these terms. Finally, even on purely scientific grounds, human reproductive cloning is a dangerous procedure: data on the reproductive cloning of animals demonstrate that only a small percentage of attempts are successful; that many of the clones die during gestation; that newborn clones are often abnormal or die; and that the procedures may carry serious risks for the mother. Such devastating consequences in humans make the procedure unacceptable.[28]

The UDHG's ban on germ-line interventions is also in conformity with most ethical and legal guidelines on the topic. The objections raised against this practice stem from the fact that, unlike the alteration of the genes in the somatic cells, which affects only the individual treated, any alteration in the germ cells (gametes)

---

(27) In 2005, the UN approved a Declaration on Human Cloning, which calls on Member States "to prohibit all forms of human cloning inasmuch as they are incompatible with human dignity and the protection of human life" (Paragraph d).
(28) US National Academy of Sciences, *Scientific and Medical Aspects of Human Reproductive Cloning*, 2002.

or in the early embryo before the stage of differentiation would be passed to the next generation. The arguments against germ-line interventions are of different nature, depending whether the purpose of the procedure is therapeutic or eugenic:

a. The objection to germ-line interventions for therapeutic purposes (i.e. for preventing the transmission of diseases) is not based on intrinsic ethical arguments, but on the risks of irreversible harm to future generations. We are increasingly aware that the interaction between genes, environment and diseases is extremely complex. Even genes that are clearly associated with diseases in one context can be beneficial in others. Thus, the most basic prudence demands that germ-line modification, which at present risks bringing more damage than benefits, should not be undertaken.[29] This is a direct application of the "precautionary principle". In addition to this, it is important to recognize that, in practice, any presumed beneficial effects of germ-line interventions would affect only a relatively few number of cases. This is why the idea of eliminating "harmful" genes from the entire human population is more utopian than real. Such a global result, if ever, could only be realized over a time scale of thousands of years and with recourse to massive coercive programs, which would be morally and legally unacceptable.

b. The objections to germ-line interventions for eugenic purposes are not merely based on risk prevention but are more substantial. They are grounded on the notion that we do not have the right to predetermine the characteristics of future individuals. This means that people should be free to develop their potentialities without being biologically conditioned by the particular conceptions of "good" and "bad" human traits that were dominant at the time of those who preceded them. In other words, genetics should not become the instrument for an intergenerational tyranny.[30] A second objection is that the procedure would profoundly affect our own self-perception as "persons", that is, as autonomous

---

(29)   CIOMS (Council for International Organizations of Medical Sciences). *Declaration of Inuyama on Human Genome Mapping, Genetic Screening and Gene Therapy*, 1990; British Medical Association, *Human Genetics. Choice and Responsibility*, Oxford, Oxford University Press, 1998, p. 198.

(30)   H. JONAS, *Technik, Medizin und Ethik*, Frankfurt, Insel, 1985, pp. 162-203.

beings, leading to consider ourselves as mere "things" or biological artifacts designed by others. A third objection is that even if social agreement on the "ideal" human being is reached, this will inevitably reinforce discrimination and stigmatization of those who do not fall into the accepted standards of genetically desirable traits.

IV. – SOLIDARITY AND INTERNATIONAL COOPERATION

Articles 17 to 19 of the UDHG deal with the issue of solidarity and international cooperation in the field of genetics. Such solidarity should take place on two different levels. First, inside each country, governments should help individuals, families and groups particularly vulnerable to genetic diseases. Second, at the international level, solidarity should be especially promoted to help developing countries to benefit from the results of genetic research. This issue needs to be addressed without delay because, without solidarity, genetic advances threaten to widen rather than narrow the gap between the rich and the poor and between developed and developing countries. Therefore, the aim behind the Declaration is that all humanity will benefit from scientific advances in this area. This means, in particular, that industrialized countries will share the results of genetic research in a free and open manner with the world's areas most in need of such scientific assistance.

Article 17 stipulates that States should take the appropriate measures to ensure the promotion of active solidarity towards individuals, families and population groups who are particularly vulnerable to genetic diseases or disabilities. In particular, States should encourage research on identification, prevention and treatment of genetic diseases, especially rare diseases, as well as endemic diseases affecting a significant number of world's population.

Article 18 provides that States should "make every effort (...) to continue fostering the international dissemination of scientific knowledge" in three specific areas: first, the human genome as a matter of general knowledge; second, human diversity; and third, in genetic research. This Article also stresses the need for scientific and cultural cooperation in this area between industrialized and developing countries.

Article 19(a) enumerates the measures that States should adopt in the context of international cooperation with developing countries. The aims of such measures are: to assess the risks and benefits pertaining to research on the human genome to be carried out and abuse to be prevented; to strengthen the capacity of developing countries to carry out research in biology and genetics, taking into account their specific problems; to allow the results and benefits of research, which is primarily carried out in the industrialized countries, could be used to promote economic and social progress for all; and to favor the free exchange of scientific knowledge and information in the areas of biology, genetics and medicine.

V. – INTERNATIONAL BIOETHICS COMMITTEE (IBC)

Article 24 of the UDHG institutionalizes the International Bioethics Committee (IBC), which had worked on an ad hoc basis since its creation in 1993. In 1997, the 29/C Resolution 17, adopted at the 29th session of the UNESCO General Conference invited the Director General to convene, as soon as possible, an ad hoc working group to redefine the integration and tasks of the Committee. The working group, composed by representatives from several Member States, met in Paris from 25 to 27 March 1998. As a result of that meeting, the working group drew up the Draft Statutes of the IBC, which were then adopted by the UNESCO Executive Board.

It is interesting to note that the IBC is currently the only global body dealing with the ethical and legal dilemmas posed by biomedical advances. According to Article 24 of the UDHG, the IBC is responsible for following up the principles set out in the Declaration and for "the further examination of issues raised by their applications and by the evolution of the technologies in question". To accomplish this task, the IBC is entitled to make recommendations, to organize appropriate consultations with parties concerned and to give advice concerning the follow up of the Declaration, "in particular regarding the identification of practices that can be contrary to human dignity".

Since the approval of its Statutes in 1998, the IBC consists of 36 experts from different countries and various disciplines, such as medicine, genetics, law and philosophy, who are appointed by the Director General. The IBC members are in a peculiar situation because they are proposed by the governments of the countries they come from, but they do not officially represent their governments. Once appointed, the IBC members act independently and on their personal capacity and conscience. On the other hand, the Committee's composition is based on the assumption that its members represent in some way the socio-cultural values from the countries they come from. Precisely for this reason the Statutes provide that the Director General, when making his choice, shall take into account the "cultural diversity" and "balanced geographical representation" of the IBC members (Article 3).

The IBC members only meet once a year. Nevertheless, the main substantial activity is developed through various working groups, which deal with specific issues and elaborate drafts reports, opinions and recommendations, to be then submitted to the plenary of the IBC. Among the reports produced by the IBC, the following can be mentioned: The Use of Embryonic Stem Cells in Therapeutic Research (2001); Report on Ethics, Intellectual Property and Genomics (2002); Human Genetic Data: Preliminary Study by the IBC on its Collection, Processing, Storage and Use (2002); Report on Pre-implantation Genetic Diagnosis and Germ-line Intervention (2003); Report on the Possibility of Elaborating a Universal Instrument on Bioethics (2003); Report on Consent (2008); Report on Human Cloning and International Governance (2009); Report on Social Responsibility and Health (2010); and The Principle of Respect for Human Vulnerability and Personal Integrity (2013).

The IBC Statutes adopted in 1998 created a parallel body, the Intergovernmental Bioethics Committee (IGBC), which comprises 36 representatives of Member States, who are elected by UNESCO General Conference (Article 11). Unlike the IBC, which is a body of independent experts, the IGBC aims to reflect the official position of States on the various bioethical issues under discussion. The States' interest in being directly involved in the discussions is perfectly understandable if one considers that UNESCO is an intergovernmental organization.

According to the Statutes, the main task of the IGBC consists in the examination of the opinions and recommendations of the IBC, particularly those relating to the follow-up of the UDHG. The IBC and the Director-General are then informed of the IGBC's point of view so that the Director-General may transmit this information, along with the opinions and recommendations of the IBC, to the Member States, the Executive Board and the General Conference of UNESCO. The IGBC may also make proposals for appropriate action regarding the IBC's opinions and recommendations. The IGBC met at least once every two years.

VI. – IMPLEMENTATION OF THE DECLARATION

The UDHG stresses that the primary responsibility for the implementation of the principles adopted lies principally with the States. In this respect, it could be said that the Declaration is ultimately no more than a call to attention to the community of States, so as to make them aware of the ethical and legal issues raised by genetic technologies.

The Declaration stresses that the governmental initiative is not restricted to the adoption of adequate legislation, but includes "all appropriate measures" aimed at the implementation of the principles adopted (Articles 20 and 22). Among the tasks assigned to States are: to foster the conditions genetic research (Articles 14 and 15); to facilitate the establishment of independent, multidisciplinary and pluralist ethics committees (Article 16); to promote the practice of solidarity towards individuals, families and population groups who are particularly vulnerable to genetic diseases (Article 17); to foster international dissemination of scientific knowledge in the field of genetics (Article 18); to encourage the sharing of benefits resulting from genetic research (Article 19); to promote bioethics education (Article 20), and to facilitate a free and open discussion on these issues in society at large (Article 21).

Although the main responsibility for the implementation of the Declaration lies with the States, the IBC has considered it necessary to suggest some concrete ways of action. For that purpose, it drew up the "Guidelines for the Implementation of the Universal Declaration on the Human Genome and Human Rights", which were approved by the Intergovernmental Bioethics Committee (IGBC) and endorsed on 16 November 1999 by the General Conference of UNESCO.

Among the various objectives and activities proposed in the Guidelines are: the dissemination of the principles set forth in the Declaration, which presupposes the translation of the

Declaration into the largest possible number of languages, as well as the organization of seminars, symposia and conferences on topics relating to the Declaration; the publishing of books on the subject; the preparation of programs of education and training in bioethics; the preparation of information kits and audio-visual materials on specific subjects of bioethics; the promotion of an exchange of ideas regarding bioethical issues at the international and regional level, in order to identify practices that could be contrary to human dignity; the effective cooperation with other international organizations dealing with the issues covered by the Declaration. Regarding this latter point, the Guidelines suggested the creation of an interagency committee within the United Nations system open to other intergovernmental organizations and responsible for the coordination of activities related to bioethics.

Following this latter suggestion, all UN agencies interested in bioethics decided in 2003 to establish the UN Inter-Agency Committee on Bioethics (UNIACB). Since then, the UNIACB has met yearly to foster better cooperation and coordination between intergovernmental organizations in this field. The committee includes the World Health Organization (WHO), the UN High Commissioner on Human Rights (UNHCHR), the International Labor Organization (ILO), and the World Intellectual Property Organization (WIPO), in addition to UNESCO.

CONCLUSION

The UDHG is the first international human rights instrument specifically dealing with the challenges posed by increasing access to human genetic information. It represents a significant effort of the international community in the search for common legal standards in this area, where the interests of present and future generations are at stake. The main originality of the Declaration is the fact that, for the first time, the human genetic structure is regarded as a common heritage that needs to be protected against improper manipulation.

The broad support that the Declaration has received from of the international community is a valuable asset and makes the instrument a good starting point for more detailed regulations at the international and domestic level. The 2003 International

Declaration on Human Genetic Data embodies a first extension of the UDHG to issues concerning the collection, handling and storage of human genetic data. Time will be necessary to assess the real impact of both instruments on national policies relating to genetics.

CHAPTER 5

GLOBAL BIOETHICS AT UNESCO: THE UNIVERSAL DECLARATION ON BIOETHICS AND HUMAN RIGHTS

Former UN Secretary General Dag Hammarskjöld often said that the UN was not created to take humanity to heaven but to save it from hell. [1] By this aphorism, he meant that, although the UN has its weaknesses and limitations, it has an irreplaceable role in our conflictive world by promoting peace, respect for human rights, and social and economic development. The UN is imperfect because it mirrors the world, with its divisions and disagreements. Nevertheless, it is the only forum where humanity speaks in its entirety and where it is able to express, as best as it can, its collective hopes and convictions.

If we consider the specific domain of bioethics, Hammarskjöld's dictum could be applied to UN agencies that are engaged in this specialty. Although they are not able to guarantee that biomedical advances will always be used for the greatest well-being of humanity, they can at least contribute to prevent their use in a manner that would be contrary to human dignity and human rights. Among the means UN agencies use to achieve their goals (in this case, the promotion of responsible biomedical research and clinical practice), the standard setting activity is one of the most salient ones.

It is precisely in such a context and with such an expectation that the Universal Declaration on Bioethics and Human Rights (UDBHR) was adopted on 19 October 2005, at the 33rd session of the General Conference of UN Education, Scientific and Cultural Organization (UNESCO) by representatives of 191 countries. This chapter aims to outline the main features of this document

---

(1) "Address at the University of California Convocation. 13 May 1954", in A.W. CORDIER and W.FOOTE (eds.), *Public Papers of the Secretaries General of the United Nations,* vol. II, New York, Columbia University Press, 1972, p. 301.

before responding to two general charges that have been leveled at UNESCO's bioethical activities and at this particular declaration.

I. – THE UNIVERSAL DECLARATION ON BIOETHICS AND HUMAN RIGHTS

It is important to stress that the drafting of the UDBHR was based upon the experience of a group of experts from different countries who sat in the International Bioethics Committee (IBC) of UNESCO. The drafting process was preceded by a report of an IBC working group that considered the feasibility of such an instrument. The group, chaired by Professors Leonardo De Castro (Philippines) and Giovanni Berlinguer (Italy), concluded by supporting the initiative and affirming the need to develop "a worldwide common sense in order to foster understanding and cohesion in relation to new ethical categories and new practical possibilities emerging from science and technology".[2] With this background in mind, the IBC, chaired at the time by Mrs Michèle Jean (Canada), prepared the preliminary draft declaration, after almost 2 years of discussions and public consultations with governmental and non-governmental organizations. Justice Michael Kirby (Australia) chaired the drafting group, which was open to all IBC members. To ensure transparency in the process, the successive versions of the document were posted on the internet as they were being developed. In January 2005, the draft was examined by the Intergovernmental Bioethics Committee (IGBC) and, finally, it was revised in two successive meetings of governmental representatives, who introduced several amendments.[3]

Despite the great number of existing international guidelines, statements and declarations relating to bioethics, the UDBHR makes its own significant contribution to this topic. It is worth mentioning that this is the first international legal, though non-binding, instrument that comprehensively deals with the linkage

---

(2) UNESCO IBC. *Report on the Possibility of Elaborating a Universal Instrument on Bioethics*, 13 June 2003.

(3) See a detailed account of the drafting process of the Declaration in H. TEN HAVE and M. JEAN, "Introduction", in H. TEN HAVE and M. JEAN (eds.), *The UNESCO Universal Declaration on Bioethics and Human Rights. Background, principles and application*, Paris, UNESCO, 2009, pp. 17-55. See also http://www.unesco.org/bioethics and then click on "Bioethics and Human Rights".

between human rights and bioethics. Regardless of the weaknesses inherent to this kind of instrument, the very fact that virtually all States reached an agreement in this sensitive area is a major achievement in itself. It should be noted that most international declarations and guidelines in this topic do not have the status of legal instruments because they have been issued by non-governmental organizations such as the World Medical Association (WMA), the Council for International Organizations of Medical Sciences (CIOMS), and other academic or professional institutions. Other documents, although adopted by intergovernmental bodies, cover only specific bioethical issues, such as the UN Declaration on Human Cloning of 2005 and the UNESCO Universal Declaration on the Human Genome and Human Rights of 1997, or are regional but not global instruments, such as the European Convention on Human Rights and Biomedicine of 1997.

The Declaration includes in its Section II important substantive principles relating to bioethics. The principles are to be understood as "complementary and interrelated" (Article 26). This means that the relationship between them has been conceived as non-hierarchical.[4] The complexity of bioethical dilemmas in real life makes it impossible to establish a clear priority of some principles over others. In case of conflict between two or more principles, the priority of one of them will be determined taken into account the particular circumstances of each case, as well as the cultural specificities of each society. However, this does not preclude that the principle of respect for human dignity, due to its inescapable overarching nature, will always play a role in every bioethical decision.

The substantive principles enumerated in the Declaration are the following:

- Respect for human dignity and human rights (Article 3.1)
- Priority of the individual's interests and welfare over the sole interest of science or society (Article 3.2)
- Beneficence and non-maleficence (Article 4)
- Autonomy (Article 5)
- Informed consent (Article 6)

---

(4) E. GEFENAS, "Article 26. Interrelation and complementarity of the principles", in H. TEN HAVE and M. JEAN (eds.), *op. cit.*, pp. 327-333.

- Protection of persons unable to consent (Article 7)
- Special attention to vulnerable persons (Article 8)
- Privacy and confidentiality (Article 9)
- Equality, justice and equity (Article 10)
- Non-discrimination and non-stigmatization (Article 11)
- Respect for cultural diversity and pluralism (Article 12)
- Solidarity and cooperation (Article 13)
- Access to health care and essential medicines (Article 14)
- Benefit sharing (Article 15)
- Protection of future generations (Article 16)
- Protection of the environment, the biosphere and biodiversity (Article 17)

Section III ("Application of the principles") is devoted to principles of a more procedural nature such as:

- The requirement for professionalism, honesty, integrity and transparency in the decision-making process regarding bioethical issues (Article 18)
- The need to establish independent, multidisciplinary and pluralist ethics committees (Article 19)
- The call for an appropriate risk assessment and management in the biomedical field (Article 20)
- The need for justice in transnational research (Article 21)

II. – THREE BASIC FEATURES OF THE DECLARATION

Three basic features of the UDBHR should be emphasized. Firstly, the principles it contains are formulated in very general terms; the declaration does not give almost any definition of their precise meaning (which are only provided, to some extent, by the explanatory memorandum that accompanied the preliminary draft declaration). This methodology, which may surprise some, is in fact a common practice in law. Except for very technical terms, lawmakers normally prefer not to define precisely most of the words they use. Rather, they tend to leave that task to common understanding and, ultimately, to courts' interpretation, in order not to be constricted in advance by rigid definitions. In the case of the UNESCO Declaration, this strategy can also be explained for practical reasons, because it would have been impossible to reach a global agreement on the precise meaning of terms like "human dignity", "autonomy", "justice", "benefit", "harm", or "solidarity", which have a long philosophical history and are, to some extent, conditioned by cultural factors. Thus, the generality in the formulation of the principles can ultimately be justified by the need to find a balance between the universalism of some bioethical norms and the respect for cultural diversity.

A second feature of the declaration relates to the nature of UNESCO itself as an intergovernmental body. This should not be forgotten because it would be a mistake to assess with purely academic criteria an instrument like the declaration, which is not the exclusive product of academic work, but rather a kind of compromise between a theoretical conceptualization made by experts and what is practically achievable given the political choices of governments.[5] We need to keep in mind that governments, not independent experts, have the last word in every declaration or convention issued by UN agencies. This is not to say that the quality of such instruments is necessarily affected negatively by the requirements of governments. It is true that the IBC draft was more precise on several points than the version adopted by governmental representatives, as Justice Kirby himself has admitted.[6] Personally, I regret for instance that the recognition of the precautionary principle as a risk management tool for public health purposes has been removed from the final version of the document. On the other hand, I acknowledge that some of the amendments introduced by governmental representatives really improved the declaration, such as the more detailed provision regarding research on persons unable to consent (Article 7) and the reference to human vulnerability (Article 8). What I intend to argue here is that the approach to bioethics followed by international instruments such as the 2005 Declaration is not

---

(5) See F. BAYLIS, "Global Norms in Bioethics. Problems and Prospects", in R. GREEN, A. DONOVAN, and S. JAUSS (eds), *Global Bioethics. Issues of Conscience for the Twenty-First Century*, Oxford, Clarendon Press, 2008, pp. 323-339.

(6) M. KIRBY, "UNESCO and Universal Principles on Bioethics: What's next?", in Twelfth session of the International Bioethics Committee (IBC), *Abstracts or Texts of the Presentations of Speakers*, Paris, UNESCO, 2005, pp. 121-136.

only an academic but also a political one, and therefore must be assessed with different, broader criteria.

A third important feature of the UDBHR is its non-binding nature. Like any declaration adopted by UN agencies, the Declaration makes up part of the so-called soft law instruments, that is, instruments that are weaker than conventions because they are not intended to oblige States to enact enforceable rules inspired by the common standards, but to encourage them to do so. This procedure permits States to take on commitments they otherwise would not have taken, because they assume just political obligations that are not legally binding. Furthermore, soft law instruments present the advantage of permitting countries to gradually become familiar with the proposed standards before they are confronted with the adoption of enforceable rules, or with the development of a binding instrument– that is, a convention. [7] In addition, it is helpful to remember that, if the same non-binding standards are reaffirmed in successive declarations, in the course of time they may become binding rules, in the form of customary law and jurisprudential criteria, as it happened with the Universal Declaration of Human Rights of 1948.

III. – Unesco's involvement in bioethics

Two serious criticisms have been leveled against the UDBHR. The most fundamental one concerns the involvement of UNESCO itself in bioethics. The other one relates to the use of a human rights framework to achieve common standards in this discipline.

Regarding the first charge, it has been advanced that UNESCO would be in an "obvious attempt at meddling in the professional domain of another UN agency, WHO" and that "it is entirely unclear why UNESCO should concern itself with such a matter".[8] Similarly, it has been argued that "UNESCO is clearly

---

(7) N. Lenoir and B. Mathieu, *Les normes internationales de la bioéthique*, 2nd ed., Paris, PUF, 2004.

(8) U. Schuklenk and W. Landman, "From the Editors", *Developing World Bioethics*, Special Issue: Reflections on the UNESCO Draft Declaration on Bioethics and Human Rights, 2005, vol. 5, n° 3, pp. iii-vi.

overstepping its mandate and encroaching on that of the World Health Organization (WHO)."[9]

In response to these objections, it should be noted, first of all, that a clear-cut division of competences between UN agencies is not always as simple as it might seem at first glance, especially in issues that are at the intersection of different disciplines. Secondly, what is really unclear is why the only UN agency specialized in sciences (both natural and human sciences) and having served for decades as a forum for philosophical discussion on cross-cultural issues would be excluded from making any contribution to the normative guidance of life sciences. It is helpful to remember here that the purpose of UNESCO is, according to its Constitution, to promote "collaboration among nations through education, science and culture in order to further universal respect for justice, for the rule of law and for the human rights and fundamental freedoms".[10] Is it really then surprising that an organization with such a mission might be interested in the establishment of some common standards for bioethics?

In addition, it is noteworthy that, since its foundation in the aftermath of the Second World War, UNESCO has been associated in the preparation of some 28 international conventions, 12 declarations and about 31 recommendations, including the Convention against Discrimination in Education (1960), the Universal Copyright Convention (1971), the Convention concerning the Protection of the World Cultural and Natural Heritage (1972), the Declaration on Principles of International Cultural Cooperation (1966), the Declaration on Race and Racial Prejudice (1978), the Declaration on the Responsibilities of the Present Generations Towards Future Generations (1997), the Recommendation on the Status of Scientific Researchers (1974), the Recommendation concerning the International Standardization of Statistics on Science and Technology (1978), and the Convention on the Protection and Promotion of the Diversity of Cultural Expressions (2005). Why could the international community not take advantage of this long experience regarding sciences, its cross-cultural effect,

---

(9) J. WILLIAMS "UNESCO's Proposed Declaration on Bioethics and Human Rights. A Bland Compromise. *Developing World Bioethics.* Special Issue: Reflections on the UNESCO Draft Declaration on Bioethics and Human Rights, 2005, vol. 5, n° 3, pp. 210-215.

(10) UNESCO Constitution, 16 November 1945 (Article 1).

and its significance for human rights in order to set up global bioethical standards?

This is especially to be considered when one reflects on the fact that the UNESCO's strong involvement in bioethics is not new. It dates back at least to 1993, when the International Bioethics Committee (IBC) was established on the initiative of Dr Federico Mayor Zaragoza, Director-General of the organization at that time. The first task of the Committee was the preparation of the preliminary draft of the Universal Declaration on the Human Genome and Human Rights, adopted in 1997. Thereafter, the IBC worked on the drafting of the International Declaration on Human Genetic Data, finalized in 2003. Additionally, since its creation, the IBC produced about 19 reports on various bioethical issues such as genetic counseling, ethics and neurosciences, confidentiality and genetic data, embryonic stem cells, ethics of intellectual property and genomics, and preimplantation genetic diagnosis and germ-line interventions. In light of this, the question is: Are there many other global intergovernmental organizations that could claim the same level of experience at the intersection of sciences, ethics and human rights? The answer, at least at this stage, seems to be "no".[11]

In reality, a conflict of competence between two or more UN agencies interested in this matter would be as absurd as a dispute between a philosopher and a physician over the "ownership" of bioethics. Of course, bioethics does not belong in exclusivity to any of them. As it is by its very nature an interdisciplinary specialty, all related professions (and likewise, all related UN bodies) have the right –and the duty– to make their specific contribution to this emerging and complex domain. It is noteworthy that UN agencies have already recognized their mutual interest in this matter and, on this ground, have established in 2003 the UN Inter-Agency Committee on Bioethics (UNIACB). Since then, the UNIACB has met once a year to improve the coordination of activities in this area.

Concerning the WHO, there is no doubt that, as it is the specialized UN agency for health, it is to have a major role in the standard-setting activities in biomedical sciences. Nevertheless, as

---

(11)   A. TAYLOR, "Globalization and Biotechnology: UNESCO and an International Strategy to Advance Human Rights and Public Health", *American Journal of Law and Medicine*, 1999, vol. 25, n° 4, pp. 479-542; S. HARMON, "The Significance of UNESCO's Universal Declaration on the Human Genome and Human Rights," *SCRIPT-ed. A Journal of Law, Technology, and Society*, 2005, vol. 2, n° 1, pp. 18-47. Available at http://www.law.ed.ac.uk/ahrb/script-ed/

some experts have pointed out, clearly, WHO cannot manage this task alone, for the following reasons:

- The field is growing, rapidly encompassing more diverse and complex concerns, due to its interdisciplinary nature.
- WHO has very limited experience in international health lawmaking.
- Such a task would deplete the organization's limited resources and undermine its ability to fulfill its well-established and essential international health functions.
- Member States are highly unlikely to limit their autonomy and freedom by granting to WHO alone such an expansive new mandate.
- Decentralization of the international lawmaking enterprise presents great advantages that cannot be ignored. [12]

Furthermore, beyond the fact that UNESCO and WHO are, after all, composed of the same Member States, there is a more substantial reason for favoring simultaneous participation of both UN agencies in the topic of bioethics: their standard-setting activities operate at different levels. While UNESCO tends to produce general normative frameworks of a predominantly philosophical and legal nature, WHO's guidelines are usually more technical and focused on specific health-related issues. Therefore, as the approach followed by both organizations is different, their respective engagement in this matter can perfectly coexist. Moreover, it is to be hoped that sincere efforts will be made to stimulate greater cooperation between both UN agencies, which could be extremely fruitful given their complementary expertise in this domain.

IV. – THE USE OF A HUMAN RIGHTS FRAMEWORK

Another criticism of the UDBHR relates to the use of a human rights framework. It has been reasoned that "human dignity and human rights, both strong features of European enlightenment philosophy, pervades this Declaration" and that UNESCO "chose an ideological framework (human rights) that does not feature particularly prominently in professional bioethical analyses". [13]

---

(12) A. TAYLOR, *Ibid.*
(13) U. SCHUKLENK and W. LANDMAN, *op. cit.*, p. iv.

In my opinion, these objections are misplaced. It is true that the current notion of human rights has its immediate origins in the insights of the European Enlightenment philosophers. But this historical circumstance is not a good enough reason to discard the idea that human beings have inherent rights, just as it would not be enough to argue that Mozart or Bach were Europeans to deny the extraordinary beauty of their works. The relevant question is whether the notion that every human being has an inherent dignity and inherent rights makes sense, no matter where this idea comes from. My personal view on this is that the current widespread conviction that people have unconditional rights simply by virtue of their humanity is one of the major achievements of human civilization, much more important than any scientific or technical development.

This does not mean to ignore the fact that in many Western nations there has been an excessive emphasis on rights and freedoms for the individual, sometimes to the detriment of family and community values, which are of paramount importance to most non-Western societies. Neither does it mean to disregard the great philosophical discussion concerning whether, or how, the recognition of universal human rights can be conciliated with cultural diversity. However, the truth is that today these controversies have lost much of their practical significance—firstly, because of the increasing number of non-Western States that are party to international human rights treaties; secondly, because human rights emerge from international law instruments with sufficient flexibility to be compatible with full respect for cultural diversity. Far from imposing one cultural standard, human rights instruments set up a minimum protection necessary for human dignity. [14]

It has to be noted that, paradoxically, some of the most severe criticisms of the universality of human rights come from Western scholars. According to Amartya Sen, these views are often based on a misconception of non-Western (largely Asian) societies, as if people in these countries had little or no interest in their rights and were only concerned with issues of social order and discipline (misconception which is of course well exploited by authoritarian regimes...). [15] In this connection, it is revealing that the only two

---

(14)   J. DONNELLY, *Universal Human Rights in Theory and Practice*, Ithaca, NY, Cornell University Press, 1989.

(15)   A. SEN, "Universal Truths: Human Rights and the Westernizing Illusion", *Harvard International Review*, 1998, vol. 20, n° 3, pp. 40-43.

papers written by non-Western authors that appear in a journal special issue on the UDBHR openly contradict the pessimistic view of the journal editorial and have a favorable opinion of the human rights approach adopted by UNESCO.[16] One of these papers even argues that the universality of the principles of human dignity and human rights... is not emphasized enough by the Declaration![17]

Furthermore, the objection that the bioethical discourse is alien to a human rights approach is simply contrary to the facts: many, if not most international policy documents relating to bioethics issued during the last decades are framed on a rights-based approach and attach utmost importance to the notion of human dignity. A paradigmatic example in this respect is the Council of Europe's Convention on Human Rights and Biomedicine. Nevertheless, this is not an exclusive feature of Western instruments. Indeed, about 200 worldwide declarations, guidelines, recommendations, opinions and codes relating to bioethics adopted by very different institutions could be cited in support of this assertion.[18] For illustrative purposes, a few examples can be mentioned. Firstly, the famous WMA Declaration of Helsinki on Research Involving Human Subjects (1964/2008), which repeatedly refers to the rights of participants and regards the protection of human dignity of research subjects as the first basic principle for medical research, along with respect for their life, health and privacy.[19] Secondly, the UN Commission on Human Rights Resolution 2003/69 of 25 April 2003 entitled "Human rights and bioethics", which strongly insists on the need to ensure the protection of human rights in this field and makes a recurring appeal to the "dignity of the human being". Thirdly, the various Statements of the Ethics Committee of the Human Genome Organization (HUGO), which emphasize the need to "adhere to international norms of human rights" and to accept and uphold "human dignity and freedom".[20]

---

(16) A. ASAI and S. OE, "A valuable up-to-date compendium of bioethical knowledge", *Developing World Bioethics* (Special Issue: Reflections on the UNESCO Draft Declaration on Bioethics and Human Rights), 2005, vol. 5, n° 3, pp. 216-219; N. JING-BAO, "Cultural values embodying universal norms: A critique of a popular assumption about cultures and human rights", *ibid.*, pp. 251-257.

(17) N. JING-BAO, *Ibid.*

(18) See University of Minnesota Human Rights Library, "Bioethics and Human Rights Links" at: http://www1.umn.edu/humanrts/links/bioethics.html

(19) World Medical Association (WMA), *Handbook of WMA Policies,* 2012. Available at: http://www.wma.net/en/30publications/10policies/index.html

(20) See http://www.hugo-international.org/comm_hugoethicscommittee.php

Why this reliance on human rights to set up global bioethical standards?

The first obvious reason is that, as biomedical activities deal with the most basic human prerogatives such as the right to life and to physical integrity, it is perfectly sound to have recourse to the umbrella of international human rights law to ensure their protection. Despite all its weaknesses, the existing human rights system, with its extensive body of international standards and wide range of mechanisms, represents a considerable achievement of our time. This is why it would be strange that a human rights framework could not be used to protect individuals from harm in the biomedical specialty.

A more practical reason for this phenomenon is that "there are few mechanisms available other than human rights to function as a global ethical foundation, a Weltethik."[21] In other words, "the human rights framework provides a more useful approach for analyzing and responding to modern public health challenges than any framework thus far available within the biomedical tradition".[22]

Regarding the idea of human dignity, it can be said that it already plays a key role in international bioethics by providing the ultimate rationale for the norms relating to this discipline. Certainly, the appeal to human dignity in international law is neither new nor specific to instruments dealing with biomedical issues. On the contrary, this notion is at the cornerstone of the universal human rights movement that emerged after the Second World War. However, recent international biolegal instruments emphasize the importance of human dignity in a more powerful way than traditional human rights law. Indeed, the contrast between the background role assigned to human dignity in international human rights instruments and the foreground role assigned to it in international biolaw could not be more impressive.[23]

The UDBHR inscribes itself in this trend when it places at the top of its principles that of "human dignity, human rights and

(21) D. THOMASMA, "Proposing a New Agenda: Bioethics and International Human Rights", Cambridge Quarterly of Healthcare Ethics, 2001, vol. 10, n° 3, pp. 299-310.

(22) J. MANN, "Health and human rights. Protecting human rights is essential for promoting health", British Medical Journal, 1996, vol. 312, pp. 924-925.

(23) D. BEYLEVELD and R. BROWNSWORD, Human Dignity in Bioethics and Biolaw. Oxford, Oxford University Press, 2002.

fundamental freedoms" (Article 3.1). Similarly, when it provides that "the interests and welfare of the individual should have priority over the sole interest of science or society" (Article 3.2). This provision, which has surprisingly also been criticized, [24] is in fact included, with almost the same wording, in several international documents relating to bioethics such as the WMA Declaration of Helsinki (Article 6), the European Convention on Human Rights and Biomedicine (Article 2) and the UNESCO Declaration on the Human Genome and Human Rights (Article 10). Through this provision, the UDBHR sought to emphasize a direct corollary of the principle of human dignity: that people should not simply become instruments for the benefit of science, because science is not an absolute, but only a means at the service of the human person. It is indeed hard to see what other bioethical principle could be more fundamental than this one.

CONCLUSION

The UDBHR is an important step in the search for global bioethical standards. Like any international instrument of this kind, it is not free from shortcomings. However, in view of the sensitive nature of bioethical issues, the simple fact that virtually all States reached a comprehensive agreement in this discipline is a major achievement in itself. Certainly, most of the declaration's principles are not original; they are derived from several existing international documents. This is why the greatest merit of this instrument is to gather those principles and to integrate them into a human rights framework. In sum, the purpose of the declaration is not to invent new bioethical principles or to provide the definitive solution to the growing list of bioethical dilemmas. Its main goal is much more modest: to assemble some basic standards in order to help States in their efforts to promote responsible biomedical research and clinical practice, in conformity with the principles of international human rights law.

---

(24) U. SCHUKLENK and W. LANDMAN, *op. cit.*, p. v.

CHAPTER 6

THE BIOMEDICINE CONVENTION: A EUROPEAN LEGAL FRAMEWORK AT THE INTERSECTION OF HUMAN RIGHTS AND HEALTH LAW

The Council of Europe's Convention on Human Rights and Biomedicine ("Biomedicine Convention" or "Oviedo Convention") is the best current example of how to promote the protection of human rights in the biomedical field at a transnational level. The importance of this instrument lies in the fact that it is *the first comprehensive multilateral treaty addressing issues at the intersection of human rights and biomedicine.* Certainly, some of the principles it establishes were already included in more general terms in previous international human rights treaties, such as the European Convention on Human Rights of 1950, and the International Covenant on Civil and Political Rights of 1966 (e.g. the rights to life and to physical integrity and privacy, the freedom from inhuman or degrading treatment and from any form of discrimination). However, the Oviedo Convention marks the first time that these rights have been developed and brought together in one single multilateral binding instrument entirely devoted to biomedical issues. This chapter aims first, to give an overview of the history of the Biomedicine Convention (I), second, to present its general features (II), and finally to summarize its provisions (III).

I. – HISTORY OF THE BIOMEDICINE CONVENTION

The Biomedicine Convention is the result of a long-term effort by the Council of Europe, which is an intergovernmental organization composed by 47 States, and whose goal is the promotion of human rights and democratic values in the European context.[1] This

---

(1) The Council of Europe should not be mistaken for the European Union. While the first is an intergovernmental organization, the second is the result of a real integration process of 27 European countries, which delegate some of their sovereign powers to the common institutions.

organization was responsible for the elaboration of the European Convention on Human Rights of 1950 and thereafter for the implementation of a series of mechanisms aimed at ensuring the respect for human rights in the Old Continent.

The Council of Europe has actually been involved in addressing bioethical issues since the 1980s. From that time, the Parliamentary Assembly, the deliberative body of the Council of Europe, as well as the Committee of Ministers, composed by all Foreign Ministers of Member States, developed an intense activity in this field. These different bodies have issued a number of recommendations on topics such as genetic engineering, embryo research, patient's rights, health databases, and common measures for the prevention and treatment of some specific diseases. A major step forward was taken in 1985 with the establishment of a multidisciplinary body, the Ad Hoc Committee of Experts on Bioethics (CAHBI), whose main task would be to give advice on the legal gaps that may result from the rapid development of biomedical sciences. The immediate origin of the Convention dates back to the 17th Conference of European Ministers of Justice in June 1990. On the proposal of Ms. Catherine Lalumière, the then Secretary General of the Council of Europe, it was decided to elaborate a Framework Convention on Bioethics. The Ad Hoc Committee of Experts on Bioethics (CAHBI) was charged with the task of examining "the possibility of preparing a framework convention, open to non-member States, setting out common general standards for the protection of the human person in the context of the development of the biomedical sciences."[2] On that basis, the Parliamentary Assembly recommended in June 1991 the elaboration of a "framework convention comprising a main text with general principles and additional protocols on specific aspects."[3] In September of that same year, the CAHBI was entrusted by the Committee of Ministers with the responsibility of preparing the draft Convention and additional protocols.[4]

In March 1992 the CAHBI (later renamed Steering Committee on Bioethics, CDBI), set up a Working Group, chaired by Dr. Michael Abrams (United Kingdom), with the mandate to prepare the draft

---

(2)   17th Conference of European Ministers of Justice, Istanbul, 5-7 June 1990, Resolution N° 3 on bioethics.

(3)   Parliamentary Assembly, Recommendation 1160 (1991).

(4)   See Explanatory Report to the Convention on Human Rights and Biomedicine, paragraph 4.

Convention. In July 1992 the Working Group presented a first draft instrument, which was submitted to public consultation and for an opinion to the Parliamentary Assembly. Taking account of this opinion and of comments of governmental experts, the CDBI produced a final draft on 7 June 1996 and submitted it again to the Parliamentary Assembly. The latter recommended on 26 September 1996 the adoption, with some amendments, of the revised draft.[5] The Convention was finally adopted by the Committee of Ministers on 19 November 1996 and opened for signature in Oviedo, Spain, on 4 April 1997. After the fifth ratification, that of Spain, the Convention entered into force in December 1999.

So far, the Biomedicine Convention has been signed by 35 countries and ratified by 29 of them, where it has entered into effect.[6] The countries which have ratified the Convention are: Albania, Bosnia and Herzegovina, Bulgaria, Croatia, Cyprus, Czech Republic, Denmark, Estonia, Finland, France, Georgia, Greece, Hungary, Iceland, Latvia, Lithuania, Macedonia, Moldova, Montenegro, Norway, Portugal, Romania, San Marino, Serbia, Slovakia, Slovenia, Spain, Switzerland, and Turkey. Notably absent from the Convention are the United Kingdom and Germany. These absences are due to different, and even opposed reasons. While the United Kingdom considered the Convention to be too restrictive, Germany viewed it to be too permissive, especially in the most controversial issues such as embryo research and non-therapeutic research on people unable to consent.[7]

II. – FEATURES OF THE BIOMEDICINE CONVENTION

The features of the Biomedicine Convention can be summarized as follows:

1. *Binding instrument.* The chief merit of the Council of Europe's efforts in this field is that it obtained the ratification by a large number of European States of the first multilateral binding instrument entirely devoted to biomedical issues. The

---

(5) Parliamentary Assembly, Opinion N° 198 (1996) on the draft convention for the protection of human rights and dignity of the human being with regard to the application of biology and medicine: convention on human rights and biomedicine.

(6) The updated list of ratifications is available at: http://www.coe.int/bioethics/

(7) M. DE WAECHTER, "The European Convention on Bioethics", *Hastings Center Report*, 1997, n° 1, pp. 13-23.

treaty nature of the European instrument means that States having ratified it are obliged to introduce implementing legislation to bring their national laws into conformity with its principles. When one considers that the (understandable) tendency of other international organizations involved in bioethics to develop soft law instruments, one cannot but be impressed by the remarkable accomplishment by the Council of Europe of having produced a legally binding instrument in this sensitive field.

2. Comprehensive approach to bioethics. The Biomedicine Convention is not focused on a specific area of bioethics (for instance, genetics, medical research, etc.) but has been conceived as a framework of principles covering the whole biomedical field. The term "biomedicine" is not used by the Convention in its narrow sense meaning that branch of medical science that applies biological principles to clinical practice, but in a very broad sense, which refers to all applications of biological and medical sciences to human beings.[8] In this regard, the Convention has the same broad approach to bioethics as the Universal Declaration on Bioethics and Human Rights of 2005. It is also important to note that this is the first time that a multilateral treaty (i.e. a binding instrument) comprehensively addresses the linkage between human rights and biomedicine. As Henriette Roscam Abbing has pointed out, the Oviedo Convention is "Health Law Convention 'pur sang' (...). Its elaboration in one single Convention is important and unique".[9] This broad approach reflects the ambitious scope of this instrument and represents, along with its binding nature, the most original feature of the Convention.

3. Framework instrument. The Biomedicine Convention has been conceived as a "framework" treaty containing general principles which have to be developed by additional protocols on specific issues.[10] Despite the apparent vagueness of the Convention's provisions, the approach followed is the most realistic way to facilitate the development of more detailed rules in the long term.

---

(8) See Explanatory Report to the Biomedicine Convention, para. 10.

(9) "In essence, therefore, the Treaty is a Health Law Convention 'pur sang' (...). Its elaboration in one single Convention is important and unique" (H. ROSCAM ABBING, "The Convention on Human Rights and Biomedicine. An Appraisal of the Council of Europe Convention", *European Journal of Health Law*, 1998, n° 5, p. 379).

(10) So far, four additional protocols have been adopted: on human cloning (1998), on organ transplantation (2002), on biomedical research (2004), and on genetic testing for health purposes (2008).

The strategy has consisted of identifying the most basic principles that are accepted by all involved countries in order to create a solid basis for further developments. Without this gradual approach, the Convention would have probably never been adopted. This is why, despite all the ambiguities and vagueness inherent to this kind of agreements, the Biomedicine Convention represents a historical step in the development of a European biomedical law.[11]

4. Minimum common standards. The Biomedicine Convention does not aim to provide precise responses to the most complex bioethical dilemmas such as the status of the human embryo, pre-implantation genetic diagnosis, abortion or assisted suicide. These controversial issues are left to each country's discretion[12]. Rather, the Convention's aim is to bring together the most basic biolegal principles on which European countries agree. This minimalist approach arises from mere *practical* reasons, and is not to be interpreted as a deliberate preference for a "liberal" bioethics, or as an encouragement of those practices that are not explicitly prohibited. A misunderstanding in this regard has been at the root of the criticisms that have been leveled against the Convention, especially in Germany, where it was regarded as too permissive on issues such as embryo research and non-therapeutic interventions on persons unable to consent,[13] or as incompatible with the Nuremberg Code and the Declaration of Helsinki.[14] The pragmatic, not ideological nature of the minimalist approach is evident if one considers that according to Article 27 each State has the right to establish stricter regulations. This provision illustrates that the Convention does not attempt to provide the maximum level of

---

(11) *Cf.* H.-L. SCHREIBER, "The European Bioethics Convention : Legal Aspects", in A. SCHAUER, H.-L. SCHREIBER, Z. RYN, J. ANDRES (eds.), *Ethics in Medicine,* Göttingen, Vandenhoeck & Ruprecht, 2001, p. 242.

(12) In this regard, the judgment of the European Court of Human Rights (Second Section) of 28 August 2012 that condemned Italy for not allowing preimplantation genetic diagnosis (PGD) is problematic since it disregards the margin of appreciation that Member States enjoy in the most contentious bioethical issues (*Costa and Pavan v. Italy*, Application 54270/10).

(13) *Cf.* K. BRAUN, *Menschenwürde und Biomedizin. Zum philosophischen Diskurs der Bioethik,* Frankfurt, Campus, 2000; M. EMMRICH (ed.), *Im Zeit der Bio-Macht. 25 Jahre Gentechnik: eine kritische Bilanz,* Frankfurt, Mabuse Verlag, 1999.

(14) B.-R. KERN, "Die Bioethik-Konvention des Europarates: Bioethik versus Arztrecht?", *Medizinrecht,* 1998, n° 11, p. 485; M. EMMRICH, "Abschied vom Nürnberger Kodex. Bioethik-Konvention: Der Triumph des utilitaristischen Denkens", in M. EMMRICH (ed.), *Im Zeitalter der Bio-Macht,* Frankfurt, Mabuse, 1999, p. 341-348.

due protection of persons' rights, but just the minimum protection resulting from the consensus among European countries.[15]

Although it would have been preferable to reach a more detailed consensus on many topics, the fact is that because of the disparity of positions regarding the more controversial issues, it was impossible to do more than was done.[16] Nevertheless, the agreement that has been reached, even if apparently vague, has an important effect. States which have ratified the Convention are not allowed to adopt a lower level of protection of human rights when they decide to legislate on this matter. Rather, they are obliged to introduce into their national law the common rules adopted in the Convention at the very least. When one considers that many European countries do not yet have specific legal provisions on several bioethical issues, the importance of setting out such a set of minimum standards should not be underestimated.[17]

5. Implementation at the national level. The responsibility for the development and effective implementation of the Convention's norms lies primarily with each State. Article 1.2 is explicit in this respect: "Each Party shall take in its internal law the necessary measures to give effect to the provisions of this Convention". Consequently, the common standards set up by the Council of Europe need the cooperation of States for their implementation. In fact, the influence of the Convention on the national legislation of a number of European countries is already evident.[18] Anyway, some of the Convention's provisions are specific enough to have

---

(15) V. BELLVER CAPELLA, "Pasos hacia una bioética universal: el Convenio Europeo sobre Derechos Humanos y Biomedicina", in C.M. ROMEO CASABONA (ed.), *El Convenio de Derechos Humanos y Biomedicina. Su entrada en vigor en el ordenamiento jurídico español,* Granada, Comares, 2002, p. 55.

(16) *Cf.* H.-L. SCHREIBER: "The Convention is, I believe, a notable milestone. It is not, of course, without its flaws. It neglects important matters (...). Still, given the degree to which opinions on basic ethical issues are divided and indeterminate, it is remarkable that the Convention has been able to establish as much as it has" ("The European Bioethics Convention: Legal Aspects", in A. SCHAUER; H.-L. SCHREIBER; Z. RYN; J. ANDRES, (ed.), *Ethics in Medicine,* Göttingen, Vandenhoeck & Ruprecht, 2001, p. 242); H. NYS, "La Convención Europea de Bioética. Objetivos, principios rectores y posibles limitaciones", *Law and Human Genome Review,* 2000, n°12, p. 86.

(17) *Cf.* L. HONNEFELDER, "Biomedizinische Ethik und Globalisierung. Zur Problematik völkerrechtlicher Grenzziehung am Beispiel der Menschenrechtskonvention zur Biomedizin des Europarates", in A. ESER (ed.), *Biomedizin und Menschenrechte,* Frankfurt, Knecht, 1999, p. 55; J. TAUPITZ and H. SCHELLING, "Mindestandards als realistische Möglichkeit. Rechtliche Gesichtspunkte in deutscher und internationaler Perspektive", in A. ESER (ed.), *ibid.,* p. 95.

(18) H. NYS, L. STULTIËNS, P. BORRY, T. GOFFIN, and K. DIERICKX, "Patient rights in EU Member States after the ratification of the Convention on Human Rights and Biomedicine", *Health Policy,* 2007, vol. 83, n°s 2-3, pp. 223-235.

self-executing effect (that is, that courts could rely on them to decide cases without the need for further national implementation measures). This is the case, for instance, regarding those norms concerning individual rights such as the right to information and the requirement of informed consent.[19] Also prohibition norms, such as the ban on genetic discrimination (Art. 11) and on sex selection in the reproductive techniques (Art. 14) have immediate efficacy.[20] Nevertheless, in the absence of penal sanctions, which are determined by each State (Article 25), their efficacy is restricted to civil and administrative remedies.

6. Judicial protection by national courts. Article 23 requires the States to "provide appropriate judicial protection to prevent or to put a stop to an unlawful infringement of the rights and principles" set forth in the Convention. Once again, the primary responsibility for ensuring the rights guaranteed by the Convention rests with each State, which should adapt their legislation to the Convention's provisions, and guarantee the effective implementation of such norms through an efficient and independent judicial system. In this respect, it is important to note that individuals do not have the right to bring proceedings before the European Court of Human Rights (ECtHR) on the exclusive ground of an infringement of the Biomedicine Convention. Some scholars view the lack of a judicial complaint procedure as a major weakness of the Convention.[21] Article 29 only allows the possibility of requesting an advisory opinion from the ECtHR on legal questions concerning the interpretation of the Convention. Moreover, only States Parties and the Steering Committee on Bioethics (CDBI) are entitled to request such advisory opinions. An individuals' access to the ECtHR would only be possible if the facts on which the request is based constitute, in addition to an infringement of the Biomedicine Convention, a violation of one

---

(19) Explanatory Report to the Biomedicine Convention, para. 20; L. Dubouis, "La Convention sur les droits de l'homme et la biomédecine", *Revue de droit sanitaire et social,* 1998, n° 2, p. 217 ; P. Fraisseix, "La protection de la dignité de la personne et de l'espèce humaines dans le domaine de la biomédecine: l'exemple de la Convention d'Oviedo", *Revue internationale de droit comparé,* 2000, n° 2, p. 390.

(20) R. O'Connell and S. Gevers, "Fixed Point in a Changing Age? The Council of Europe, Human Rights, and the Regulation of New health Technologies", in M.L. Flear, A.-M. Farrell, T. K. Hervey, T. Murphy (eds.), *European Law and New Health Technologies,* Oxford, Oxford University Press, 2013, p. 53.

(21) H. Roscam Abbing, "The Convention on Human Rights and Biomedicine. An Appraisal of the Council of Europe Convention", *op. cit.,* p. 379.

of the rights recognized by the European Convention of Human Rights of 1950.[22] At this stage it is important to point out that a number of judgments of the ECtHR already make explicit reference to the Biomedicine Convention.[23]

7. Relative rights. Like most international human rights instruments, the Biomedicine Convention allows certain restrictions on the rights recognized, insofar as they are "prescribed by law and are necessary in a democratic society in the interest of public safety, for the prevention of crime, for the protection of public health or for the protection of the rights and freedoms of others" (Article 26.1). This article restates the provisions of the analogous Article 8.2 of the European Convention of Human Rights that are relevant to biomedical issues.[24] In this respect, it should be pointed out that in order to prevent arbitrary use of this power, there is a long line of European Court of Human Rights jurisprudence emphasizing that such restrictions to the rights guaranteed by the 1950 Convention must be "proportionate to the legitimate aim pursued".[25] This jurisprudence is certainly also applicable to the interpretation of the Biomedicine Convention.[26] Moreover, the Explanatory Report to the Convention provides some examples of possible rights' restrictions: compulsory isolation of a patient with a serious infectious disease; confinement without consent of a person who, due to his or her mental disorder, could be a source of serious harm to others; compulsory genetic testing carried out in the context of judicial proceedings to establish parentage or to identify the author

---

(22)   Explanatory Report to the Biomedicine Convention, Paragraph 165.

(23)   ECtHR, *Glass v. UK* (Appl. N° 61827/00), 9 March 2004 (parental consent to medical treatment of child); *Vo v. France* (Appl. N° 53924/00), 8 July 2004 (legal status of the unborn child); *Evans v. UK* (Appl. N° 6339/05), 10 April 2007 (frozen embryos, consent to IVF, and genetic parenthood); *Özalp v. Turkey* (Appl. N° 74300/01), 11 October 2007 (forced gynaecological examination following arrest); *Juhnke v. Turkey* (Appl. N° 52515/99), 6 May 2008 (forced gynaecological examination following arrest). See J. SANDOR, "Human rights and bioethics: competitors or allies? The role of international law in shaping the contours of a new discipline", *Medicine and Law*, 2008, vol. 27, n° 1, pp. 15-28.

(24)   Article 8, paragraph 2 of the European Convention on Human Rights provides that: "There shall be no interference by a public authority with the exercise of this right except such as is in accordance with the law and is necessary in a democratic society in the interests of national security, public safety or the economic well-being of the country, for the prevention of disorder or crime, for the protection of health or morals, or for the protection of the rights and freedoms of others". See analogous provisions in Articles 4, 12(3), 19(3), 21 and 22(2) of the International Covenant on Civil and Political Rights (ICCPR) of 1966.

(25)   ECtHR, *W v. the United Kingdom* (Application 9749/82) 8 July 1987, p. 27, § 60 (b) and (d); *Olsson v. Sweden* (Application N° 10465/83), 24 March 1988, pp. 31-32, § 67.

(26)   *Cf.* Explanatory Report to the Biomedicine Convention, paragraph 159.

of a crime.[27] Nevertheless, it is important to note that, according to Article 26.2, the above mentioned restrictions are not applicable to some Convention's provisions that contain unconditional norms: Article 11 (Non-discrimination), Article 13 (Interventions on human genome), Article 14 (Sex selection), Article 16 (Protection of persons undergoing research), Article 17 (Protection of persons not able to consent to research), Articles 19 and 20 (Organ and tissue removal from living donors for transplantation purposes) and Article 21 (Prohibition of financial gain).

III. – CONTENT OF THE BIOMEDICINE CONVENTION

The Biomedicine Convention consists of a preamble and 28 articles, organized into 14 chapters. The general norms are contained in Chapter I, which consists of Articles 1 to 4; Chapters II to VII set up substantive provisions relating to specific bioethical issues, while Chapters VIII to XIV include the procedural norms. This section will provide an overview of the key provisions of the Convention.

A. – *Human dignity, primacy of the person and equity*

The notion of *human dignity* is clearly the bedrock of the Oviedo Convention. According to the Explanatory Report, "the concept of human dignity (...) constitutes the essential value to be upheld. It is at the basis of most of the values emphasized in the Convention."[28] Recalling the history of the instrument, one of the members of the drafting group recognizes that "it was soon decided that the concept of dignity, identity and integrity of human beings/individuals should be both the basis and the umbrella for all other principles and notions that were to be included in the Convention."[29]

---

(27) Explanatory Report to the Biomedicine Convention, paragraphs 149-153.
(28) Explanatory Report to the Biomedicine Convention, paragraph 9.
(29) J. KITS NIEUWENKAMP, "The Convention on Human Rights and Biomedicine", in J. DAHL RENTDORFF and P. KEMP (eds.), *Basic Ethical Principles in European Bioethics and Biolaw*, vol. II, Report to the European Commission, Center for Ethics and Law, Copenhagen, and Institut Borja de Bioètica, Barcelona, Guissona, Barnola, 2000, p. 329.

Interestingly, the *title* itself of the Convention, in its complete form, includes the notion of human dignity.[30] The Preamble refers three times to this concept: the first, when it recognizes "the importance of ensuring the dignity of the human being"; the second, when it recalls that "the misuse of biology and medicine may lead to acts endangering human dignity"; the third, when it expresses the resolution of taking the necessary measures "to safeguard human dignity and the fundamental rights and freedoms of the individual with regard to the application of biology and medicine." Moreover, the *purpose* of the Convention is defined by reference to the notion of human dignity. According to Article 1, the Convention aims to "protect the dignity and identity of all human beings and guarantee to everyone, without discrimination, respect for their integrity and other rights and fundamental freedoms with regard to the application of biology and medicine." This article deserves a particular explanation. The twofold distinction it makes between, on the one hand, the dignity and identity of "human beings," and on the other hand, the integrity, rights and freedoms of "everyone" might appear peculiar. After all, are not all human beings persons? The question which arises is: Why was it necessary to mention them separately as if they were two different entities? In fact, the odd wording of Article 1 is due to the fact that the Convention lacks precise definitions of the terms "persons" and "human being", since the task of defining those basic terms is left to domestic law. In this regard, Article 1 is a good example of a deliberate ambiguity in the elaboration of a legal text. Since there was no consensus among the drafters of the Convention concerning the legal status of the human embryo and the beginning of personhood, it was decided to use two different expressions, simultaneously namely, "everyone" (in French "toute personne") and "human being" (in French "être humain"), to refer to the subject of the protection granted by the Convention, without specifying if both concepts are synonymous or not. Mrs Johanna Kits Nieuwenkamp, former member of the draft commission, states that it was decided "to tie up the notions of dignity and identity with the concept of 'human being', that is from conception, and the notion of integrity with the concept of 'everyone', i.e. born persons".[31]

---

(30) "Convention for the protection of human rights and *dignity* of the human being with regard to the application of biology and medicine".

(31) J. KITS NIEUWENKAMP, "The Convention on Human Rights and Biomedicine", *op. cit.*, p. 330. In this sense, the Explanatory Report, which is not a binding document for the

As a direct corollary of the idea of human dignity, Article 2 assigns the highest priority to the interests and welfare of the individual, whose respect "shall prevail over the sole interest of society or science". The primacy of human beings means that no reason of economic efficiency or scientific progress can be used as a justification for an instrumentalization of people. Similar provisions can be found in the Declaration of Helsinki on biomedical research of 1964/2008 and in the Universal Declaration on the Human Genome and Human Rights of 1997.[32]

Article 3, which is also directly based on the idea of human dignity, requires States to take adequate measures to provide "equitable access to health care of appropriate quality". This means not only the absence of unjustified discrimination in the access to health care services, but also the active involvement of States in ensuring at least a minimum of medical care to their citizens. This Article relates to the "right to health care", which is one of the most basic economic, social and cultural rights, often referred to as "second generation of human rights".[33] The drafters of the European instrument were aware that resources allocated to health care will always be scarce or, at the very least, limited. For this reason, Article 3 stipulates that such measures will be adopted taking into account the "available resources" of each state.[34] In addition, the Explanatory Report clarifies that Article 3 is not to be understood as creating an individual right on which each person may rely in legal proceeding against the state, but rather as urging States to make the necessary efforts to ensure equitable access to health care.[35]

States Parties, affirms that "it was acknowledged that it was a generally accepted principle that human dignity and the identity of the human being had to be respected *as soon as life began*" (Paragraph 19) (emphasis is ours).

(32) See Principle 2 in chapter 1.

(33) See Principle 5 in chapter 1.

(34) This specification seems to be inspired on Article 2 of the International Covenant on Economic, Social and Cultural Rights of 1966, which provides that each State shall undertake to take steps "to the maximum of its available resources, with a view to achieving progressively the full realization of the rights recognized in the present Covenant" (such as the right to health).

(35) Explanatory Report to the Biomedicine Convention, paragraph 26.

B. – *Informed consent*

Articles 5 to 9 of the Convention deal with the requirement for informed consent for any biomedical intervention. These provisions embody a widely accepted principle of biomedical ethics, according to which medical interventions can only be carried out after the patient or the research subject have been informed of the purpose, nature, risks and consequences of the intervention, and have freely consented to it. This principle was already enshrined in the International Covenant on Civil and Political Rights of 1966.[36] However, the Covenant only requires informed consent for medical research, and not for all biomedical intervention: "no one shall be subjected without his free consent to medical or scientific experimentation" (Article 7). As mentioned above, the particular importance of the Biomedicine Convention lies precisely in the fact that informed consent is required for the first time as a general principle for any biomedical intervention in an international binding instrument.

The information provided to patients and research subjects should include "the purpose and nature of the intervention" as well as its "consequences and risks" (Article 5). The Explanatory Report stresses that Article 5 only mentions the most important elements of informed consent, but that additional information may be required according to the circumstances. For instance, "information on the risks involved in the intervention or in alternative courses of action must cover not only the risks inherent in the type of intervention contemplated, but also any risks related to the individual characteristics of each patient, such as age or the existence of other pathologies".[37] In addition to this, the information must be provided in a way that makes it easy for patients and research subjects to understand.[38]

The Convention does not require any particular procedure for consent, which can be explicit or implied, written or verbal. Nevertheless, written consent is requisite for biomedical research (Article 15.5) and living organ donation (Article 19.2). The determination of the conditions for the validity of the consent

---

(36) "No one shall be subjected without his free consent to medical or scientific experimentation" (International Covenant on Civil and Political Rights, Article 7).

(37) Explanatory Report to the Biomedicine Convention, paragraph 35.

(38) *Id.*, paragraph 36.

is left to the discretion of each State (Article 6.2). In the case of individuals who are unable to consent, such as minors and persons suffering from mental disorders, biomedical interventions must be aimed at benefiting them directly (id., para. 1) and carried out with the consent of their legally authorized representatives (id., paras. 2 and 3). The requisite of direct benefit clearly excludes interventions such as organ donation and non-therapeutic research which are, by definition, carried out in the interest of third parties. Nevertheless, there are some exceptions to this requirement, according to Article 17.2 and Article 20.2, which will be considered below.

Article 9 recognizes the value of advance directives, which are intended to communicate the wishes regarding treatment or refusal of certain kinds of treatment, in preparation for a time when the person might be unable to make medical decisions (for instance, if he or she is in coma). According to this provision, such wishes "shall be taken into account", which means that there may be legitimate reasons for not following the patient's directives, for instance, if they have been formulated a long time before the intervention and medical technology has since then made significant progress. [39]

C. – Right to privacy, right to know and right not to know

Article 10 of the Biomedicine Convention deals with the right to privacy of health information and two rights deriving from it: the right to be informed ("right to know") and the right not to be informed ("right not to know") about one's health condition.

The Convention makes a specific application of the more general right to privacy set out in Article 8 of the European Convention on Human Rights to the field of personal health information. [40] This is fully justified: given the sensitive nature of personal health information, it is universally accepted by ethical and legal standards that health care professionals have a duty of confidentiality towards their patients. This duty is however not absolute. According to the above mentioned Article 26.1, a disclosure could be justified if it

---

(39) *Id.*, paragraph 62.
(40) Article 8 of the European Convention on Human Rights: "Everyone has the right to respect for his private and family life, his home and his correspondence".

aims to prevent harm to third persons (for instance, the spouse of a patient suffering from a serious contagious disease).

The "right to respect for private life in relation to information about [one's] health" is formulated in very general terms by the Convention. Article 10 does not provide any guidance, beyond the "right to know" and the "right not to know", as to what this right to privacy of health information means. However, as the Explanatory Report points out, the European Convention for the Protection of Individuals with regard to Automatic Processing of Personal Data of 1981 has already dealt with this issue. This latter instrument states in Article 6 that personal health information constitutes a "special category of data" that needs particular protection and provides specific norms about the access to personal records and how personal information can be stored and disclosed.[41]

Article 10.2 stipulates that "everyone is entitled to know any information collected about his or her health". This is an innovative norm in international conventional law.[42] The right to be informed about one's health status is a logical consequence of the full recognition of the patient as a "person", that is, as an autonomous being. If we accept that patients have the right to take decisions about their medical care, then we have to accept that they are entitled to receive the information that will enable them to take such decisions. The right to know is indeed a constitutive element of the doctor-patient relationship which has emerged in the last decades and is in stark contrast to the old paternalistic model that allowed doctors to make decisions on behalf of patients.

In addition to the right to know, Article 10.2 guarantees the right not to know: "However, the wishes of individuals not to be so informed shall be observed." The use of the term "wishes" in the formulation of this right makes it clear that the right not to know is an expression of autonomy, i.e. of the legitimate desire of a person not to receive potentially harmful information about his or her health status, especially when no treatment or preventive measures are available. This is why the claim that this provision is "contrary to human rights" is unjustified.[43] Certainly, the right

---

(41) See Articles 5, 7 and 8.

(42) L. DUBOUIS, "La Convention sur les droits de l'homme et la biomédecine", *op. cit.*, p. 215.

(43) Gilbert Hottois criticizes this provision as "directly opposed to human rights philosophy and to ethics" ("A Philosophical and Critical Analysis of the European Convention

not to know, as is the case with most rights, is not absolute. There may be situations in which the interest in not knowing would not be justified because non-disclosure would pose a serious risk to patients' relatives, who, in the absence of that information, would be deprived of preventive measures, for instance, in case of transmissible diseases such as AIDS.[44]

D. – Genetics, medically assisted reproduction and germline interventions

Chapter IV of the Convention (Articles 11 to 14) contains three prohibitions which relate to genetic discrimination (Articles 11 and 12), germ-line interventions (Article 13), and the use of assisted procreation techniques with the purpose of choosing a future child's sex, except when serious hereditary sex-related disease is to be avoided (Article 14). The Additional Protocol of 1998 added a fourth ban: that on human reproductive cloning. This is the first time that such prohibitions have been included in a multilateral treaty.

Concerning genetic discrimination, Article 11 provides that "[a] ny form of discrimination against a person on grounds of his or her genetic heritage is prohibited." The European Convention on Human Rights of 1950 already prohibited discrimination on several grounds and included at the end the sentence: "and for any other reason" (Article 14). Although this expression could have been interpreted as covering genetic discrimination, the drafters of the Biomedicine Convention considered it pertinent to refer explicitly to genetic discrimination. According to the Explanatory Report, this norm only proscribes "unfair discrimination". This means that "positive measures which may be implemented with the aim of re-establishing a certain balance in favor of those at a disadvantage because of their genetic inheritance" are not prohibited.[45]

Article 12, complementing Article 11, stipulates that predictive genetic testing "may be performed only for health purposes or for scientific research linked to health purposes, and subject to appropriate genetic counseling". This means that, for instance,

---

of Bioethics", *Journal of Medicine and Philosophy,* 2000, n° 2, p. 140).

(44) See Explanatory Report to the Biomedicine Convention, paragraph 70.

(45) *Id.*, paragraph 77.

employers and insurance companies are not allowed to request genetic testing from their employees, job or insurance applicants, even with their consent, if the test is not aimed at promoting the health of those individuals.[46] In other words, genetic testing is not justified if it only serves the interest of employers or insurers. Nevertheless, employers are allowed to require genetic testing from employees or job applicants if it aims to prevent potential harm to these individuals. For example, a company could require a genetic test with the aim of identifying if some job applicants have a serious risk of developing a disease due to exposure to a chemical material that is produced or used by the company.[47]

Article 13 of the Convention bans germ-line interventions and limits the use of somatic gene therapy to preventive, diagnostic and therapeutic applications: "An intervention seeking to modify the human genome may only be undertaken for preventive, diagnostic, or therapeutic purposes and only if its aim is not to introduce any modification in the genome of its descendants". The distinction between germ-line interventions and somatic gene therapy is common in bioethical discussion. Germ-line interventions introduce modifications on the gametes or in the early embryo, and may cause irreversible damage to future generations thereby raising the issue of eugenics. Although this procedure could theoretically be used for preventing the transmission of diseases to future generations, the risk of irreversible damage seems at present disproportionate in comparison with its potential benefits. In view of these concerns, there is widespread agreement that germ-line interventions should not be undertaken.[48] On the other hand, somatic cell gene therapy is much less problematic as it only affects the individual treated by the intervention, even if there could be a risk of indirect alteration of germ cells as a side-effect of somatic cell gene therapy.[49]

---

(46) "Article 12 prohibits the carrying out of predictive tests for reasons other than health or health-related research, *even with the assent of the person concerned*" (Explanatory Report to the Biomedicine Convention, paragraph 85).

(47) "This means that in particular circumstances, when the working environment could have prejudicial consequences on the health of an individual because of a genetic predisposition, predictive genetic testing may be offered without prejudice to the aim of improving working conditions. The test should be clearly used in the interest of the individual's health" (Explanatory Report to Biomedicine Convention, paragraph 85).

(48) See Principle 12 in Chapter 1 of this book.

(49) According to the Explanatory Report to the Biomedicine Convention, Article 13 "does not rule out interventions for a somatic purpose which might have unwanted side-effects on the germ cell line. Such may be the case, for example, for certain treatments of

Article 14 bans *sex selection*, that is, the use of in vitro fertilization to help choose the sex of a child, "except where serious hereditary sex related disease is to be avoided." Similar provisions can be found in several national European laws dealing with assisted procreation.[(50)] The rationale behind this norm is that choosing a child's sex for other than medical reasons seems to turn the procreative process into a consumer experience and is an encouragement of commodification of children. An additional argument, although it is probably not relevant to the European context, is that the possibility of sex selection would have a direct impact on the sex ratio of populations, in particular in countries where males are favored in accordance with traditional social and economic pressures. The exception for medical reasons is made on the grounds that there are some genetic diseases that affect only males, for instance haemophilia and Duchenne's muscular dystrophy, and therefore it is possible, either by sperm sorting or by preimplantation genetic diagnosis (PGD), to guarantee that the child will not be a male.

E. – *Cloning*

The *human cloning* issue was not covered by the Biomedicine Convention. It is worth remembering that the draft Convention was finalized in November 1996, a few months before the announcement of the birth of Dolly, the first cloned mammal. This is why the Council of Europe decided to ban the procedure through an Additional Protocol specifically devoted to this topic, which was urgently prepared and opened for signature in Paris on 12 January 1998. Article 1.1 of the Protocol defines human cloning as "[a]ny intervention seeking to create a human being genetically identical to another human being, whether living or dead". Article 1.2 explains that the expression "human being genetically identical" to another human being means "a human being sharing with another the same nuclear gene set". The use of the expression "human being", instead of that of "person", which was included in the draft

---

cancer by radiotherapy or chemotherapy, which may affect the reproductive system of the person undergoing the treatment" (Paragraph 92).

(50) See, for instance, German Embryo Protection Law of 1990, Art. 3; Spanish Law on Assisted Reproductive Techniques of 26 May 2006, Art. 26.c.10; Danish Law on Assisted Procreation of 1997, Art. 8; Norwegian Law on the Medical Use of Biotechnologies of 1994, Art. 4.3.

version of the Protocol, seems to reflect the concern about the need to include the embryo, which is logical given that the cloning procedure takes place at the embryonic stage.[51]

This interpretation of the Protocol would imply that, whatever the final purpose of the procedure, any creation of human embryos by cloning is forbidden. On the other hand, the Protocol appears to leave the question open because, according to the Explanatory Report, the meaning of the expression "human being" is left to domestic law.[52] Therefore some States could claim that the Protocol contains a comprehensive ban on the creation of cloned embryos for both reproductive and research purposes, while others States could adopt the stance that it only deals with reproductive cloning. However, even if it is accepted that the Protocol is focused on reproductive cloning, the issue becomes complicated because Article 18.2 of the Convention prohibits *any* creation of human embryos for research purposes, regardless of the procedure used to obtain them. It is true that the announcement of the first successful cloning of a mammal (the sheep Dolly) was made in February 1997, when the drafting of the Convention had already concluded (although it was not open for signature until April 1997). On this ground, it is argued that the notion of "embryo" that the drafters had in mind was the result of the fertilization of an egg by a sperm cell, and therefore an extensive interpretation of Article 18.2 would not be permissible.[53] However, on the other hand, it can be claimed that including cloned embryos in the protection granted by Article 18.2 is not an "extensive" interpretation of this provision, but a literal interpretation of it, since embryos obtained by cloning are really embryos. Moreover, from a purely moral point of view, one may wonder why embryos obtained by cloning would have less value that those created by in vitro fertilization.

Concerning the reasons for the ban on reproductive cloning, the Preamble of the Protocol and the Explanatory Report to it indicate

---

(51) As mentioned above, Article 1 of the Convention employs the expression "human being" with this broad meaning. The Explanatory Report to the Additional Protocol seems to support this interpretation (see Paragraph 2).

(52) Explanatory Report to the Additional Protocol on the Prohibition of Cloning Human Beings, Paragraph 6.

(53) I. ERNY and C. DE SOLA, "La convention d'Oviedo sur les droits de l'homme et la biomédecine", in H. GAUMONT-PRAT (ed.), *Mélanges en l'honneur de Jean Michaud. Droit et bioéthique*, Bordeaux, Les Études Hospitalières, 2012, p. 460. See also: C. DE SOLA, "Convenio de derechos humanos y biomedicina", in C. ROMEO CASABONA (ed.), *Enciclopedia de Bioderecho y Bioética*, vol. I, Granada, Comares, 2011, p. 490.

that human cloning is an "instrumentalisation of human beings", which is "contrary to human dignity"; it poses "serious difficulties of a medical, psychological and social nature" for the individuals involved; it is "a threat to human identity", because "it would give up the indispensable protection against the predetermination of the human genetic constitution by a third party", and it reduces human freedom because it is preferable "to keep the essentially random nature of the composition of their own genes" instead of having a "predetermined genetic make-up".

F. – Biomedical research

Articles 15 to 18 of the Convention lay down general rules for *biomedical research*. The principle is that scientific research may be carried out freely, but always subject to the legal provisions that protect human beings (Article 15). According to Article 16, the conditions for research on human beings are: research subjects should give their free, explicit and informed consent; no alternative of comparable effect may exist (for example, animal research); the risks for the research subject should not be disproportional to the potential benefit of the research; the research project should be approved by an independent body, which shall assess its scientific merit and its ethical acceptability. Article 17 regulates research on persons unable to consent. The general rule is that this kind of research may only be carried out when it has the potential to produce a real and direct benefit to the health of the person concerned (Article 17.1). However, research without direct therapeutic benefit is permitted in certain cases if the research entails "only minimal risk and minimal burden" for the individual (Article 17.2). This was one of the most controversial provisions of the document.[54] The Convention assumes that these kind of minor procedures (for example, taking a single blood sample from a newborn) do not constitute an instrumentalization of persons and may contribute in a decisive way to diagnostic and therapeutic progress for the benefit of sick children.[55]

---

(54) Some have argued that this provision contradicts the principles of human dignity and non-discrimination emphatically affirmed by the Convention: "Quite in opposition to its anti-utilitarian commitment, the Convention permits instrumentalization of human beings unable to consent" (C. DESKELKAMP-HAYES, "Respecting, Protecting, Persons, Humans, and Conceptual Muddles in the Bioethics Convention", *Journal of Medicine and Philosophy*, 2000, n° 2, p. 159).

(55) *Cf.* Explanatory Report to the Biomedicine Convention, Paragraphs 111 and 112.

G. – *Embryo research*

Article 18 deals with the controversial issue of *embryo research*. It should be noted that the Convention does not take a position on the debate about the status of the human embryo. The response to this issue is left to each State, in conformity with its national law. This also explains the contradictory wording of Article 18.1 which stipulates: "Where the law allows research on embryos in vitro, it shall ensure adequate protection of the embryo." It is indeed unclear how the protection of the embryos could be compatible with their use as research material, which necessarily implies their destruction.

The only limit to the practice of embryo research can be found in Paragraph 2 of the same article, which forbids the deliberate creation of embryos for research purposes. It is important to note that it is not the research itself which is forbidden, but the deliberate creation of embryos with that aim. As mentioned above, the controversial issue remains whether Article 18.2 also includes "therapeutic cloning" (i.e. the creation of embryos by cloning in order to use them in research) or not.

H. – *Organ donation and non-commercialization of body parts*

Articles 19 and 20 of the Convention set up the conditions for organ and tissue donation by living donors for the purpose of transplantation: organs from living persons should not be used where an appropriate organ from a cadaver is available; no alternative therapeutic method of comparable effectiveness should exist; informed consent must be explicit and specific, and must be given either in written form or before an official body. The removal of organs or tissue from persons unable to consent is therefore forbidden. However, an exception is permitted for regenerative tissue (e.g. bone marrow), if the recipient is a sibling of the donor and there is no compatible donor available (Article 20.2).

Articles 21 and 22 prohibit any financial gain from the human body and its parts. This principle is a consequence of the concept of human dignity. The idea behind this is that organs and tissues, are not "commodities", and therefore should not be bought or sold, or give rise to financial gain for the person from whom they have been removed or for a third party. Especially in order to prevent organ trafficking and the exploitation of potential donors, payment for organs and tissues is illegal in almost all countries and condemned by several international guidelines. [56] The Biomedicine Convention does not exclude however that technical acts (sampling, testing, pasteurisation, purification, storage, culture, transport, etc.), which are performed on the basis of human materials, may legitimately give rise to reasonable remuneration. [57] The controversial issue of patenting of human genes is not covered by the Convention.

CONCLUSION

The Biomedicine Convention represents a milestone in the efforts of the European institutions to guarantee the protection of human rights in the biomedical field. Its importance lies, first, in the fact that it is the first multilateral *binding* instrument entirely devoted to biomedical law; and second, in the comprehensive approach it takes to the matter. In addition to this, the human rights framework adopted by the Convention seems the best strategy for regulating biomedical research and practice at a transnational level. It should be noted that even among European countries, which share many common values, there are profound disagreements about key bioethical issues. This is why the adoption of a binding instrument in this sensitive field represents a remarkable accomplishment.

The framework nature of the Biomedicine Convention is another important feature of this instrument. Far from intending to provide the ideal solution to the growing list of bioethical challenges, the Convention aims to establish some common minimal principles to prevent practices that would most seriously infringe on human rights and human dignity. The importance of setting general principles in this field should not be underestimated, since they are conceived to constitute a first step towards promoting more concrete regulations both through additional protocols, and especially by means of national measures. After all, the primary agents for the realization of human rights are national governments, not international organizations. Thus, if

---

(56) See Principle 11 in Chapter 1 of this book.
(57) Explanatory Report to the Biomedicine Convention, Paragraph 132.

it is within the context of appreciating the need to accommodate diverse social, cultural and legal backgrounds, the Biomedicine Convention is a great achievement in itself. Furthermore, the development of additional protocols on specific topics will improve the continued importance and relevance of this instrument into the future.

Section III

THE APPLICATION OF
THE COMMON PRINCIPLES
TO SPECIFIC ISSUES

CHAPTER 7

POPULATION BIOBANKS
AND HUMAN RIGHTS

Population biobanks (i.e. large-scale collections of human biological samples, of the genetic data derived from them, and associated health data) have the potential to contribute to identify genetic predispositions to complex diseases that are not caused by single genetic mutations, but rather result from an interaction of environmental, lifestyle and genetic factors. By bringing together several streams of information about individuals, population biobanks are expected to provide an unprecedented insight into the role of gene-environment interaction in the disease process. Furthermore, they are viewed as an important research tool in the field of pharmacogenetics, which is intended to tailor drugs to particular constitutions and to screen for genetic suitability before prescribing, since this kind of research needs the access to large pools of genetic information. Therefore, we can reasonably expect that the current trend towards the establishment of large-scale biobanks will contribute in the next decades to fight diseases at a population level and to help to develop more personalized medicines.

On the other hand, large-scale biobanks create a number of challenging ethical and policy dilemmas, in particular regarding informed consent for future use of the biological samples, confidentiality issues, feedback to participants, benefit sharing and risk of discrimination practices. These issues, which are posed by any collection of human genetic data, become especially acute in the case of population biobanks. The key question is therefore: how to conciliate the benefits of the genetic revolution with respect for human rights? In other words, "who should have access to genetic information?"[1]

This chapter examines some of these challenges and illustrates them by using the experiences of Iceland and Estonia during

---

(1) B.M. KNOPPERS, "Who should have access to genetic information?", in J. BURLEY (ed.), *The genetic revolution and human rights,* New York, Oxford University Press, 1999, pp. 38-53.

the 2000s. Both countries were the first to attempt to establish population biobanks, and to pass specific laws to address the new dilemmas. The Icelandic biobank failed a few years after having been launched for the reasons that will be described below, while the Estonian project still continues, although with adaptations. Since the approaches followed by these two countries were quite different, the comparative analysis of both experiences helps to better understand the issues at stake.

I. – TWO POPULATION BIOBANKS

A. – *The Icelandic population biobank*

In December 1998, without any previous public debate, the Icelandic Parliament passed a law innocuously called Healthcare Sector Database Act that stirred considerable controversy in Iceland and around the world. The law created a nationwide centralized database of medical records of the whole Icelandic population to be used for genetic research. According to Article 1, the database's purpose was "to increase knowledge in order to improve health and health services". In more precise terms, Article 10 stipulated that the database would be used "to develop new or improved methods of achieving better health, prediction, diagnosis and treatment of disease, to seek the most economic ways of operating health services, and for making reports in the health sector." Based on this Law, the Health Minister granted in January 2000 an exclusive 12-year license to operate the database to the Icelandic subsidiary of the American bio-tech company deCODE Genetics.

There were several reasons for choosing Iceland for this project. First, the Icelandic population seems to be more genetically homogenous than any other developed society thanks to thousand years of relative isolation. Icelanders descend from 9th and 10th century Nordic settlers and were almost isolated from the rest of the world until the beginning of the 20th century. The assumption was that detecting disease causing mutations would be easier in a homogenous gene pool and in a population exposed to similar environmental factors. [2]

---

[2]   Some scholars claim that the supposed "genetic homogeneity" of the Icelandic population is not supported by evidence. See E. ARNASON, "Genetic Heterogeneity of Icelanders", *Annals of Human Genetics*, 2003, vol. 67, issue 1, pp. 5-16. See also A. ABBOTT, "DNA study deepens rifts over Iceland's genetic heritage", *Nature*, 2003, vol. 421, p. 678.

Another reason for choosing Iceland was that genealogy has been very popular among Icelanders for centuries. The country possesses an extensive record of genealogical information that enables scientists to link together genealogy and medical records in a way that is not available in other countries. In addition, Icelandic population of about 300'000 inhabitants is large enough to make research valuable but still small enough to be manageable. Finally, the national health coverage that exists since 1915 provides extensive and detailed medical records of the Icelandic population.

The Icelandic database was from the very beginning very controversial. Part of the reason for this was that deCODE was authorized not only to collect new health data from volunteers but also the already existing patient records from Iceland's national healthcare system without the explicit consent of patients. The law presumed the consent of all Icelanders for their data to be entered into the database unless they voluntarily opted out by filling out a form and sending it to the Director General of Public Health. deCODE assumed that it would be easy to conclude financial agreements with hospitals and physicians to obtain the transfer of their patients' data, but soon it perceived that this was a miscalculation, as many doctors refused to "sell" the medical records of their patients.

In addition, the Healthcare Sector Database Act did not contain any provision regarding the deletion of the respective information from the database once individuals have notified their wish to opt out. The government informed that opt-outs were only relevant for future recording into the database, but previously entered data would not be removed.[3] The absence of a real informed consent process stirred a controversy in the country. The Association of Icelanders for Ethics in Science and Medicine (*Mannvernd*) leaded the opposition to the project. The Icelandic Medical Association also opposed the presumed consent model and many doctors refused to hand over their patients' records without their consent. The World Medical Association supported the Icelandic Medical Association's opposition to the database and declared that the Icelandic legislation "violates the WMA's commitment to confidentiality, the principles of real and valid consent, and the freedom of scientific

---

(3) See H. JÓNATANSSON, "Iceland's Health Sector Database: A Significant Head Start for the Biological Grial or an Irreversible Error?", *American Journal of Law and Medicine*, 2000, 26, p. 48.

research".[4] In 2002 the WMA adopted a Declaration on Health Databases that implicitly condemned the Icelandic experience.[5]

Another reason for the opposition to the project was the confidentiality issue. Although the Healthcare Sector Database Act stipulated that the database would only contain "non-personally identifiable health data" (Articles 1, 7 and 10), critics of the project claimed that confidentiality safeguards were not secure enough, because the one-way coding of personal identifiers did not really render the data non-personally identifiable.[6] It should be noted that the law did not provide any clear guidance as to what information from medical records would be encrypted prior to transfer to the database. According to the Annex to the licence, the only data that would be encrypted were the patients' names and their addresses. But the medical records include other personal information, such as age, city of residence, profession, marital status and the indication of a particular disease. In a small country like Iceland, all this information, if combined, could have allowed to establish which data belongs to which individual, particularly in cases of rare conditions. Therefore, since an indirect identification of individuals was theoretically possible, it was argued that the Icelandic database violated the European Directive 95/46 on data protection that requires the explicit informed consent for the storage and use of personally identifiable information.[7]

Taking into account the possibility of indirect identification, Iceland's Supreme Court ruled on 27 November 2003 in favor of an 18-year-old girl who did not want her dead father's health records

---

(4) World Medical Association (WMA), *Workgroup report on patient confidentiality and personal health information*, 1999, cited by V. ENGLISH et al., *Journal of Medical Ethics*, 2000, 26, pp. 215-216.

(5) World Medical Association (WMA), Declaration on ethical considerations regarding health databases, 2002.

(6) E. ARNASON, "Personal Identifiability in the Icelandic Health Sector Database", *Journal of Information, Law and Technology (JILT)*, 2002, n° 2. Available at: http://www2.warwick.ac.uk/fac/soc/law/elj/jilt/2002_2

(7) According to Article 2(a) of the Directive, "an identifiable person is one who can be identified, *directly or indirectly*, in particular by reference to an identification number or to one or more factor specific to his physical, physiological, mental, economic, cultural or social identity" (emphasis is ours) (Directive 95/46/EC of the European Parliament and of the Council of 24 October 1995 on the Protection of Individuals with Regard to the Processing of Personal Data and to the Free Movement of Such Data). See H. JÓNATANSSON, "Iceland's Health Sector Database: A Significant Head Start for the Biological Grial or an Irreversible Error?", *American Journal of Law and Medicine*, 2000, 26, pp. 31-67; R. ADALSTEINSSON, "The Constitutionality of the Icelandic Act on a Health Sector Database", in J. SANDOR (ed.), *Society and Genetic Information. Codes and Laws in the Genetic Era*, Budapest, Central European University Press, 2003, pp. 203-211.

to be entered into the database. The Director General of Public Health had rejected her request arguing that data were personally non-identifiable and therefore, she had no interest in opposing to the storage of her father's data. The court found that the one-way encryption system was, in general, a sufficiently safe mechanism for data protection, but in this case, the possibility of an indirect identification was higher because the law allowed health data to be linked with genetic and genealogical data. Consequently, including the records in the database might allow the plaintiff to be identified as an individual at risk of any heritable disease her father might be found to have had. According to the decision, although the Act repeatedly stipulated that health information should be non-personally identifiable, "it is far from being adequately ensured that this objective will be achieved." The Health Sector Database was therefore considered unconstitutional because it failed to adequately protect confidentiality.

A third reason that played a role in the controversy around the project was the idea that a for-profit company should not have a monopoly on the storage and exploitation of Icelanders health data that belong to the national health system. The rationale behind this criticism was that health issues of an entire nation should not be managed with purely commercial criteria, but should be guided by the idea of public interest. It is worthy of note that the licensee was explicitly authorized by Article 10 of the law to use the database for purposes of financial profit. This is why, when it was known that deCODE, after having paid an initial fee of about 700-thousand U.S. dollars to the government in exchange of the license, had concluded an agreement with the Swiss-based pharmaceutical company Roche to sell for 200 million U.S. dollars the rights to develop and market drugs resulting from the findings of the database, the controversy became even more passionate. The circumstance that the licensee was an American company increased the criticism of the project, because the exploitation of the database was regarded as a "theft" of national common-pool resources, comparable to the depletion by foreign companies of key fishing stocks of the continental shelf surrounding Iceland that was denounced in the 1970's. [8]

---

(8) J.H. BARKER, "Common-pool resources and population genomics in Iceland, Estonia, and Tonga", *Medicine, Health Care and Philosophy*, 2003, vol. 6, pp. 133-144.

In May 2000 the Healthcare Sector Database Act was completed by a second law, the Biobanks Act, which included rules for the storage of biological samples to obtain genetic sequences. On the basis of this law, deCODE was granted a license to operate also the biobank and to link the information it will contain with the data entered into the Healthcare Database, as well as with Iceland's extensive public genealogical records. Although the Act mandated the "informed consent of the persons giving the biological sample", this requirement did not apply to samples that have been collected in the past for clinical purposes, in which case patients' consent was presumed (Article 7). The only condition for use of the samples for "other purposes than those for which [they] were originally collected" was the approval by the Data Protection Authority and the National Bioethics Committee (Article 9). Concerning the withdrawal of consent, although the law provided that "a donor of a biological sample may at any time withdraw his/her consent (...) and then the biological sample will be destroyed" (Article 7), it added that "material that has been produced from a biological sample by performance of a study or the results of studies already carried out shall however not be destroyed" (ibid). The importance of confidentiality safeguards was vaguely mentioned by Article 11 and there was no provision specifying levels of coding and anonymization of data.

In 2004, the Icelandic biobank project was in serious trouble, both in legal and financial terms.[9] The judgment of the Constitutional Court declaring the unconstitutionality of the Healthcare Sector Database Act was a hard blow for the project. In addition, many hospitals and physicians refused to provide their patients' data to the database. For these reasons, deCODE decided to abandon the initial project of a population-based biobank and started to collect data from donors on a voluntary basis. In this way, it collected the genetic data of 140,000 Icelanders and started to market genetic tests directly to the public for predisposition to a number of diseases. At the same time, it invested in basic research to uncover the genetic origins of conditions such as breast and prostate cancer, heart disease, and diabetes. This produced a number of publications in renowned scientific journals, but never generated

---

(9) A. ABBOTT, "Icelandic database shelved as court judges privacy in peril", *Nature*, 2004, vol. 429, p. 118.

a profit. In 2009 a press release announced that the company had filed for bankruptcy.[10]

B. – *The Estonian population biobank*

Trying to learn from the mistakes of the Icelandic experience, Estonia launched in 2002 the Estonian Genome Project (EGP). The legal framework for the project was provided by the Human Genes Research Act of 2000. Simultaneously, the government founded the Estonian Genome Project Foundation (EGPF), a non-profit organization that would be in charge of carrying out the project in order to create a database of health, genetic and genealogical data of a high proportion of the Estonian population (about one million people, which represent 70% of the whole population of the country). By the end of 2002, the first samples and health data of volunteers began to be entered into the database. Unfortunately, the collection of samples was much slower than initially expected, partly due to financial problems. The initially promising public-private partnership failed in 2003, after three years of venture capital financing the project. When private investors started to postpone payments and discuss changing objectives, the project almost collapsed because of a lack of available funding. At the end of 2005 the government decided to provide public funding and ensured in this way the continuation of the project. In 2007 the Parliament amended the Human Genes Research Act in order to enable the reorganization of the public foundation into an institution affiliated with the University of Tartu (Estonian Genome Center at the University of Tartu, EGCUT).[11] The aim became less ambitious: instead of one million, only samples from some 100'000 participants will be included, about 10% of Estonia's population. In 2012, the biobank contained samples from around 52'000 donors.[12]

Despite the highs and lows that the Estonian project has experienced during its short history, the approach it has taken is

---

(10) N. WADE, "A Genetics Company Fails, Its Research Too Complex", *New York Times*, November 17, 2009.

(11) R. EENSAAR, "Estonia: Ups and down of a biobank project", in H. GOTTWEIS and A. PETERSEN (eds.), *Biobanks: Governance in Comparative Perspective*, New York, Routledge, 2008, p. 56.

(12) A. METSPALU, "The Estonian Biobank", 3.10.2012. Available at: http://www.geenivaramu.ee/info/the-estonian-biobank.html

ethically preferable to the Icelandic one. First, the Estonian Human Genes Research Act places a strong emphasis on individuals' rights. Participation in the project is strictly voluntary and informed consent is required for the collection of biological samples, health information and genealogical data (Art. 9.1). The information in this informed consent is specified to include not only the means and risks of obtaining the sample but also all the rights to which participants are entitled. The law guarantees the confidentiality of data through high-level technical encoding of personal identifiers (Arts. 22 to 24). All research studies have to be previously approved by an ethics committee (Art. 29).

Participants are entitled to a number of rights: the right to have access to their information stored in the database (Art. 11.2);[13] the right not to know their genetic data (Art. 11.1); the right to genetic counseling (Art. 11.4); the right to submit additional information on themselves to the database (Art. 11.5); the right to withdraw their consent until their tissue samples or health data are coded (Art. 12.4.7). Once the coding is done, participants can demand the destruction of the information that enables decoding of personal identifiers (Art. 10), but the biological sample could only be destroyed in the exceptional case that the donor's identity was unlawfully disclosed (Art. 12.6).[14] The law includes also specific norms to prevent genetic discrimination in insurance and employment contracts (Arts. 25 to 27). If one considers that the Icelandic Healthcare Sector Database Act only contained one provision (Art. 8) that vaguely referred to the "rights of patients" (and only aimed at presuming their consent!), the contrast with the Estonian law could not be more striking. Interestingly, the legal framework of the Estonian project was developed with the help of international experts, such as Bartha M. Knoppers, and took

---

(13) The access of participants to their genealogies is however excluded by Article 11.2.

(14) This limit to the right to withdraw consent could a priori be seen as contrary to the European Biomedicine Convention, which provides that "the person concerned may freely withdraw consent at any time" (Art. 5). However, the project's supporters argued that the right to withdraw consent at any time had been recognized having in mind biomedical research that operates on the human body and therefore entails some risk to the physical integrity of participants, but this is not the case of research that only deals with biological samples and genetic data, especially since they have been anonymized (A.NÓMPER and K. KRUUV, "The Estonian Genome Project", in J. SANDOR (ed.), *Society and Genetic Information. Codes and Laws in the Genetic Era,* Budapest, Central European University Press, 2003, p. 222). In support of this interpretation, the International Declaration on Human Genetic Data of 2003 stipulates that a withdrawal of consent is possible unless data "are irretrievably unlinked to an identifiable person" (Art. 9).

into account international legal instruments like the European Convention on Human Rights and Biomedicine and the Universal Declaration on the Human Genome and Human Rights. [15]

Concerning the confidentiality issue, as mentioned above, the Estonian Human Genes Research Act provides that all data in the biobank "shall be processed in compliance with the highest standards of data protection" (Art. 22). In this respect, several safeguards are put in place to prevent indirect identification. Each tissue sample, description of DNA, health information and genealogy is given a unique 16-digit code (Art. 23.1). This code replaces any information that could enable identification, such as name, address, personal identification number and date of birth (Art. 23.2). The same code is to be noted on the consent form and therefore the consent will be the only possible key for decoding (Art. 23.3). In order to prevent indirect identification of a donor, the database operator may release information from the database as a set of data and on the condition that samples or data concerning at least five donors are issued at a time (Art. 22.4). In the interests of greater security, the database operator "may give an additional code" to coded tissue samples, coded genetic data and coded genealogical data (Art. 23.4).

The different approach of the Estonian project, when compared to the Icelandic biobank, is also visible in the non-profit nature of the foundation that managed it until 2007 (Estonian Genome Foundation). The members of the Foundation's board of directors were appointed by the government and by the Estonian Academy of Sciences. Certainly, the commercial dimension of the planned research was not a priori excluded from the project. However, the non-profit nature of the database's owner showed well that it was not conceived to be managed will purely commercial criteria, but taking mainly into consideration the public interest. A good illustration of this is the fact that the law allows the use of the database for academic research free of charge (Art. 19).

---

(15) A. RANNAMÄE, "Estonian Genome Project. Large scale health status description and DNA collection", in B.M. KNOPPERS (ed.), *Populations and Genetics: Legal and Socio-Ethical Perspectives*, Leiden, Martinus Nijhoff Publishers, 2003, p. 23.

II. – ETHICAL AND POLICY DILEMMAS RAISED
BY POPULATION BIOBANKS

The Icelandic and Estonian experiences illustrate well the ethical and policy challenges posed by large collections of human biological samples and derived genetic data, in particular regarding informed consent, confidentiality, the risk of genetic discrimination and stigmatization, feedback to participants, and issues of property and benefit sharing. This section aims to summarize these challenges.

A. – *Informed consent*

There is international consensus that for most medical research to be ethical, participants must be informed about the scope and potential risks of the research, and voluntarily consent to be in the study. There is a priori no obvious reason for departing from this principle when creating collections of human biological samples for research purposes.[16] Applying the traditional requirement of specific informed consent not only to the initial collection of samples, but also to every new project intending to use those samples would clearly meet classic consent norms. However, this solution becomes problematic in large-scale biobanks, which have thousands of samples and are conceived to develop decades-long projects. Requiring them to obtain a renewal of donors' consent for each new project would entail prohibitively high costs and would render biobanks virtually useless. In addition, this may even contradict the wishes of participants who are willing to provide their samples for future, unspecified research and would prefer not to be re-contacted for every specific project. It is also to note that the risks in biobank research are minimal for participants. While traditional biomedical research create some risks for the health and physical integrity of participants, genetic research is

---

(16) See for instance, Universal Declaration on the Human Genome and Human Rights of 1997, Article 5; International Declaration on Human Genetic Data of 2003, Article 8; European Commission Experts Group, The 25 recommendations on the ethical, legal and social implications of genetic testing, Brussels, 2004, Recommendation 23; World Medical Association (WMA), Declaration on ethical considerations regarding health databases, 2002, paras. 16-21; Human Genome Organization (HUGO) Statement on Human Genomic Databases of 2002, Recommendation 4.

conducted on the collected biological samples and on the genetic data derived from them. [17]

It is therefore not surprising that the model of "broad consent", as opposed to the "specific consent model", is emerging as an accepted solution for population biobanks. [18] The UK Biobank, which is the first population-based biobank to be successful, is known for its bold move to a broad consent model. [19] In 2002, the UK Human Genetics Commission (HGC) had already recognized that "repeated processes of re-consent for subsequent use are impractical and, moreover, may be considered as unnecessary invasive". [20] Therefore, the HGC considered that "it is acceptable to seek general consent in cases where there is to be irreversible or reversible anonymization of data and samples". [21]

Also the German National Ethics Council supports a broad consent model in biobank research. It acknowledges that a requirement to obtain fresh consent for any new project may give raise to problems in the case of large-scale biobanks. Therefore, "it must be made possible for donors to consent to the use of their samples and data for undefined research projects to be specified only at some future data". [22]

The broad consent model has been proposed by several international guidelines such as the WHO guidelines for genetic research, [23] the CIOMS guidelines for biomedical research, [24] the

---

(17) The specific risk of genomic research relates to the confidentiality of the data, and the potential discrimination or stigmatization of people or groups of people.

(18) B. ELGER, *Ethical issues of human genetic databases. A challenge to classical health research ethics?*, Farnham, Ashgate, 2010, p. 254 ; M. HANSSON, J. DILLNER, C. BARTRAM, J. CARLSON, and G. HELGESSON, "Should donors be allowed to give broad consent to future biobank research?", *Lancet Oncology*, 2006, vol. 7, 266-269; K. STEINSBEKK and B. SOLBERG, "Biobanks: When is Re-consent Necessary?", *Public Health Ethics*, 2011, vol. 4, n° 3, pp. 236-250.

(19) "Because it will be impossible to anticipate all future research uses, consent will be sought for research in general that is consistent with UK Biobank's stated purpose (rather than for specific research)" (*UK Biobank Ethics and Governance Framework*, 2007).

(20) UK Human Genetics Commission (HGC), *Inside Information. Balancing interests in the use of personal genetic data,* May 2002, London, pp. 94-95.

(21) *Ibid.*

(22) German National Ethics Council, *Biobanks for research. Opinion,* Berlin, Nationaler Ethikrat, 2004, p. 51.

(23) "A blanket informed consent that would allow use of a sample for genetic research in general, including future as yet unspecified projects, appears to be the most efficient and economical approach, avoiding costly re-contact before each new research project" (World Health Organization, Proposed International Guidelines on Ethical Issues in Medical Genetics and Genetic Services, 1998, Section 11).

(24) Council for International Organizations of Medical Sciences (CIOMS), *International Ethical Guidelines for Biomedical Research Involving Human Subjects* 2002: "Medical records

Statement on DNA Sampling of the Human Genome Organization (HUGO),[25] the UNESCO International Declaration on Human Genetic Data of 2003,[26] and the 2001 Report on Genetic Databases prepared for the World Health Organization Regional Office for Europe.[27]

Nevertheless, the consent issue in biobank research is still debated among experts. In this regard, it has been noted, not without humor, that this controversy is so difficult to resolve that "even authors of the same publications and guidelines are divided on the subject".[28] The problem is that broad consent is not, strictly speaking, an *informed* consent at all. As Arnason argues, "the more general the consent is, the less informed it becomes. It is misleading to use the notion of informed consent for participation in research that is unforeseen and has not been specified in a research protocol".[29] Similarly, some scholars claim that the broad consent model distorts the original concept of informed consent, and propose the concept of an authorization model whereby

---

and biological specimens taken in the course of clinical care may be used for research without the consent of the patients/subjects only if an ethical review committee has determined that the research poses minimal risk, that the rights or interests of the patients will not be violated, that their privacy and confidentiality or anonymity are assured, and that the research is designed to answer an important question and would be impracticable if the requirement for informed consent were to be imposed" (Guideline 4).

(25) "Research samples obtained with consent and stored may be used for other research if; there is general notification of such a policy, the participant has not yet objected, and the sample to be used by the researcher has been coded or anonymized. For the use of research samples obtained before notification of a policy, these samples may be used for other research if the sample has been coded or anonymized prior to use" (Human Genome Organization Ethics Committee, *Statement on DNA Sampling. Control and Access*, 1998).

(26) According to the 2003 International Declaration on Human Genetic Data, genetic data and samples "should not be used for a different purpose that is incompatible with the original consent, unless the prior, free, informed and express consent of the person concerned is obtained (...) or unless the proposed use, decided by domestic law, corresponds to an important public interest reason and is consistent with the international law of human rights" (Art. 16a). Although the wording of this provision is ambiguous, it seems that a general consent for future uses of data and samples may be permissible.

(27) WHO Regional Office for Europe, *Genetic Databases: Assessing the Benefits and the Impact on Human and Patients' Rights*. A Report for the World Health Organization's European Partnership on Patients' Rights and Citizens' Empowerment, May 2001. The report suggests that "participants should be informed of the possibility of future uses of data, beyond the limits of the present consent" (p. 12), but recognizes that "in some cases it might be desirable to seek broad, open-ended consent to future research, the purposes, limits or consequences of which are currently unknown. In such cases, blanket future consent is only permissible where anonymity can be guaranteed, and there is no risk that unexpected results will filter back to the subjects concerned" (p. 14).

(28) B. ELGER, *op. cit.*, p. 142.

(29) V. ARNASON, "Coding and consent: moral challenges of the database project in Iceland", *Bioethics*, 2004, vol. 18, pp. 27-49.

participants in genetic research are able to exercise a certain amount of control over future uses of samples and genetic data. This authorization could take the form of a directive that gives participants the ability to specify in advance the uses for which they do or do not wish to give informed consent in the future.[30] It has also been pointed out that, in a broad consent model, donors could be consenting to future unknown research which they may morally oppose (for instance, embryonic stem cells research).[31]

B. – Confidentiality of data

Because of the significant harm that misuse of health information can cause to individuals, it is widely accepted by ethical and legal standards that health care professionals have a duty of confidentiality towards their patients. This is a fundamental principle of the fiduciary nature of the doctor-patient relationship and also applies to biomedical research. In the context of biobanks for research purposes, the duty of confidentiality presupposes that researchers are not allowed to disclose participants' genetic information to third parties without donors' consent[32], provided that such consent is in accordance with law.[33]

While all forms of personal health information have a sensitive nature, this is, for various reasons, especially true of personal genetic information.[34] The UNESCO International Declaration

---

(30) T. CAULFIELD, R. UPSHUR and A. DAAR, "DNA databanks and consent: A suggested policy option involving an authorization model", *BMC Medical Ethics* 2003, vol. 4, p. 1. See also T. CAULFIELD and J. KAYET, "Broad Consent in Biobanking: Reflections on Seemingly Insurmountable Dilemmas", *Medical Law International*, 2009, vol. 10, n° 2, pp. 85-100; H. GREELY, "The Uneasy Ethical and Legal Underpinnings of Large-Scale Genomic Biobanks", *Annual Review of Genomics and Human Genetics*, 2007, vol. 8, pp. 343-364.

(31) K. MASCHKE, "Biobanks: DNA and Research", in M. CROWLEY (ed.), *From Birth to Death and Bench to Clinic: The Hastings Center Bioethics Briefing Book for Journalists, Policymakers, and Campaigns*, Garrison, NY, The Hastings Center, 2008, pp. 11-14.

(32) See Universal Declaration on the Human Genome and Human Rights, (Article 7; Council of Europe's Convention on Human Rights and Biomedicine, Article 10.1; WMA Declaration of Helsinki (1964-2008), Paragraph 23); World Medical Association (WMA), *Declaration of the Rights of the Patient* (1981-2005), Article 8.

(33) This means that, in order to protect vulnerable individuals against undue pressures, domestic law can prohibit disclosure to third parties, even with the consent of data subjects. See Article 14 of the UNESCO International Declaration on Human Genetic Data.

(34) This does not necessarily mean falling into a "genetic exceptionalism", *i.e.* the idea that genetic information is a completely separate category of personal data. Genetic information is not but a kind of personal health information. However, it has some peculiarities and raises particular issues that deserve specific solutions. See: European Commission Experts Group, *The 25 recommendations on the ethical, legal and social implications of genetic testing*,

on Human Genetic Data of 2003 has summarized such reasons: "Human genetic data have a special status because: "i) they can be predictive of genetic predispositions concerning individuals; ii) they may have a significant impact on the family, including offspring, extending over generations, and in some instances on the whole group to which the person concerned belongs; iii) they may contain information the significance of which is not necessarily known at the time of the collection of the biological samples; iv) they may have cultural significance for persons or groups" (Article 4). Two additional reasons for a special consideration of genetic information are provided by a report of the UK Human Genetics Commission: First, unlike other health data, genetic data provide uniquely identifying information because, with the exception of identical twins, each individual has a unique genetic make-up. Second, genetic information can be obtained from a very small amount of biological material (from a hair, a blood sample, etc.), without a lengthy observation or study and even without the knowledge of the person. [35]

Most guidelines on biomedical research accept the coding of genetic data as a sufficient measure to protect confidentiality. [36] In this regard, an important terminological clarification is needed. Although coding is often referred to by guidelines as "anonymization" of data, one has to be aware of the fact that this term is somehow misleading since codes allow to identify individuals, provided there is access to the original encoding. This is why some guidelines prefer to use the expressions "reversible anonymization", or "pseudo-anonymization". Certainly, irreversible anonymization is to some extent impossible in the case of genetic data. Since an individual's unique identity is embedded within DNA, this identity could theoretically be revealed if an anonymized sample were matched up with another sample that has not been anonymized. [37] Despite this eventuality, which is

---

Brussels, 2004, Recommendation n° 3, p. 9 and the more detailed Report on *Ethical, legal and social aspects of genetic testing: research, development and clinical applications*, elaborated by the same body, Brussels, 2004, pp. 41-45.

(35) UK Human Genetics Commission (HGC), *op. cit.*, pp. 28-32.

(36) See for instance, the CIOMS guidelines, according to which "secure coding" seems to be the generally accepted and sufficient protection, if combined with "restricted access to the database" (Council for International Organizations of Medical Sciences (CIOMS), *International Ethical Guidelines for Biomedical Research Involving Human Subjects* 2002, guideline 18).

(37) UK Human Genetics Commission (HGC), *op. cit.*, p. 91.

likely to be rare, the concept of "anonymization" (with the meaning of "coding") is regarded as valid by most guidelines.[38] The fact is that in the large-scale databases that are being established, genetic data are at some point coded, so that it may be linked to health, genealogical and lifestyle information. This possibility of re-linking the participants identifying information with their data and samples can be explained by the need to follow up participants' health, to eliminate redundant data (e.g. duplicate cases), to verify correctness and completeness of data against original records, to establish correct linkages among databases, and to find specific data or samples if participants withdraw.[39]

Obviously, since the anonymization of samples and data is aimed to protect confidentiality, it is essential for the relevant codes to satisfy certain quality criteria and for them not to be easily breakable. Nevertheless, guidelines do not provide a detailed guidance as to what degree of anonymization or coding is considered adequate. They tend to stipulate that the issue cannot be decided in general, but depends on the particular circumstances of the planned research.[40]

The goal of confidentiality safeguards is to prevent a misuse of genetic information to discriminate against people. The principle of non-discrimination on genetic grounds means that, for instance, employers and insurance companies are not allowed to use genetic information to affect the hiring of an individual, or the conditions of employment or of insurance. This principle is already included in several international instruments.[41] Unlike genetic discrimination, which can be prevented by law, the risk that people may be stigmatized by the results of genetic research is much more difficult to avert. Stigmatization of a certain category of people (for instance, an ethnic group) is a phenomenon that may result

---

(38) UK Biobank Governance Framework, 2007, C; UK Human Genetics Commission (HGC), *op. cit.*, p. 17.

(39) UK Biobank Governance Framework, 2007, C.2.

(40) The use of non-coded data is allowed if required by the nature of the research, provided that such procedure is approved by an ethical review committee and other confidentiality safeguards are established. See Article 14(d) of the 2003 International Declaration on Human Genetic Data, which stipulates that genetic data and samples "can remain linked to an identifiable person, only if necessary to carry out the research and provided that the privacy of the individual and the confidentiality of the data or biological samples concerned are protected in accordance with domestic law".

(41) See Universal Declaration on the Human Genome and Human Rights, Article 6; International Declaration on Human Genetic Data, Article 7(a); Council of Europe's Convention on Human Rights and Biomedicine, Article 11.

from the knowledge that it has a higher probability of developing a certain disease (e.g. Tay-Sachs disease in Ashkenazi Jews or sickle cell anemia in Africans). Since the risk of stigmatization is especially serious in the case of population-based genetic studies, it is strongly recommended to pay "appropriate attention" to the interpretation of such studies' findings.[42]

C. – Feedback to participants

Large-scale biobanks are designed for research, not for clinical purposes, and therefore usually do not offer any feedback to participants concerning their own individual risks discovered in the course of the research. The Estonian Genome Project is an exception in this regard, as it allows disclosure of information to participants and their physicians for clinical purposes. But most population biobanks exclude to give feedback, not only because this is not their goal, but because of the practical difficulties to re-contact participants and to ensure genetic counselling to them. Since the information would be communicated outside of a clinical setting and would not have been evaluated in the context of the full medical record of the subject, such feedback would have a questionable value and could even be harmful by causing undue alarm.[43] This is why the informed consent forms for biobank research usually include the statement that no individual medical information will be returned to the subject. Since subjects have agreed to participate knowing that there will be no feedback, it could be argued that they do not have a right to feedback.

This does not exclude that when research findings show that a number of participants are at particular risk of a condition, this should be reported in a general feedback to all participants, for instance, through the use of newsletters.[44] In any case, it is important to ensure from the outset of the enrolment process that participants are aware of the fact that no information about individual risks will be disclosed to them.

---

(42) See International Declaration on Human Genetic Data, Article 7(b).
(43) UK Biobank Ethics and Governance Framework, 2007, para. B.3.
(44) See UK Human Genetics Commission, *op. cit.*, p. 106.

This absolute lack of feedback, even in extreme situations, has been criticized by Greely as "immoral, possibly illegal, and certainly unwise".[45] He claims that we have here a special application of the duty to rescue, which means that a person is obliged to save another one when he can do this without undue risk or difficulty. In his view, biobank researchers are not merely bystanders or spectators of the risks that can be discovered by analyzing participants' samples. Researchers are accepting benefits of information and samples in a situation where participants trust them, and therefore have a duty to protect them from harm if they can do this without undue difficulty.[46] Similarly, it has been argued that research subjects have volunteered to participate for the public good and therefore, if information is discovered which could be potentially life-saving or significantly relevant to their health, to withhold it could be regarded as a harm.[47]

On the other hand, the possibility of a feedback raises also the question of participants' right not to know their predisposition to genetically-related diseases. This is especially relevant when no treatment or preventive measures are available, and therefore the disclosure of information would be more harmful than helpful. The right not to know is recognized by several international instruments and guidelines adopted since the end of the 1990s.[48]

D. – Issues of property and benefit-sharing

The establishment of population biobanks has raised concerns about the "privatization" of human genetic data and their exploitation for commercial purposes. The Icelandic case, as mentioned above, was paradigmatic in this regard, as a monopoly was granted to a single for-profit company to make profit with health data and genetic information of an entire nation. The unease with a purely for-profit approach to the management of population biobanks is even greater if one assumes that the

---

(45) H. GREELY, *op. cit.*, p. 359.

(46) *Ibid.* See also V. RAVITSKY and B. WILFOND, "Disclosing individual genetic results to research participants", *American Journal of Bioethics*, 2006, vol. 6, issue 6, pp. 8–17.

(47) R. CHADWICK, "The right to know and the right not to know. Ten years on", in C. REHMANN-SUTTER and H. MÜLLER (eds.), *Disclosure Dilemmas. Ethics of Genetic Prognosis after the 'Right to Know/Not to Know' Debate*, Farnham, Ashgate, 2009, p. 12.

(48) See chapter 8.

human genome should be regarded as a "common heritage of humanity"[49] and that genomic databases should be treated as "global public goods".[50] It results from this that one of the key issues in this domain is to find the proper governance strategy that ensures a good balance between the private and public domain in managing such infrastructure for research.

Various alternatives to the proprietary model have been proposed for managing biobanks. One of the most promising ones is that of a *trust*. In the fiduciary relationship of a trust, one person, trustee, holds title to the property vested by the settlor but has as an obligation to use it for the benefit of another, the beneficiary. In our case, the settlor would be the source of the samples and the beneficiary would be the patients. Advantages of the trust model include the fact that it respects altruism of donors while ensuring that their good will is not misused, that the repository would have a duty to make the property in human material productive, and that fiduciary law recognizes the power imbalance between the settlor/beneficiaries and the trustee.[51]

In this regard, the UK Biobank is a good mixture of public funding (the Medical Research Council, the Department of Health and the Scottish Government) and medical charity funding (the Wellcome Trust). The legal owner of the database and the sample collection is UK Biobank Limited, a charity operating as a company limited by guarantee. It serves as the steward of the resource, maintaining and building it for the public good. The resource is available to scientists from the UK and outside, whether employed by universities, government, charities or commercial companies, subject to verification that the research is health-related, is in the public interest, and has relevant ethics approval.[52]

---

(49) See Universal Declaration on the Human Genome and Human Rights, Article 1; Human Genome Organization (HUGO) Ethics Committee, Statement on benefit-sharing, 9 April 2000.

(50) B.M. KNOPPERS and C. FECTEAU, "Human Genomic Databases: A Global Public Good?", *European Journal of Health Law*, 2003, vol. 10, pp. 27-41.

(51) See D.E. WINICKOFF and R.N. WINICKOFF, "The Charitable Trust as a Model for Genomic Biobanks", *The New England Journal of Medicine*, 2003, vol. 349, pp. 1180-1184; German National Ethics Council (Nationaler Ethikrat) and French National Advisory Committee on Ethics (Comité consultatif national d'éthique), "Joint declaration by the NER and the CCNE supplementing their Opinions on biobanks", 2003, in German National Ethics Council, *Biobanks for research*, Berlin, 2004, pp. 101-102.

(52) UK Biobank Governance Framework, 2007, II.B.

Another concern relates to the question whether benefits resulting from biobanks findings should be shared with participants and if so, what could be a fair way of sharing. The issue is complex because it appears to contradict a long ethical tradition according to which research subjects are not allowed to receive payments for their participation in a study if such rewards are "so large as to persuade them to take undue risks" or if "they undermine a person's capacity to exercise free choice".[53] This principle is clearly aimed to avoid coercion and to prevent the exploitation of the poor. However, one has to bear in mind that genetic research puts the issue in a different light than traditional biomedical research because participants in genetic studies are not assuming any particular bodily risk and, after all, they are making their biological samples and data available to the database. Therefore, why could not they somehow benefit from the profit resulting from research based on the use of their material and data?

Alas, the issue is not that simple because, in addition to the norm that proscribes payment to research subjects, there is the more general principle of non-commercialization of body parts, which is included in several international instruments.[54] This means that body parts and samples should not be bought or sold, or give rise to financial gain for the donor or for a third party.[55] In this regard, the Estonian Human Genes Research Act explicitly proscribes the payment of fees to donors of samples (Article 15.3). Similarly, the UK Biobank Governance Framework stipulates that participants will not be offered any material financial or other inducement to contribute to the biobank, but only will be reimbursed for reasonable expenses incurred through participation (such as travel and parking).[56]

---

(53) See Council for International Organizations of Medical Sciences (CIOMS), *International Ethical Guidelines for Biomedical Research Involving Human Subjects* 2002, guideline 7.

(54) See Council of Europe's Convention on Human Rights and Biomedicine, Article 21; Universal Declaration on the Human Genome and Human Rights, Article 4.

(55) This principle does not exclude however that technical acts (sampling, testing, pasteurisation, purification, storage, culture, transport, etc.), which are carried out on the basis of human materials, may legitimately give rise to reasonable remuneration for those who performed such acts. See Explanatory Report to the European Biomedicine Convention, Paragraph 132.

(56) UK Biobank Governance Framework, 2007, I.B.8.

In this regard, there has been criticism that data collected in developing countries turn to profit for the sponsors and bring no benefit to the community from which the samples and data are obtained. Moreover, there is the fear that in this scenario even an apparently generous benefit-sharing would be "merely bribing people to become commodities".[57] Despite this criticism, it seems fair to promote some form of benefit-sharing at a population level, especially if it translates into long-term infrastructure improvements, rather than allowing a community to contribute to a research project without obtaining any benefit. In this respect, it has been said that "in population studies, benefit to the population has become one of the critical issues in determining the ethical justification for the study itself, and sharing benefits with the population is critical in preventing exploitation".[58] Several proposals have been made suggesting various ways in which benefits can be shared at a population level. For instance, the Human Genome Organization Ethics Committee proposed that 1 to 3 % of the profit from genetic research should be returned to healthcare infrastructure and/or to humanitarian efforts.[59] Also UNESCO has suggested various forms of benefit-sharing with the society from which the data are obtained.[60]

CONCLUSION

Large-scale biobanks pose new challenges to human rights, especially regarding informed consent, confidentiality of data, discrimination on genetic grounds, feedback to participants, and issues of property and benefit-sharing. The comparison of the Icelandic and the Estonian shows that the new ethical and legal issues should be adequately addressed at the very beginning of the process. In sum, in the search for solutions to the emerging dilemmas it appears especially important to ensure an open, public, and transparent debate about the implications of genetic databases; to require an explicit and specific informed consent of

---

(57) D. DICKENSON, "Consent, Commodification and Benefit-Sharing in Genetic Research", *Developing World Bioethics,* 2004, vol. 4, n° 2, p. 119.

(58) G.J. ANNAS, "Reforming Informed Consent to Genetic Research", *Journal of the American Medical Association* (JAMA), 2001, vol. 286, n° 18, p. 2327.

(59) Human Genome Organization (HUGO) Ethics Committee, *Statement on benefit-sharing,* 9 April 2000.

(60) See 2003 International Declaration on Human Genetic Data, Article 19(a).

participants, at least for the initial collection of data; to recognize the right of participants to decide not to receive potentially harmful information about themselves; to apply high-quality confidentiality safeguards; to prevent genetic discrimination; to involve independent ethics committees to guarantee compliance with ethical and legal standards; to avoid the creation of databases based on purely commercial criteria and to establish some mechanism of benefit-sharing with society.

CHAPTER 8
THE RIGHT NOT TO KNOW ONE'S GENETIC STATUS

The claim for a "right not to know" might sound strange. Over the last decades it has been strongly stressed that the patient has the right to be informed about the risks and benefits of a treatment or intervention and, on this basis, to consent –or not– to them. Having affirmed the patient's "right to know" as a fundamental ethical and legal principle, we are now faced with the apparently opposite demand. This takes place particularly in the field of genetics: as the predictive power of genetic tests increases, more and more people come to know that they are at risk from a serious disease with no real chance of reducing that risk or of obtaining an effective treatment. To illustrate the problem, let us consider the following examples:

- Anne, a 35 year old woman and mother of two children, has a family history of breast cancer. Urged by her relatives, she decided to undergo the BCRA1/2 testing. If Anne has the mutation, she has 80% risk of developing breast cancer. Three days later, depressed by the difficult decisions she would have to make in case the mutation was found, she asked the doctor not to inform her about the test results.

- Peter, a 29 year old married man, is invited to participate in a research study about the mutations that may cause Alzheimer's disease (the most common cause of dementia) because a member of his family has been diagnosed with this disorder. DNA samples will be coded, but the unit's director will keep a confidential list of the names of each participant. Although this is a research study and not a clinical genetic test, the laboratory offers Peter the possibility to be informed about the result of the analysis, in case it indicates the presence of a mutation. This information may be helpful in predicting his risk of developing Alzheimer's disease or of having children with this disorder. However, Peter does not want to know the results and therefore does not sign the request to be informed.

Far from being purely academic, both scenarios happen in the daily routine of genetic testing and research. In order to understand the refusal of Anne and Peter to have access to their genetic information, one has to consider that the burden of knowledge may become unbearable for them, leading to a severe psychological depression and having a negative impact on their family life and on their social relationships in general. For many people, the discovery that they have a genetic condition that places them at a high risk of suffering certain untreatable diseases could so depress them that the quality, joy and purpose of their lives would literally evaporate.[1] Now, in such situations, "it may not be justifiable to take away hope from a person by exposing them to knowledge they do not want".[2] Therefore, it seems reasonable to allow these persons to choose not to receive that potentially harmful information and to continue their lives in peace.

This chapter argues that autonomy, understood in a wide sense, provides a theoretical basis for a right not to know one's genetic status. The discussion will focus on predictive testing of adults, and not on other types of genetic testing (diagnostic testing, preimplantation genetic diagnosis, prenatal testing and newborn screening), which raise other specific ethical issues. It is also worth mentioning here that, although the interest in not knowing may be greater in the case of single gene disorders (when a particular mutation is causally sufficient for a disease to occur) than in polygenic disorders, it is not the purpose of this chapter to enter in a detailed discussion of the issues raised by each type of genetic testing. Rather, what is intended is to provide a broad philosophical and legal analysis of the debate regarding the right not to know one's genetic status.

After summarizing the objections made against the right not to know (I), it will be recalled that various recent ethical and legal instruments explicitly recognize this claim (II). Then, this chapter will attempt to respond to those objections (III), and will suggest

---

(1) R. WACHBROIT, "Disowning Knowledge: Issues in Genetic Testing", in V. GEHRING and W. GALSTON (eds.), *Philosophical dimensions of public policy*, New Brunswick, N.J., Transaction Publishers, 2002, pp. 239-245.

(2) R. CHADWICK, "The philosophy of the right to know and the right not to know", in R. CHADWICK, M. LEVITT, and D. SHICKLE (eds.), *The Right to Know and the Right not to Know*, Aldershot, Ashgate, 1997, p. 18; *Id.*, "The right to know and the right not to know. Ten years on", in C. REHMANN-SUTTER and H. MÜLLER (eds.), *Disclosure Dilemmas. Ethics of Genetic Prognosis after the 'Right to Know/Not to Know' Debate*, Farnham, Ashgate, 2009, pp. 9-18.

some conditions that should be fulfilled for the exercise of the right not to know (IV).

I. – OBJECTIONS TO THE RIGHT NOT TO KNOW

Several criticisms have been formulated against the formal recognition of a right not to know one's genetic status. The main practical objection is that this right is not feasible because, in order to decide not to receive some information, the person should previously be informed of the possibility of having a particular health risk. Now, this is precisely what the individual wanted to avoid. [3]

A most fundamental objection is that, according to a long and well established philosophical tradition, knowledge is always good in itself and therefore a "right to remain in ignorance" appears as a contradiction; that is, as an irrational attitude, which is incompatible with the notion of «right». [4] Let us recall that, according to Aristotle "all men by nature desire to know" and this desire is one of the features that distinguishes humans from other animals. [5] The Enlightenment's philosophers considered also human progress in direct connection with an increasing access to knowledge. In the words of Kant, "*Sapere aude!*" ("Have courage to use your own understanding!") was indeed the motto of the Enlightenment. [6] Adopting this latter perspective, a contemporary philosopher acidly criticizes the recognition of the right not to know as "directly opposed to human rights philosophy and to ethics". [7]

The right not to know would be also contrary to the recent evolution of the doctor-patient relationship, which tends to abandon the old paternalism that allowed the doctor not to tell the truth to the patient. Moreover, the claim not to know would be contrary to the doctor's "duty to disclose" risks to patients. Therefore such a

---

(3) D.C. WERTZ and J.C. FLETCHER, "Privacy and Disclosure in Medical Genetics Examined in an Ethics of Care", *Bioethics*, 1991, vol. 5, pp. 212-232; C.M. ROMEO-CASABONA, "Human Rights Issues in Research on Medical Genetics", in *Ethics and Human Genetics*. Strasbourg, Council of Europe Editions, 1994, pp. 167-174.

(4) D. OST, "The 'right' not to know", *The Journal of Medicine and Philosophy*, 1984, vol. 3, pp. 301-312; J. HARRIS and K. KEYWOOD, "Ignorance, information and autonomy", *Theoretical Medicine and Bioethics*, 2001, vol. 22, pp. 415-436

(5) ARISTOTLE, *Metaphysics*, I, 1.

(6) I. KANT, *What is Enlightenment?*, 1.

(7) G. HOTTOIS, "A Philosophical and Critical Analysis of the European Convention of Bioethics", *Journal of Medicine and Philosophy*, 2000, vol. 2, pp. 133-146.

claim would represent a return to a paternalistic attitude given that it put persons in a state of ignorance, depriving them of choice.[8] For the same reason, the right not to know is criticized as being opposed to patient's *autonomy*, given that the exercise of autonomy depends on the ability to understand relevant information and only on this basis to consent to treatment.[9]

Another objection refers to the harm to others that may result from the ignorance of one's genetic status: the individual who chooses not to know his or her genetic makeup —thereby putting him or herself in a position of being unable to disclose that vital information to family members— could be said to be harming others and acting against solidarity. The same thing could be said about an individual who refuses to participate in a population screening program because of a claimed right not to know.[10]

II. – ETHICAL AND LEGAL RECOGNITION OF THE RIGHT NOT TO KNOW

In spite of the criticisms leveled against it, the right not to know has been recognized by various international instruments relating to biomedicine.

For instance, the UNESCO's Universal Declaration on the Human Genome and Human Rights (1997) provides that: "The right of every individual to decide whether or not to be informed of the results of genetic examination and the resulting consequences should be respected" (Article 5.c). The International Declaration on Human Genetic Data (2003) develops further this principle. According to Article 10, "When human genetic data (...) are collected for medical and scientific research purposes, the information provided at the time of consent should indicate that the person concerned has the right to decide whether or not to be informed of the results. This does not apply to research on data irretrievably unlinked to identifiable persons (...). Where appropriate, the right not to be informed should be extended to identified relatives who may be affected by the results".

---

(8) M. CANELLOPOULOU BOTTIS, "Comment on a View Favoring Ignorance of Genetic Information: Confidentiality, Autonomy, Beneficence and the Right not to Know", *European Journal of Health Law* 2000, vol. 7, n° 2, pp. 173-183.

(9) J. HARRIS and K. KEYWOOD, *op. cit.*, pp. 418-19.

(10) R. CHADWICK, *The philosophy of the right to know*, p. 20.

The European Convention on Human Rights and Biomedicine (1997) stipulates that "Everyone is entitled to know any information collected about his or her health. However, the wishes of individuals not to be so informed shall be observed" (Article 10.2). The Explanatory Report to the Convention justifies the right not to know by saying that "patients may have their own reasons for not wishing to know about certain aspects of their health".[11] The Additional Protocol concerning Genetic Testing for Health Purposes (2008) reiterates this point in Article 16.3.[12]

Other important international ethical guidelines also recognize the right not to know. The "Declaration on the Rights of the Patient" (Lisbon Declaration) adopted by the World Medical Association in 1981 and amended in 2005, provides that "the patient has the right not to be informed on his/her explicit request, unless required for the protection of another person's life" (Article 7d). The WHO "Guidelines on Ethical Issues in Medical Genetics and the Provision of Genetic Services" (1997) states that "the wish of individuals and families not to know genetic information, including test results, should be respected, except in testing of newborn babies or children for treatable conditions" (see Table 7 in these Guidelines).

It is important to note that in all the aforementioned international instruments, an explicit choice is necessary for the functioning of the right not to know: the European Biomedicine Convention refers to individual's "wishes"; both UNESCO Declarations mention the individual's "decision"; the WMA Declaration points out the necessity of an "explicit request" of the patient; the WHO Guidelines refers to the "wishes" of individuals and their families.

The right not to know is also enshrined in a number of national laws. According to the Belgian Law on Patients' Rights (2002), "The information will not be provided to the patient if he or she expressly so requests, unless the non-disclosure of this information

---

(11) Council of Europe, *Explanatory Report to the Convention on Human Rights and Biomedicine*, paragraph 67.

(12) Article 16.4 of the Additional Protocol specifies that both the right to know and the right not to know may be restricted "in the interests of the person concerned". Strangely, there is no mention of the potential interest of third parties (i.e. family members) in receiving that information. The Explanatory Report to the Additional Protocol indicates that "information on the health of a person who has expressed a wish not to know is sometimes particularly important for him or her. For example, knowing that he or she has a predisposition to a disease might be the only way to enable him or her to take measures to prevent that disease or delay its development (...)" (Paragraph 135).

causes a serious harm to the patient or a third party, and provided that the physician has previously consulted another professional practitioner about this and heard the opinion of the patient's trustee" (Article 7.3). The French Law on Patient's Rights (2002) stipulates that "Everyone has the right to be informed on his/her health status... The person's will to remain ignorant of diagnostic and prognostic information should be respected, except when third parties are exposed to a risk of transmission" (Art. 1111-2, Public Health Code). The Spanish Law on Patient's Autonomy (2002) provides that "When patients explicitly express their wish not to be informed, such a wish must be respected" (Art. 9.1). According to the Swiss Law on Human Genetic Testing (2004), "Every person has the right to refuse to be informed about his/her genetic status, except in the situation referred to in art. 18.2". This latter provision stipulates that "The physician must immediately disclose the results of the test to the individual in case of an imminent physical danger to him/herself, or to the embryo or the fetus, which could be avoided". The German Law on Genetic Diagnosis (2009) provides that "The results of a genetic test should not be disclosed to the concerned persons if they have decided (...) that they should be destroyed, or if they have withdrawn their consent to the test" (Art. 11.4).

III. – The right not to know: an expression of "autonomy"

The main thesis of this chapter is that the claim for not knowing one's genetic status, far from being contrary to *autonomy* —understood as an individual's self-determination— may be indeed considered a legitimate expression of this basic bioethical principle. In other words, the choice of not knowing the results of genetic tests does not entail a paternalistic attitude because the challenge to medical paternalism is precisely based on the idea that people should be free to make their own choices with respect to information. If we understand autonomy in this wider sense, then the decision not to know should be, at least in principle, as fully respected as the decision to know. [13]

---

(13) J. HUSTED, "Autonomy and a right not to know", in R. CHADWICK, M. LEVITT, and D. SHICKLE (eds.), *The Right to Know and the Right not to Know*, Aldershot, Ashgate, 1997, pp. 55-68; T. TAKALA, "Genetic Ignorance and Reasonable Paternalism", *Theoretical Medicine and Bioethics*, 2001, vol. 22, pp. 485-491.

Thus, the possibility to choose not to know the results of genetic tests may constitute an *enhancement of autonomy*, because the decision to know or not to know is not taken out of the hands of the patient by the doctor. Precisely with this broad understanding of autonomy, the right not to know is widely recognized, for example, by the German legal literature as a part of the "right to informational self-determination" (*Recht auf informationelle Selbstbestimmung*). [14]

In addition to this, it should be noted that there is not an absolute "duty to disclose" information to patients, neither on legal nor on ethical grounds. On the contrary, it is the responsibility of the health care professional to assess the amount of information an individual wants and is able to deal with at a particular time. [15]

If this understanding of autonomy is correct, it can be argued that the theoretical foundation of the right not to know lies on the respect for individual *autonomy*, even if the ultimate foundation of this right is the individual's *interest in not being psychologically harmed*. Both grounds are indeed situated at a different level. Autonomy is the immediate source of the right not to know, but what is in the end protected is the psychological integrity of the person. Certainly, patients do not need to prove the harmful effects of genetic information, because each of them is the only entitled to recognize what information may be psychologically harmful. In any case, the recognition of the potentially negative effect of genetic information helps to better understand what the right not to know tends to protect and what, ultimately, justifies this claim. [16] We deal here with the oldest principle of medical ethics: "first, do not harm" (*Primum non nocere*), which is formulated in modern times in the so called "principle of non-maleficence" that certainly includes patient's psychological integrity. [17]

---

(14) G. WIESE, "Gibt es ein Recht auf Nichtwissen?", in E. JAYME *et al.* (eds.), *Festschrift für Hubert Niederländer*, Heidelberg, Carl Winter, 1991, pp. 475-88; J. TAUPITZ, "Das Recht auf Nichtwissen", in P. HANAU, E. LORENZ, H. MATTHES (eds.), *Festschrift für Günther Wiese*, Neuwied, Luchterhand Verlag, 1998, pp. 583-602.

(15) British Medical Association, *Human Genetics. Choice and Responsibility*, Oxford, Oxford University Press, 1998, pp. 86-88.

(16) J. WILSON, "To know or not to know? Genetic ignorance, autonomy and paternalism", *Bioethics*, 2005, vol. 19, n⁰ˢ 5-6, pp. 492-504.

(17) T. BEAUCHAMP and J. CHILDRESS, *Principles of Biomedical Ethics*, 5ᵗʰ ed., New York, Oxford University Press, 2001, p. 117.

The criticism that the right not to know is contrary to the requirement of informed consent is misplaced. The right to remain in ignorance about one's genetic make-up should not be mistaken for a *waiver* of informed consent. In the exercise of a waiver, a patient voluntary relinquishes the right to an informed consent and relieves the physician from the obligation to inform. It seems to be a consensus among ethicists that the acceptance of waivers of consent is a dangerous practice.[18] But in the case of the right not to know the informed consent exists, insofar as the person is perfectly aware that he or she will undergo a genetic test that may indicate a risk of developing a disease. In this case, the individual just refuses to be informed of the test outcome. Thus, the ignorance does not concern the *medical practice* itself, for which a valid informed consent has been given, but only its *result*.

Consequently, the individual does not receive any particular medical treatment on the basis of ignorance. A different situation may arise in the emerging area of pharmacogenetics. What if a patient arguing the right not to know refuses the test that can determine if a particular drug may have an adverse effect and in spite of that demands the medicine? In such a case the pharmacogenetic test, as far as it has been proved to be effective, should perhaps be considered as a part of the treatment itself. Therefore, it would be a breach of the physician's duty of care to prescribe a drug for a patient who intends to use it without the test having been performed. In other words, in the absence of the test, the requirement of informed consent for the treatment would not be met. This conclusion is especially valid since information about drug response could hardly be considered contrary to the patient's interests.

What about the argument that the right not to know is intrinsically not feasible because its exercise always requires a previous knowledge? Certainly, for the exercise of this right the person should have, at least, a general and abstract knowledge of the risk. We know that we are all at risk of developing genetic diseases, particularly when we have a family history of a particular genetic condition. But some risks may be so remote in our perception as to seem virtually inconceivable. In contrast, a genetic testing, which may determine individuals likely to suffer from a serious

---

(18) *Ibid.*, p. 93.

disorder or even the certainty that the disease will emerge (in the case of a single gene disorder), makes those vague concerns look much more real. This is precisely why an individual's refusal to know the results of genetic tests might make sense.

One has to recognize however that the refusal to be informed about one's genetic status may in some cases be problematic, because genetic information is not only an individual, but also a family affair. Tests results may alert family members about a serious risk, giving them the opportunity of changing their life plans, or eventually of preventing or treating a disease. The familial nature of genetic information has even led some ethicists to argue that the concept of "genetic privacy" is a contradiction in terms.[19] In any case, the question is: how can the right not to know be harmonized with the potential interest of a patient's relative in knowing?

As it has already been pointed out, some legal and ethical regulations try to give an answer to this difficult dilemma: the right not to know (like most rights) is *not absolute* because its exercise is conditioned by the fact that *there is no risk of serious harm to other persons*.[20] That means that the disclosure to family members, if ever, could be accepted as an exceptional measure, as long as two conditions are fulfilled: firstly, the disclosure is necessary for avoiding a serious harm to them; secondly, some reasonable form of cure or therapy is available. However, we should not forget that we are dealing with unsolicited genetic information. We are indeed not sure that relatives really want to receive that information. This is why we should be extremely prudent before any unsolicited approach is made.

Those "other persons" that the exercise of the right not to know should not harm could be society in general. Public health interests may in particular circumstances justify limitations on the right to ignore one's genetic makeup as they may justify limitations to confidentiality, for instance, in the case of infectious diseases. Surely, the circumstances in which the right not to know and confidentiality can be breached in the interest of public health should be well defined by law. Particularly important in this context

---

(19)   A. SOMMERVILLE and V. ENGLISH, "Genetic privacy: orthodoxy or oxymoron?", *Journal of Medical Ethics* 1999, vol. 25, pp. 144-150.

(20)   See Council of Europe, Explanatory Report to the Biomedicine Convention, paragraph 70; WMA Declaration of the Rights of the Patient, Article 7.d.

are population genetic screening programs, which can contribute to the prevention of genetic diseases. For example, potential parents could be alerted to the risks they may take if they marry and have children with a person who also carries the genetic trait. However, such programs face significant challenges in terms of informed consent, privacy and risks of stigmatization of ethnic groups. In addition, there is the fear that public screening programs could encourage eugenic practices, like systematic abortion of affected fetuses.[21] In summary, we have to make a substantial effort in this area to ensure an adequate balance between the respect for individuals' rights and the benefits of using genetic information for the common good of society.

IV. – THE WISH OF NOT KNOWING SHOULD BE EXPLICIT

Graeme Laurie has argued that, in addition to autonomy, the right not to know might be based on a particular form of *spatial privacy*, the so-called "psychological spatial privacy", which encompasses separateness of the individual's psyche. This aspect of spatial privacy tends to safeguard *one's own sense of the self* and to provide a larger protection of the interest in not knowing than simple *choice*, especially in those cases in which no explicit choice has been made.[22]

Laurie's concern is perfectly understandable: it is true that even if no wish has been expressed, the interest in not knowing can also be compromised by unsolicited revelations of genetic information. This circumstance leads the author to advocate a "prima facie" respect for the interest in not knowing, even in absence of an explicit choice.[23] This means, in practice, an *inversion of the burden of proof*: it is not the person interested in not knowing who should express his or her wish but, on the contrary, it is the individual who intends to disclose the information who, before any

---

(21) R. HOEDEMAEKERS and H. TEN HAVE, "Geneticization: The Cyprus Paradigm", *Journal of Medicine and Philosophy*, 1998, vol. 23, n° 3, pp. 274-287.

(22) G. LAURIE, "In Defence of Ignorance: Genetic Information and the Right not to Know", *European Journal of Health Law*, 1999, vol. 6, issue 2, pp. 119-132; *Id.*, "Protecting and Promoting Privacy in an Uncertain World: Further Defences of Ignorance and the Right not to Know", *European Journal of Health Law*, 2000, vol. 7, pp. 185-191; *Id.*, "Challenging Medical-Legal Norms. The Role of Autonomy, Confidentiality, and Privacy in Protecting Individual and Familial Group Rights in Genetic Information", *The Journal of Legal Medicine*, 2001, vol. 22, pp. 1-54.

(23) G. LAURIE, "In Defence of Ignorance...", p. 127.

disclosure, should be sure that some special conditions are fulfilled (for example, the severity of the condition, the availability of a cure, the nature of the testing and the question of how the individual might react if exposed to unwarranted information).[24] Therefore, this position "places the onus of justifying disclosure firmly on the shoulders of those who would do so".[25]

The appeal to privacy in order to call for an attitude of prudence in the disclosure of genetic information is fully justified, especially when there are doubts about the patient's will. Moreover, the "privacy approach" provides an insightful explanation of what is at stake in this issue. It is true that when there is no previously expressed wish in respect of the information, the potential interference is primarily with the spatial privacy interests –or let's say, with the psychological integrity– of the individuals in question, rather than with their autonomy *per se*.[26]

However, what is difficult to accept in Laurie's view is the assumption that those individuals who have not made any explicit choice of not knowing their genetic status (which means almost everybody) want to ignore it. In the case of competent patients, this assumption can hardly be harmonized with their right to know, as well as with the duty to inform that, in principle, the health care professional has towards them. Both competing rights –to know and not to know– cannot be the rule. Surely, to determine which right should prevail will depend on the circumstances of each case, but law and ethics need *rules* to operate in a coherent manner; and the rule in this field is that patients have a right to know their health status. This is why the right not to know may only be accepted as an *exception,* at least with regard to competent persons. The situation is probably different in the testing of minors, in which case genetic tests for adult onset genetic disorders should perhaps be simply banned, particularly when no cure is possible.[27]

In brief, therefore, the argument of this chapter is that the right not to know cannot be *presumed*, but should be "activated" by the

---

(24) *Ibid.*, pp. 128-129; G. LAURIE *et al.*, *Genetic Databases. Assessing the Benefits and the Impact on Human & Patient Rights.* Report for Consultation to the WHO. Geneva, WHO, May 2001, Recommendation 16

(25) G. LAURIE, *Genetic Privacy. A Challenge to Medico-Legal Norms,* Cambridge, Cambridge University Press, 2002, p. 259.

(26) *Ibid,* p. 210.

(27) S. MCLEAN, "The genetic testing of children: some legal and ethical concerns", in A. CLARKE (ed.), *The genetic testing of children,* Oxford, Bios, 1998, pp. 17-26.

explicit will of the person.[28] Let us recall that, for those cases in which the interest in not knowing seems clear, but no explicit choice has been made, we already have the concept of "therapeutic privilege", which allows physicians to withhold information if, based on sound medical judgment, they believe that divulging the information would be harmful to a depressed or unstable patient, especially when there is currently no effective treatment.[29] But this is different to recognizing a *right* not to know, because the violation of a right (in this case, by disclosure of the unsolicited information) means that the professional could eventually incur civil liability. Now, such a serious consequence in cases in which patients had not expressed their interest in not knowing seems a step too far.

Thus, the exercise of an autonomous choice is necessary for the functioning of the right not to know, because it is impossible to determine a priori the wish of the patient. Precisely, one of the particularities of this right consists in the fact that it almost entirely depends on the subjective perceptions of the individual, who is, in fact, the best interpreter of his or her best interest. It should be noted that the problem of genetic tests is raised not so much by the information itself (which is neutral) but by the *effect* that that information may have on the person who has been tested. That effect varies greatly from individual to individual. This is why the previous informed consent should be as comprehensive as possible, in order to know in advance the patient's interests and possible fears.

It could be argued that this autonomy-based approach is unrealistic, because it ignores the fact that people are not always free to decide according to their real interests.[30] For instance, various forms of coercion, in a more or less subtle way, may lead individuals to choose to know their genetic makeup, when in fact they would prefer to ignore it. The most obvious example is the requirement of genetic tests as a condition of employment or insurance. Nevertheless, the factual possibility of coercion in certain circumstances is not *per se* a sufficient reason to deny people the right to self-determination regarding genetic information. It is true that coercion may happen in the field of genetic testing,

---

(28) J. TAUPITZ, *op. cit.*, p. 592.
(29) T. BEAUCHAMP and J. CHILDRESS, *op. cit.*, p. 84.
(30) G. LAURIE, *op. cit.*, p. 209.

but it may happen in all areas of clinical and research activities as well. If we consider that the likelihood of coercion is very high in certain circumstances, what we can do (as many ethical guidelines suggest) is simply to prohibit the requirement of genetic tests by insurance companies or employers and the requirement to disclose results of any previously undertaken genetic tests. Or at least we can put additional safeguards in place to ensure that people are free from coercion and are not exposed to unjustified discrimination. However, the risk of coercion should not lead us to deny that competent people, with appropriate genetic counseling, are in principle able to decide whether they want to know their genetic status or not.

Do third parties like patients' relatives have a right not to know? In this case one has to recognize that such a right is even difficult to conceive. First, for a practical reason: how can patients' relatives exercise this right, if they probably even ignore that a family member has been tested? Moreover, against *whom* would they have this right? Against the doctor who, having tried to help them, disclosed that information? Against the family member who was tested and had revealed, for example at a family gathering, that he or she is at risk of a genetic illness? Would such a general right not to know not be a serious obstacle to confidence within the family? In addition to this, how can doctors assume that patients' relatives do not have interest in knowing genetic information, which may be extremely important to them? Certainly, doctors should in principle avoid disclosing information about patients to individuals with whom they do not have any professional relationship. Healthcare professionals have a duty of confidentiality towards their patients. But if in a particular case a doctor considers in good faith that he or she is morally obliged to disclose that information to patients' relatives —for example, because a reasonable treatment or preventive measure is available— it would be an exaggeration to make him or her legally responsible on the basis of a supposed right not to know of those individuals. On the other hand, if there is no treatment or preventive measure for the disease, it is hard to imagine why healthcare professionals would be so interested in disclosing genetic information to patients' relatives. If such a thing could come to happen, the doctor would be violating without justification his or her professional duties. However, we do not need to postulate that third parties have a "right not to know" their genetic makeup, which would be an excessively strong argument, in order to protect them from unjustified invasions of their privacy.

One could theoretically imagine a solution to this complex dilemma with the creation of a public register –similar to those that exist for organ donation– where people can express in advance their wish to know or not to know their genetic status. Of course, those who do not register a refusal would not be automatically presumed to be interested in knowing their genetic makeup. The only purpose of such a register would be to give people a means to specify in advance their preferences concerning genetic information and, at the same time, to facilitate the task of doctors, who could consult that register before making any unsolicited disclosure. Nevertheless, for the moment we are still very far from a general solution of this kind. Therefore, it seems that at present the right not to know can only operate within the doctor-patient relationship and as the result of an explicit choice made in that context. In summary, autonomy —that is, explicit will— is the best guarantee that we do not make a mistake in deciding for others whether they have interest in knowing their genetic status or not.

Conclusion

The increasing access to personal genetic information leads lawmakers to recognize new rights in order to protect people from harm. The right not to know is one of them. This claim is based on individuals' autonomy and on their interest in not being psychologically harmed by the results of genetic tests. Such a right, as an exception to both the patient's right to know and the doctor's duty to inform, needs to be "activated" by the explicit will of the patient. In addition, this right has two characteristics: firstly, it can only operate in the context of the doctor-patient relationship; secondly, it is a relative right, in the sense that it may be restricted when disclosure to the individual is necessary in order to avoid serious harm to third parties, especially family members, which means that some form of prevention or treatment is available.

CHAPTER 9

BIOMEDICAL RESEARCH: REGULATORY DISCREPANCIES BETWEEN THE COUNCIL OF EUROPE AND THE EU

This chapter aims first to outline the *human rights* approach to biomedical research adopted by the Council of Europe's Convention on Human Rights and Biomedicine (Biomedicine Convention),[1] and to contrast it with the more *market-oriented* provisions of the Clinical Trials Directive of the European Union.[2] While this difference of approach is understandable in the light of the dissimilar objectives of both European bodies, it has resulted in some unfortunate regulatory inconsistencies which might lead to less protection of research participants, in particular those who are most vulnerable. Second, this chapter aims to illustrate these normative discrepancies by comparing the requirements for biomedical research contained in both instruments.

I. – Two approaches to biomedical research in Europe

The regulation of medical research on human subjects is always placed in a context of tension between two fundamental aspirations of every society. On the one hand, there is the legitimate desire to contribute to people's health and quality of life through the development of new preventive, therapeutic, and diagnostic tools. This aspiration justifies the widely held view according to which biomedical research activities should enjoy the greatest possible freedom to advance and develop new procedures and techniques. On the other hand, there is also the conviction that medical research, like any other activity within society, does not have absolute autonomy to operate at the margin of respect for

---

(1) See chapter 6 of this book.

(2) Directive 2001/20/CE of the European Parliament and of the Council of 4 April 2001 on the approximation of the laws, regulations and administrative provisions of the Member States relating to the implementation of good clinical practice in the conduct of clinical trials on medicinal products for human use.

human dignity and human rights. This is so because science is not an end in itself, but rather a means to promote the well-being of society and of every individual. In other words, medicine exists to serve people, not people to serve medicine. Consistently with this, modern societies have made serious efforts to ensure, first, that participants in biomedical research understand the nature, risks, benefits and alternatives of the prospective research and freely consent to it; second, that they are not exposed to disproportionate risks; and third, that a qualified independent body will review compliance with the two aforementioned requirements, as well as the fulfilment of other conditions (for instance, scientific validity of the planned research; respect for the privacy of participants, etc.).

The first international set of principles for research involving human subjects was the Nuremberg Code, which was drafted in 1947 by the Allied Military Tribunal that judged and convicted the Nazi physicians who had used the prisoners of concentration camps as subjects of brutal experiments. The Nuremberg Code embodies the idea that there are certain principles for the protection of research subjects that are non-negotiable. In this regard, Jay Katz says that:

"The Nuremberg Code is a remarkable document. Never before in the history of human experimentation, and never since, has any code or any regulation of research declared in such relentless and uncompromising a fashion that the psychological integrity of research subjects must be protected absolutely."[3]

Since the Nuremberg Code, scientists have been strictly required to comply with some basic conditions for conducting research on human beings. Regarding the requirement of informed consent, the Nuremberg Code emphasizes from the very beginning that "voluntary consent of the human subject is absolutely essential", and that that "the person involved should have legal capacity to give consent; should be so situated as to be able to exercise free power of choice (...); and should have sufficient knowledge and comprehension of the elements of the subject matter involved as

---

(3) J KATZ, "The Consent Principle of the Nuremberg Code: Its Significance Then and Now", in G.J. ANNAS and M.A. GRODIN (eds), *The Nazi Doctors and the Nuremberg Code*, New York, OUP, 1992, p. 227.

to enable him to make an understanding and enlightened decision" (Principle 1).

The Nuremberg Code also requires that research "should be so conducted as to avoid all unnecessary physical and mental suffering and injury" (Principle 4); that it should not be conducted "where there is an a priori reason to believe that death or disabling injury will occur" (Principle 5); and that "the degree of risk to be taken should never exceed that determined by the humanitarian importance of the problem to be solved by the experiment" (Principle 6).

In contemporary societies, research on human beings is unconceivable if these basic requirements are not fulfilled. This is of course also the case of Europe, where specific policies regarding this issue have been adopted, not only at the domestic level, but also at the level of the common institutions, namely, the European Union and the Council of Europe. It should not be forgotten that, after all, Europe was at the very centre of the tragic event from which both modern medical ethics and international human rights law emerged: *the Second World War.* As George J. Annas points out emphatically, "World War II was the crucible in which both human rights and bioethics were forged, and they have been related by blood ever since".[4]

The establishment of the Nuremberg Code marked the birth, not only of modern medical ethics, but also of modern human rights law. Only one year after the Code was developed, the most significant event in human rights in the modern era occurred: the adoption of the Universal Declaration of Human Rights (UDHR) in 1948. This document, which would become the cornerstone of the entire international human rights system, did not only pave the way for the adoption of more than seventy treaties, which are applied today on a permanent basis at global and regional levels. It also served as a model for many constitutions and laws throughout the world, and helped to ground uncountable decisions of national and international courts.

The historical relationship between bioethics and human rights is much closer than generally believed. Robert Baker asserts that the UDHR was in part informed by the revelations that led to

---

(4) G.J. ANNAS, *American Bioethics. Crossing Human Rights and Health Law Boundaries,* New York, Oxford University Press, 2005, p. 160.

the adoption of the Nuremberg Code. Indeed, he claims that "the details revealed daily at Nuremberg gave content to the rights recognized by Articles 4 through 20 of the Declaration".[5]

Regarding the specific topic with which this chapter is concerned, it is interesting to note that the first issue with which both new disciplines —modern medical ethics and human rights law— were confronted was precisely *medical research on human beings*. It is therefore not surprising that many, if not most, international instruments relating to biomedical research appeal to a human rights framework to set up minimal common standards in this field. But beyond this coincidence of history, there are various substantive reasons explaining this phenomenon: first, biomedical practice is *per se* directly related to the most basic human rights, such as the right to life, to physical and mental integrity, to privacy, etc. Thus, it is perfectly sound to have recourse to the umbrella of international human rights law to ensure the protection of such basic human claims in this field. Second, the human rights framework facilitates the formulation of transnational standards, because international human rights law is based on the assumption that basic rights transcend cultural diversity. Third, there are few mechanisms available other than human rights to respond to emerging bioethical challenges at a transnational level. As Mann, a prominent public health expert has observed, "the human rights framework provides a more useful approach for analysing and responding to modern public health challenges than any framework thus far available within the biomedical tradition."[6]

At present, biomedical research is simultaneously regulated in Europe by two different bodies, the Council of Europe (henceforth CoE) and the European Union (henceforth EU), each of them adopting a different approach to the matter. The norms of the CoE's Biomedicine Convention dealing with research on human subjects put clearly the emphasis on promoting the dignity and rights of research participants. All the provisions of this instrument are like an extension of this basic objective. It is not by chance that the title itself of the Convention explicitly refers to human rights and the

---

(5) R. BAKER, "Bioethics and Human Rights: A Historical Perspective", *Cambridge Quarterly of Healthcare Ethics,* 2001, vol. 10, issue 3, pp. 241-252.
(6) J. MANN, "Health and human rights. Protecting human rights is essential for promoting health", *British Medical Journal,* 1996, vol. 312, pp. 924-925.

purpose itself of the Convention is defined by reference to human rights (Article 1).

The importance of the Biomedicine Convention lies precisely in the fact that it is the only intergovernmental *binding* instrument that comprehensively addresses the linkage between human rights and biomedicine. Moreover, it is probably not exaggerated to say that the Biomedicine Convention and its Additional Protocol on Biomedical Research of 2005 represent *the most elaborate and systematic effort ever undertaken at a transnational level to address by means of legally binding instruments the challenges to human rights posed by biomedical research.*

The Convention's purpose, as indicated by its Preamble, is to give a specific application in the field of biomedicine to the general rights contained in the European Convention on Human Rights. [7] The Convention can indeed be regarded as an *extension* of human rights law into the biomedical field.

Article 15 of the Biomedicine Convention is coherent with the priority assigned to human rights when it states that "scientific research in the field of biology and medicine shall be carried out freely, subject to the provisions of this Convention and the other legal provisions ensuring the protection of the human being." Similarly, the Explanatory Report to the Convention stresses that "the whole Convention, the aim of which is to protect human rights and dignity, is inspired by the principle of primacy of the human being, and all its Articles must be interpreted in this light" (para. 22). On this basis, the specific rules contained in the Biomedicine Convention to protect the rights of patients and research subjects are explicitly recognized as being able to guide the interpretation of the European Convention on Human Rights in cases where the European Court of Human Rights considers that there has been a violation of one of the rights recognized by the latter instrument. [8]

In contrast to the human rights approach of the Council of Europe's Biomedicine Convention, the European Union is in this specific field mainly concerned with the harmonization of the administrative provisions governing clinical trials for medicinal products. This is the key objective of the Directives adopted in

---

(7) A. PLOMER, *The Law and Ethics of Medical Research: International Bioethics and Human Rights,* London, Cavendish, 2007, p. 21.

(8) Explanatory Report to the Biomedicine Convention, para. 165.

this area, namely, the Directive 2001/20 on Clinical Trials, and its "offspring", the Directive 2005/28 on Good Clinical Practice. Certainly, as we will see below, the Clinical Trials Directive also includes substantive provisions relating to informed consent of participants, to the proportionality of risks, to the confidentiality of personal data, to the need of the favourable opinion of an ethics committee, etc. However, these elements do not seem to embody the main objective of this document. Rather, they clearly play a secondary role in a regulation which is "market oriented" in that it is primarily linked to the control of the medicinal products' market in Europe.[9] This particular approach has been explained on the grounds that "the initial impetus for the Clinical Trial Directive came from the pharmaceutical industry, which desires a harmonized process and set of standards for the granting of REC [Review Ethics Committees] approval for clinical trials."[10]

During the long gestational process of the Directive, which lasted approximately ten years, the official documents which were released routinely stressed that the intention was to protect participants, while facilitating high-quality research and a competitive industry. However, as Liddell *et al.* note, "it is difficult to shake the feeling that the voices of industry received more than due attention".[11] In this regard, it is revealing that the principal instrument on which the Directive was inspired was not the Declaration of Helsinki, but the European Good Clinical Practice guidelines, which are based on the ICH-Guidelines for Clinical Trials.[12] The ICH process (which stands for "International Conference on Harmonisation of Technical Requirements for Registration of Pharmaceuticals for Human Use") is led by pharmaceutical industry associations. It aims to negotiate guidelines on the authorization of medicines acceptable to industry and the regulatory authorities of the United States, Europe, and Japan in order to lessen the barriers to global trade. Furthermore, it is also interesting to note that the

---

(9) D. SPRUMONT and A. GYTIS, "The Importance of National Laws in the Implementation of European Legislation of Biomedical Research", *European Journal of Health Law*, 2005, vol. 12, n° 3, p. 250.

(10) D. BEYLEVELD and S. SETHE, "The European Community Directives on Data Protection and Clinical Trials", in E. EMANUEL *et al.* (eds), *The Oxford Textbook of Clinical Research Ethics*, Oxford, Oxford University Press, 2008, p. 184.

(11) K LIDDELL *et al.*, "Medical Research Involving Incapacitated Adults: Implications of the EU Clinical Trials Directive 2001/20/EC", *Medical Law Review*, 2006, vol. 14, n° 3, pp. 367-417.

(12) *Ibid.*

Clinical Trials Directive was drafted not by units in the European Commission responsible for health or human rights such as, for instance, the Directorate-General for Health and Consumers, but by the DG for Enterprise and Industry.[13]

It is therefore not surprising that the Directive was received with satisfaction by the pharmaceutical industry. On the other hand, researchers from public and academic institutions were critical of the stringent application processes and bureaucratic procedures put in place by the new regulation, which have significantly increased the trial costs that can almost exclusively be afforded by big companies. In this regard, there is evidence that the number of non-commercial clinical trials has dramatically fallen since 2004.[14]

The contrast between the philosophies that inspire the European Union and the Council of Europe regarding biomedical research could not be more striking. At the risk of oversimplifying the comparison, it could be said that, while the EU emphasizes freedom of research in a rather utilitarian manner, the Council of Europe is essentially concerned with the protection of research subjects, relying for that purpose, at least to some extent, on a deontological (i.e. Kantian) approach.

This difference of perspectives becomes more understandable if one remembers the history of each organization. On the one hand, the European Union has its origins in the "European Coal and Steel Community" formed among six countries in 1951, and in the "European Economic Community" (EEC) created in 1957. The purpose of these structures was of economic nature, namely the creation of a *single market* within Europe. On the other hand, the Council of Europe was established to promote *respect for human rights* in the Old Continent. To achieve this purpose, this body adopted the European Convention on Human Rights of 1950 and various mechanisms aimed at ensuring respect for human rights in Europe, such as the European Court of Human Rights, which was established in 1959. Certainly, the European Union has also a jurisdictional instance, the European Court of Justice, which is based in Luxembourg. However, its role is totally different from

---

(13) *Ibid.*
(14) R. HOEY, "The EU Clinical Trials Directive: 3 years on", *Lancet*, 2007, vol. 369, pp. 1777-78; M. HARTMANN and F. HARTMANN-VAREILLES, "The Clinical Trials Directive: How Is It Affecting Europe's Noncommercial Research?", *PLos Clin Trials*, 2006, vol. 1, issue 2, e13.

that of the European Court of Human Rights. The Luxembourg court was not created to guarantee respect for human rights, but rather *to make sure that EU legislation is interpreted and applied in the same way in all EU countries.*

As the European Union and the Council of Europe have different objectives, it is perfectly understandable that they adopt a different approach to biomedical research. This is not in itself problematic. It is the logical consequence of the complementary nature of both institutions. Furthermore, the efforts to make the European pharmaceutical research more competitive by establishing uniform procedures for the ethical review of clinical trials are perfectly legitimate. This chapter does not intend to criticize such a goal, or to disapprove the difference *per se* of the approaches adopted by the EU and the CoE to regulate this matter. Rather it aims to point out that such difference is problematic when it results –as it unfortunately does– in significant regulatory discrepancies between the regulations adopted by both European bodies, especially when they may lead to lower protection of vulnerable research participants.

II. – SIMILARITIES AND DIFFERENCES BETWEEN THE COE'S AND THE EU'S REGULATIONS

At first sight, there are no major discrepancies between the regulations of the Council of Europe and the European Union regarding the requirements for biomedical research. Moreover, the conditions that are set out in the CoE and EU above mentioned instruments are basically the same that can be found in virtually all ethical and legal guidelines relating to this matter. As mentioned above, there are at least three basic requirements that make biomedical research ethical, two internal and one external. The two internal conditions are: a) research subjects must give their free, explicit and informed consent (subjective condition); b) the risks for the research subject should not be disproportional to the potential benefits of the research (objective condition). The external requirement is that the research project should be approved by an independent body, which must assess its scientific merit and its ethical acceptability.

The need for *informed consent* means that medical interventions can only be carried out after the individual has been informed of the purpose, nature, risks and consequences of the intervention, and has freely consented to it. As pointed out above, this requirement has its origins in the "Nuremberg Code" of 1947, having thereafter been endorsed by the Declaration of Helsinki of the World Medical Association, the first version of which dates back to 1964. However, both documents do not have the status of legal instruments *per se.* The first international legally binding instrument that requires the consent of participants in medical research is the International Covenant on Civil and Political Rights of 1966, which provides in Article 7 that "[n]o one shall be subjected without his free consent to medical or scientific experimentation". However, it is interesting to note that it only refers to *free* consent, and there is no mention of the need that the consent should also be *informed,* as the Biomedicine Convention does. Indeed, according to Article 5 of this latter document, the participants must be informed about "the purpose and nature of the intervention" as well as its "consequences and risks". The consent must be given in writing (Article 16.5). In the case of individuals who are not able to give consent for themselves, such as minors and persons suffering from a mental disorder, the consent of their legally authorized representatives is needed (Article 6.2). All these provisions are developed in detail by the Additional Protocol on Biomedical Research of 2005. For instance, Article 13 contains a long enumeration of the information that must be provided to research participants.

Also the Clinical Trials Directive requires the informed consent of research subjects. Article 3, entitled "Protection of clinical trials subjects", provides that the trial subject, or his legal representative in case the person is unable to consent, must be informed of "the nature, significance, implications and risks" of the trial (para. d), as well as of its "objectives, risks and inconveniences", (...) "the conditions under which it will be conducted" (...), and of his "right to withdraw from the trial at any time" (para. b). The consent must, in principle, be given in writing (para. d).

There is wide agreement that research on human beings should not pose *disproportionate risks* to participants, to their life and physical and mental integrity. Otherwise such research would constitute an unacceptable instrumentalization of human beings and therefore would be contrary to human dignity. In this regard, Article 16(ii) of the Biomedicine Convention provides that risks should not be *"disproportionate* to the potential benefits of the research". Similarly, the Clinical Trials Directive stipulates that a clinical trial may be undertaken only if "the foreseeable risks and inconveniences have been weighed against the anticipated benefit for the individual trial subject and other present and future patients" (Article 3.2(a)).

In addition to the internal (subjective and objective) conditions for conducting research on human beings, there is an external requirement: the proposal must be approved by an *independent body* (i.e. a review committee, or review board), which must examine its scientific merit and its ethical acceptability. This is a fundamental condition because research on human beings is ethically justifiable only if it offers a prospect of contributing to people's health and is carried out in conformity with scientific criteria and in ways that respect and protect the rights of participants. All these elements cannot be assessed by the same team which is conducting the research, but should be evaluated by a third, impartial party. This requirement can be found in Article 16(iii) of the Biomedicine Convention, in Articles 9 to 12 of the Convention's Additional Protocol on Biomedical Research, as well as in Article 6 of the Clinical Trials Directive.

In spite of the apparent similarities between the two above mentioned instruments, a careful analysis of them reveals serious differences between them, in particular regarding the protection of the most vulnerable research subjects.[15] These normative discrepancies can be summarized as follows:

A. – *Benefit for the individual versus benefit for the group*

Biomedical research may present the prospect of a direct benefit to the participants themselves, or just to the age or health status category to which they belong (e.g. "children", "pregnant women", etc.), or simply to society at large. The question of *who* the potential beneficiaries of the research outcomes will be is to such an extent important that the consent cannot be considered really "informed" if the point has not been clearly understood by participants.[16]

---

(15)   See A. ALTAVILLA, "Clinical Research with Children: The European Legal Framework and its Implementation in French and Italian Law", *European Journal of Health Law*, 2008, vol. 15, pp. 109-125.

(16)   Council for International Organizations of Medical Sciences (CIOMS), *International Ethical Guidelines for Biomedical Research Involving Human Subjects*, 2002, Guideline 5.

According to the Biomedicine Convention, in the case of individuals who are not able to give a valid consent, such as minors and adults suffering from mental disorder, biomedical interventions must be aimed at benefiting them *directly* (Article 6.1). This condition excludes in such cases non-therapeutic research which is, by definition, carried out in the interest of third parties. The requirement of direct benefit can be exceptionally waived when the research entails *minimal risk and minimal burden* for the participant (Article 17.2(ii)).

It makes sense to allow different levels of risk according to whether or not research offers a direct benefit to the participant. Regarding competent participants, it is reasonable that research without the prospect of direct benefit can only be undertaken within certain limits, in particular, if it entails "no more than *acceptable risk* and *acceptable burden* for the individual".[17] On the other hand, when the research may be of direct benefit to the health of participants, "then a higher degree of risk and burden may be acceptable, provided that it is in proportion to the possible benefit."[18]

Regarding participants unable to consent, such as children or individuals with mental disorders, an even stricter regulation is needed since they lack self-determination. Such individuals need to be especially protected from the instrumentalization that would result from exposing them to research presenting more than a minimal risk and which only aims to benefit other individuals or the progress of science in general. In this regard, as it has been stated in relation to research on children, it seems well that "parental consent is not sufficient if proposed non-therapeutic research involves more than minimal risk to the child."[19]

The Clinical Trials Directive is in this regard particularly unsatisfying. As a legal expert has pointed out, "the provisions [of the Directive] are couched in a language so convoluted as to make it unintelligible".[20] According to Article 4 on clinical trials on minors, "some direct benefit for the group of patients [must be]

---

(17)   Additional Protocol on Biomedical Research, Article 6.
(18)   *Ibid.*
(19)   J.K. MASON, A. McCALL SMITH, and G. LAURIE, *Law and Medical Ethics,* Oxford, Oxford University Press, 2006, p. 687.
(20)   V. JUNOD, *Clinical drug trials. Studying the safety and efficacy of new pharmaceuticals,* Brussels, Bruylant, 2005, p. 398.

obtained from the [pediatric] clinical trial." (para. e). In addition, the clinical trial "must relate directly to a clinical condition from which the minor concerned suffers or be of such nature that it can only be carried out in minors" (*idem*). The key question is: does the "group of patients" referred to in Article 4(e) necessarily include the subject himself? One may infer that the answer is in the negative when comparing this provision with Article 5 on clinical trials on incompetent adults, which explicitly requires that there should be "grounds for expecting that administering the medicinal product to be tested will produce a benefit to the patient outweighing the risks or produce no risk at all" (para. i). It is indeed unclear why a similar provision is lacking in the norms relating to research on children. Should one conclude that the principle, emphatically enunciated by Article 4(i) of the Directive, that "the interests of the patient always prevail over the interest of science or society", is a mere rhetorical statement when applied to minors?

B. – *Minimal risks versus minimization of risks*

Closely related to the aforementioned issue is the requirement that non-therapeutic research on participants unable to consent can only be conducted when it does not involve more than a *minimal risk and a minimal burden* for the individual. This principle, which can be found in Article 17.2 of the Biomedicine Convention, is based on the assumption that certain very minor procedures (for example, taking a single blood sample from a newborn) do not constitute an unfair instrumentalization of incompetent persons, and may contribute in a decisive way to diagnostic and therapeutic progress for the benefit of other individuals in the same condition.[21]

This provision was often criticized on the grounds that it fails to offer a definition of "minimal risks and minimal burden". The Additional Protocol on Biomedical Research attempts to clarify this point. According to Article 17 of this latter document, "minimal risk" means that the research "will result, at the most, in a very slight and temporary negative impact on the health of the person concerned" (para. 1). The expression "minimal burden" is used to indicate that it is expected "that the discomfort will be, at the most, temporary and very slight for the person concerned" (para. 2).

---

(21) Explanatory Report to the Biomedicine Convention, paras. 111 and 112.

The Explanatory Report to the Additional Protocol on Biomedical Research provides very concrete examples of research with minimal risk and minimal burden, which include obtaining bodily fluids without invasive intervention, e.g. taking saliva or urine samples or cheek swab; taking small additional tissue samples, for example during a surgical operation; taking a blood sample from a peripheral vein or taking a sample of capillary blood; minor extensions to non-invasive diagnostic measures using technical equipment, such as sonographic examinations, taking an electrocardiogram following rest, one X-ray exposure, and carrying out one computer tomographic exposure or one exposure using magnetic resonance imaging without a contrast medium.[22]

It is noteworthy that the last version of the Declaration of Helsinki (2008) also includes the requirement for minimal risk as it provides that "a potential research subject who is incompetent (...) must not be included in a research study that has not the likelihood of benefit for them unless (...) the research entails only minimal risk and minimal burden" (para. 27). Similarly, the CIOMS Guidelines stipulate that, in the case of research with individuals unable to consent, "the risk from research interventions that do not hold out the prospect of direct benefit for the individual subject should be no more likely and not greater than the risk attached to routine medical or psychological examination of such persons".[23]

In contrast to this, the Clinical Trials Directive omits any reference to minimal risk and minimal burden. Articles 4(g) and 5(f) only include the requirement that clinical trials must be designed "to minimise pain, discomfort, fear and any other foreseeable risk in relation to the disease and developmental stage." Strangely, this provision only appears in the above mentioned articles, which cover research on persons unable to consent. This may give inadvertent readers of the Directive the impression that a lower level of risk is required in such cases, and that special protection is granted to vulnerable individuals. However, this would be a misleading interpretation of those provisions, because "minimizing risk" is not synonymous with "minimal risk". The minimization of risks is

---

(22) Explanatory Report to the Additional Protocol to the Convention on Human Rights and Biomedicine Concerning Biomedical Research, 2005, para. 100.

(23) Council for International Organizations of Medical Sciences (CIOMS), *op. cit.*, Guideline 9. It should be noted however that the same Guideline 9 allows slight or minor increases above such minimal risk "when there is an overriding scientific or medical rationale for such increases and when an ethical review committee has approved them."

a *general requirement* for every research on human subjects, not only on persons unable to consent but also on competent adults. The Additional Protocol on Biomedical Research explicitly refers to it when it provides that "all reasonable measures shall be taken to ensure safety and to minimise risk and burden for the research participants" (Article 21). Similarly, the Declaration of Helsinki (2008) states that "every precaution must be taken (...) to minimize the impact of the study" on the physical, mental and social integrity of research subjects (para. 23).

The general requirement of the minimization of risks in biomedical research is often formulated by saying that the research should present "a favourable risk-benefit ratio"[24] or, in other words, that the risks should be *proportionate* to the expected benefits. This means that, while the "minimization of risk" is a *relative* notion, as much dependent on the particular circumstances of each research study and on the expected benefits, the requirement of "minimal risk" embodies an *objective* standard. It is precisely because it is objective that it is possible to provide concrete examples of risks that are regarded as "minimal", as the Explanatory Report to the Additional Protocol on Biomedical Research does (para. 100).

C. – *Respect for the minor's objection*

Although children cannot give a valid consent for participating in medical research, and the permission of their parents or legal representatives is always required, this does not mean that they should be totally excluded from the informed consent process. On the contrary, the willing cooperation of the children should be sought, after they have been informed to the extent that their maturity and intelligence permit. Some children can understand the basic implications of participating in a research trial and go through the necessary procedures. They may also be able to express a refusal. Such refusals should always be respected, even if the parents have given permission, unless the child needs a treatment which is not available outside the context of the research, the research offers a direct therapeutic benefit, and there is no acceptable alternative therapy.[25] In this regard, the Declaration of Helsinki states that

---

(24) E. EMANUEL, D. WENDLER and C. GRADY, "What Makes Clinical Research Ethical?", *JAMA*, 2000, vol. 283, n° 20, pp. 2702-2711.

(25) Council for International Organizations of Medical Sciences (CIOMS), *op.cit.*, Guideline 14 and commentary.

"the potential subject's dissent should be respected" (para. 28). Other recent guidelines emphasize the importance of respecting child's refusal to participate or continue in a research study.[26]

Consistently with this requirement, the Biomedicine Convention sets out the general principle, which is valid for both clinical and research interventions, that "the opinion of the minor shall be taken into consideration as an increasingly determining factor in proportion to his or her age and degree of maturity" (Article 6.2). Regarding research on persons unable to consent, Article 17.1(v) provides that it can only be undertaken "if the person concerned does not object". This means that the wish of the individual "prevails and is always decisive."[27] The Additional Protocol on Biomedical Research specifies that the "objection to participation shall not lead to any form of discrimination against the person concerned, in particular regarding the right to medical care" (Article 15.3).

In contrast, the Clinical Trials Directive is rather unclear about the imperative of respecting the child's objection to participate in a clinical trial. Article 4(c) only provides that the wish of the minor to refuse participation or to be withdrawn from the clinical trial at any time will be "considered" by the investigator. This norm offers little guidance as to the value of the minor's refusal and opens the door to potential abuse. This is especially a cause for concern when one considers that the Directive does not exclude minors from participating in research without direct benefit to them and entailing more than minimal risk. It should be noted that Article 5(c), which deals with the refusal to participate in a clinical trial made by an incapacitated adult, also states that such refusal will be simply "considered" by the investigator.

D. – Inducements to participating in research

The promise of financial incentives to participate in research is prohibited by most ethical and legal regulations on the grounds that they compromise the voluntariness of subjects' consent decisions, may lead to exploitation of people in need, and can persuade potential participants to take risks against their better judgment. Nevertheless, a distinction is commonly made between "due"

---

(26) J.K. Mason, A. McCall Smith, and G. Laurie, *op. cit.,* p. 688.
(27) Explanatory Report to the Convention on Human Rights and Biomedicine, para. 108.

and "undue" inducements. In this regard, the CIOMS Guidelines stipulate that

> "Subjects may be reimbursed for lost earnings, travel costs and other expenses incurred in taking part in a study; they may also receive free medical services. Subjects, particularly those who receive no direct benefit from research, may also be paid or otherwise compensated for inconvenience and time spent. The payments should not be so large, however, or the medical services so extensive as to induce prospective subjects to consent to participate in the research against their better judgment ("undue inducement")" [28]

Similarly, the Convention's Additional Protocol on Biomedicine Research provides that the ethics committee, at the time of reviewing a research project, must come to the conclusion that "no undue influence, including that of a financial nature, will be exerted on persons to participate in research. In this respect, particular attention must be given to vulnerable or dependent persons" (Article 13). The Explanatory Report to the Protocol specifies that compensation to the participants, and eventually to their representatives, is not regarded as "undue influence" if it is "appropriate to the burden and inconvenience [to which they are exposed]" (para. 64). However, such financial influence becomes "undue", and therefore must not be exerted, when "it is provided at a level that might encourage participants to take risks that they would not otherwise find acceptable" (ibid.). It will be up to the ethics committee to decide, case by case, whether the promised payment or any other kind of influence on potential participants becomes "undue" (ibid.).

The Clinical Trials Directive is not satisfactory in this regard. Certainly, it provides that "no incentives or financial inducements" can be offered to minors or to incapacitated adults (Articles 4(d) and 5(d)). However, it should be noted that this requirement does not appear among the general conditions for the protection of research subjects. It is difficult to believe that this was an accidental omission, since the point was carefully included in the two Articles dealing with persons unable to consent. Thus, one may infer that the promise of financial incentives are regarded by the Directive as legitimate without limits, insofar as participants are competent adults, and

---

(28) Council for International Organizations of Medical Sciences (CIOMS), *op. cit.*, Guideline 6.

regardless if they are vulnerable for some other reason (educational, socio-cultural, economic, etc.). This contradicts most guidelines on biomedical research, which set up a general rule to protect all potential research participants from exploitation or coercion, not only those who are unable to consent.

E. – *Clinical equipoise*

The principle of "clinical equipoise" stipulates that a patient should not be involved in a randomised-clinical trial (i.e. a trial that randomly assigns patients to two or more treatments) unless there is a state of genuine uncertainty within the expert medical community about the comparative therapeutic merits of each arm of the trial. This means that, as a trial begins, treatments (including any placebo arm) must be regarded as having equal merit in treating a particular condition. The expression "clinical equipoise" was first used by Benjamin Freedman in 1987.[29] The rationale for observing this principle is that it ensures that patients involved in studies are not prescribed treatments that are *known* to be less effective that some other treatments for their condition.[30] It provides a moral foundation to the requirement that the health care of subjects should not be disadvantaged by research participation. At the same time, it aims to make physicians' role as *scientists* dedicated to conducting the best studies to gain knowledge compatible with their role as *healers* dedicated to adapting treatments to each patient's needs, goals and values.[31]

The requirement of clinical equipoise is endorsed by the Declaration of Helsinki (2008), which states, as a general principle, that "the benefits, risks, burdens and effectiveness of a new intervention must be tested against those of the best current proven intervention" (para. 32). Similarly, the CIOMS Guidelines stipulates that "as a general rule, research subjects in the control group of a trial of a diagnostic, therapeutic, or preventive

---

(29) B FREEDMAN, "Equipoise and the ethics of clinical research", *New England Journal of Medicine*, 1987, vol. 317, n° 3, pp. 141-145.

(30) K LIDDELL *et al.*, *op. cit.*

(31) L KOPELMAN, "Research methodology. II Clinical trials", in S. POST (ed.), *Encyclopedia of Bioethics*, 3rd ed., vol. 4, New York, Macmillan, 2004, pp. 2334-2342.

intervention should receive an established effective intervention" (Guideline 11).

Similarly, the Biomedicine Convention's Additional Protocol on Biomedical Research endorses the principle of clinical equipoise in Article 23, entitled "Non-interference with necessary clinical interventions", which states that "in research associated with prevention, diagnosis or treatment, participants assigned to control groups shall be assured of proven methods of prevention, diagnosis or treatment" (para. 2).

Unlike the abovementioned guidelines and regulations, which clearly support the principle of clinical equipoise, the relevant provision of the Clinical Trials Directive is drafted in obscure terms. Article 3.2(a) stipulates that "(...) a clinical trial may be initiated only if the Ethics Committee and/or the competent authority comes to the conclusion that the anticipated therapeutic and public health benefits justify the risks and may be continued only if compliance with this requirement is permanently monitored."

Some authors have pointed out the serious interpretative difficulties posed by this norm, as it allows "the benefit to the public to outweigh any degree of risk to the individual" and "no mention is made of clinical equipoise, nor it is stated that the risks should be necessary, proportionate or minimised".[32] Trying to understand why the principle of clinical equipoise was overlooked in this way, they suggest the explanation that "those drafting the Directive were strongly influenced by the pharmaceutical industry which, preferring the ease of placebo-controlled trials, downplayed the importance of clinical equipoise."[33]

F. – *Independence of ethics committees*

The credibility of the review of medical research projects largely depends on the *independence* of the committee responsible for conducting such a review. This means, concretely, that any conflict of interest should be avoided. For instance, the members of the review board must be independent from the research team, and any direct financial or other material benefit they may derive

---

(32)   K LIDDELL *et al.*, *op. cit.*
(33)   *Ibid.*

from the research should not be contingent on the outcome of their review. [34]

Article 16(iii) of the Biomedicine Convention states that each research project should be submitted for independent examination of its scientific merit and ethical acceptability to a competent body. Developing on this principle, Article 10 of the Additional Protocol on Biomedical Research provides that "[p]arties to this Protocol shall take measures to assure the independence of the ethics committee. That body shall not be subject to undue external influences" (para. 1). Furthermore, the members of the ethics committee "shall declare all circumstances that might lead to a conflict of interest. Should such conflict arise, those involved shall not participate in that review" (para. 2).

This is another issue in which the diversity of approaches followed by the EU and the CoE becomes visible. The Clinical Trials Directive just mentions in passing, in the definition of terms, that the ethics committee is an "independent body" (Article 2(k)), but avoids explaining or developing this fundamental element. This omission is especially notable given that a large (if not the largest) part of the Directive is precisely devoted to the functioning and tasks of ethics committees. This is not to suggest that the drafters of the Directive acted consciously *against* the requirement that review boards must perform their task in complete independence from any external influence. But, what is clear, is that the Directive does not focus on this essential feature of ethics committees, but rather on the *rapidity* of the decision making process. According to Article 6.5, ethics committees have a maximum of 60 days to give an opinion and, in the case of multi-centre clinical trials, there must be only one opinion of an ethics committee in each member state (Article 7). Some have expressed the view that these two requirements clearly reflect the interests of the pharmaceutical industry and that "the limits are arguably too tight and restrictive to be suitable in all cases if the safety and rights of research subjects are paramount". [35]

---

(34) Council for International Organizations of Medical Sciences (CIOMS), *op. cit.*, Guideline 2.

(35) D. BEYLEVELD and S. SETHE, *op. cit.*, p. 185.

CONCLUSION

This comparative analysis of the two main European regulations relating to biomedical research, namely, the Council of Europe's Biomedicine Convention and the EU's Clinical Trials Directive, reveals significant discrepancies between them. Although it is understandable that each European body focuses on different regulatory aspects of biomedical research, since each of them has its own objectives and competences, it is a matter for concern that the difference of approaches has resulted in a number of normative discrepancies, which may lead to watered-down protection for research participants, in particular, the most vulnerable ones.

This contrast shows that any legal regulation of biomedical research is necessarily confronted with the tension between the two above mentioned paradigms: the protection of participants' rights, and the promotion of medical (in particular, pharmaceutical) research. Nevertheless, although every society is interested in supporting both objectives, both of which aim to contribute to the common good, it is clear that in case of conflict, the first one should have the priority.

The principle of primacy of the human being over science and society is a direct corollary of the requirement of respect for human dignity. This principle, which surprisingly can be found not only in the Biomedicine Convention (Article 2) but also in the Clinical Trials Directive (ironically, in the provisions dealing with research on minors and incapacitated adults: Articles 4(i) and 5(h)), aims to emphasize one fundamental idea: that science is not an end in itself but only a means for improving the well-being of individuals. Thus, people should not be reduced to mere instruments for the benefit of science. Certainly, the very fact that we live in a society means that we should in some way contribute to the common good, according to our capacities and preferences. However, in democratic societies, people do not live for the sake of society or science, but have their own purpose, which greatly transcends the boundaries of social or scientific interests.

CHAPTER 10

REGULATING ADVANCE DIRECTIVES AT THE COUNCIL OF EUROPE

It is now widely accepted that patients' right to informed consent presupposes the possibility for them to refuse treatments, especially when these are perceived by them as excessive, futile or psychologically harmful. Both consent and refusal of consent are envisaged today as two different expressions of the same patients' right to self-determination. Thus, refusals of medical treatments are also to be respected, even if they might adversely affect patients' health or shorten their life.

But a problem emerges when patients have lost their decision-making capacity due to a condition that is not likely to be reversible (e.g. persistent vegetative state, severe head injury, dementia, etc.). Who shall decide for them in such cases? Which criteria should be used in the decision-making process? What if family members disagree about treatments to be provided or withheld? What if doctors and patient's relatives have different views on what is best for the patient? Here is where the potential utility of advance directives comes into play; they can take two different forms, which are not necessarily exclusive of each other, since they both can be combined in the same document:

a. The *living wills,* which are (usually written) instructions that specify ahead of time personal preferences regarding the provision –or the withholding– of particular treatments in the event that the individual becomes unable to make decisions in the future;

b. The *lasting (or durable) powers of attorney for health care,* which allow individuals to appoint someone as a "health care proxy" (for example a trusted relative or friend) to make health care decisions on their behalf once they lose the ability to do so.

The key issue is however whether or to what extent domestic legislation recognizes the validity and efficacy of advance directives. At present, European countries have very different or no legal standards at all on this matter. The current situation may create problems with the increasing cross-border movement of EU citizens. In addition, the growing of the aging population of European societies is likely to create an increased demand for advance directives in the next years. What seems to be clear is that a reliable solution has to be found to solve the practical problem posed by advance directives made in one European country and implemented in another.

This chapter first outlines the strengths and shortcomings of Article 9 of the European Biomedicine Convention, which specifically deals with advance directives. Then it analyzes the Council of Europe's Recommendation (2009)11 on continuing powers of attorney and advance directives for incapacity.

I. – ADVANCE DIRECTIVES IN THE BIOMEDICINE CONVENTION

There is a striking contrast between the decades-long attention paid to advance health care planning in the United States and the only recent interest given to it in Europe. In the U.S., the public debate about the scope and legal efficacy of advance directives started around thirty years ago. The American lawyer Luis Kutner seems to have been the first to suggest the concept of living wills in 1967.[1] The Congress passed in 1990 the *Patient Self-Determination Act,* which requires hospitals to ask every patient on admission whether they have completed an advance directive (either a living will or a durable power of attorney, or both) and, if so, to bring a copy to the hospital. If the patient does not have an advance directive but would like more information about these documents, hospitals must also provide the information. At present, all U.S. states have specific laws recognizing the use of advance directives and often provide a model document that may (or in some states *must*) be followed.[2]

---

(1) A. MacLean, "Advance Directives and the Rocky Waters of Anticipatory Decision-Making", *Medical Law Review,* 2008, vol. 16, n° 1, p. 1.

(2) See the complete list of model documents state by state at: http://www.uslegalforms.com/livingwills/ (accessed on 21 May 2013). In the US operates a privately held organization (U.S. Living Will Registry) that electronically stores advance directives and makes them available to health care providers across the country. See http://www.uslivingwillregistry.com/ (accessed on 21 May 2013).

In contrast, the attention given to advance directives in most European countries is very recent. Only in the last few years some of States have enacted specific laws to regulate this matter, while others are still reluctant to do so.[3] The fact is that it is still unusual in Europe to base clinical decisions regarding incompetent patients on their previously expressed wishes.

The Biomedicine Convention only covers this issue in Article 9, which provides that:

> "The previously expressed wishes relating to a medical intervention by a patient who is not, at the time of the intervention, in a state to express his or her wishes shall be taken into account."

This provision is very important as it marks the first recognition of the value of advance directives in a common European binding instrument. Although European countries are not obliged under Article 9 to give legally binding force to advance directives, they must *at least* recognize their advisory effect. Professor Adriano Bompiani, who was directly involved in the drafting of the Convention as Italian representative, has pointed out that the expression "taken into account" used in Article 9 was adopted as a way to find a balance between, on the one hand, due consideration of the patient's wishes expressed in advance, and on the other, a technical, objective assessment of the current clinical situation of the patient and of the elementary duties of the doctor to choose the more adequate treatment according to the current circumstances.[4]

While this compromise formula is understandable in the light of the conflicting views of European countries on this matter, the fact is that the wording of Article 9 is problematic in the sense that the expression "to take into account", without any additional clarification, is too ambiguous and can be interpreted in very different ways.[5] It would have been preferable to have clearer guidance for doctors as to what extent, or under what conditions,

---

(3) R. ANDORNO, N. BILLER-ANDORNO and S. BRAUER, "Advance Health Care Directives: Towards a Coordinated European Policy?", *European Journal of Health Law*, 2009, vol. 16, n° 3, pp. 207-227.

(4) A. BOMPIANI, *Consiglio d'Europa, diritti umani e biomedicina. Genesi della Convenzione di Oviedo e dei Protocolli*, Rome, Edizioni Studium, 2009, p. 86.

(5) See D. MANAÏ, "Images du droit du patient au miroir de la Convention européenne pour les droits de l'homme et la biomédecine", in F. WERRO (ed.), *L'européanisation du droit privé? Vers un code civil européen?*, Fribourg, Editions Universitaires de Fribourg, 1998, p. 120; H.-L. SCHREIBER, "The European Ethical Convention: Legal Aspects", in A. SCHAUER,

patients' wishes expressed in advance must be implemented. It is obvious that if health care professionals could arbitrarily decide, without giving any serious reason, not to comply with patients' preferences, the patient's effort of making an advance directive becomes useless. This is the key point of the current controversy, which becomes also visible in the use of the wording "previously expressed wishes" instead of "advance directives" in the title of Article 9. This latter expression, which does appear neither in the Convention nor in its Explanatory Report, was avoided on the grounds that it presupposes the *binding* nature of such documents.

Another shortcoming of Article 9 is that it is exclusively focused on living wills, but totally ignores the other form that advance directives may take (the continuing power of attorney). This becomes especially clear when one reads the Explanatory Report to the Convention, which never refers to the possibility of appointing a health care proxy.[6] The Council of Europe's Recommendation (2009)11, as will be mentioned hereafter, attempts to fill this lacuna.

It should also be mentioned that the Explanatory Report to the Convention does not resolve the ambiguity of Article 9. It only states that the expression "taken into account" "does not mean that previously expressed wishes should necessarily be followed" and provides two examples to illustrate why in some circumstances the practitioner may have good reasons not to comply with the patient's wishes on the grounds that they do not apply anymore to the situation at hand: a) when they have been expressed a long time before the intervention; b) when medical technology has made significant progress since the time when the advance directive was signed and it can be reasonably assumed that, in the present circumstances, the will of the patient would have been different.[7] In light of these examples it would seem that the spirit of Article 9 is that doctors cannot act arbitrarily, i.e., they need to have *good reasons* to disregard the patient's legitimate wishes expressed in an advance directive. The problem is that this basic principle has not been explicitly included in the Convention itself, nor there is

---

H.L. SCHREIBER and Z. RYN (eds.), *Ethics in Medicine,* Göttingen, Vandenhoeck & Ruprecht, 2001, p. 247.

(6)   See paragraphs 60 to 62.

(7)   Explanatory Report to the Biomedicine Convention, paragraph 62.

any indication as to what reasons can be validly given by health care professionals for not complying with the patient's explicit will.

Therefore, the key point is whether it would be possible (and desirable) to reach at least a minimum consensus among European countries on the two following issues:

- *The minimal formal requirements for the validity of advance directives* such as for instance the individual's legal capacity and freedom of choice at the time of its drafting; his/her incompetence at the time of its implementation; absence of revocation in the meantime; the need of a previous consultation with a health care professional, etc.

- *The legal effect of advance directives,* which directly relates to extent to which doctors are obliged to comply with patients' preferences and the *reasons* they can legitimately give for not doing so. Among the possible reasons the following can be mentioned: that the patient's will is contrary to law; that the document was written too many years before its implementation; that there have been significant advances in medical sciences that are relevant to the advance directive in question; that there are some serious evidence suggesting that the patient would have a different view had he/she had adequate knowledge of the current circumstances.

II. – THE RECOMMENDATION (2009)11

A. – *General features of the recommendation*

The Council of Europe's Committee of Ministers adopted on 9 December 2009 the Recommendation (2009)11 on "continuing powers of attorney and advance directives for incapacity". This document is of great relevance regarding advance directives as it seeks to fill the two above mentioned gaps of the Biomedicine Convention –the vagueness of Article 9 regarding the legal efficacy of living wills, and the lack of regulation of continuing powers of attorney.

Before focusing on the analysis of the Recommendation, two preliminary remarks ought to be made. The first is that the scope of the recommendation is actually much broader than health care, since it also covers decisions regarding welfare, and economic and financial matters. The second is that the Recommendation uses the expression "advance directives" in a narrow sense, as a synonym for "living wills". Continuing powers of attorney are treated as a separate category. In order to avoid misunderstandings, this paper will use below the expression "advance directive" in this narrow meaning.

The Recommendation consists of a preamble and seventeen principles. It makes it clear from the very beginning that its overarching scope is "to promote self-determination of capable adults in the event of their future incapacity, by means of continuing powers of attorney and advance directives" (Principle 1.1). "Self-determination", which is mentioned five times in the whole Recommendation, clearly embodies the key value of this document.

The preamble draws attention to previous international and regional instruments relating to this matter, in particular, to the Recommendation (99)4 of 23 February 1999 on principles concerning the legal protection of incapable adults. This latter document is recognized as a "valuable and up-to-date international instrument" in this field. However, it is also recognized that there is a need to build upon the principles of subsidiarity and necessity already contained in the Recommendation (99)4, and to "supplement" it by giving prominence to the principle of self-determination. There is indeed a substantive difference between both documents: the 1999 Recommendation deals with measures of protection provided by *competent authorities* (i.e., courts), while the 2009 one covers decisions made privately by the *individuals concerned themselves*, either by appointing a proxy or by making an advance directive. According to the Recommendation, this new strategy for protecting the interests of incapacitated adults should be given priority over other measures of protection (Principle 1.1), not only more because it is more in line with the principle of self-determination, but also because it avoids time-consuming and sometimes costly, sensitive and burdensome judicial and administrative proceedings.[8]

Nevertheless, the two means of self-determination covered by the 2009 Recommendation do not seem to be put on an equal level: the document appears to give preference to the use of surrogate decision-making over living wills: while most of its provisions

---

(8) The Preamble notes that "that in some member states continuing powers of attorney are a preferred alternative to court decisions on representation".

(Principles 3 to 13) concern continuing powers of attorney, living wills receive little attention: only the last four principles (14 to 17) deal with them, and in a very succinct way. It is true that continuing powers of attorney cover a broad spectrum of possible uses (financial, economic, welfare and medical ones) and therefore need to be regulated in more detail, while living wills are particularly (though not exclusively) conceived to serve health care purposes. [9] But there are more substantive reasons explaining this disparity. First of all, European States are well familiarized with the use of powers of attorney, which have a very long tradition in the continent (beginning with the contract of *mandatum* in Roman law), even if only recently they began to be used for making decisions about medical treatment. In contrast, living wills are an entirely new way of stating health care preferences ahead of time. Secondly, the implementation of living wills raises difficult (and sometimes unsolvable) problems of interpretation, which do not exist, or are less serious, with surrogate decision-making. Thirdly, some States are concerned with the possibility that living wills could be misused, leading to the neglect of vulnerable or elderly patients, even maybe for purely economic reasons. In addition, it must be noted that over the last years, doubts have been raised about the real utility of living wills, especially when they are drafted in general terms (as it is often the case). Looking back at the long, and according to them, unsuccessful experience with living wills in the United States, some experts suggest that it is time to change the strategy and give priority to continuing powers on attorney, or at least to a combination of living wills and continuing powers of attorney. [10]

B. – *Continuing powers of attorney*

As mentioned above, one of the well-known problems with living wills is the difficulty of drafting a sufficiently specific document without knowing the particular condition in which one will be placed. When there is already a diagnosis that makes a serious condition predictable, the spectrum of decisions regarding

---

(9) The Explanatory Memorandum to the Recommendation is explicit in this regard: "The most important type of legally regulated advance directives concerns health issues" (n° 65).

(10) A. FAGERLIN and C.E. SCHNEIDER, "Enough. The Failure of the Living Will", *Hastings Center Report*, 2004, vol. 34, n° 2, pp. 30-41.

alternative treatments is relatively limited and easy to handle. But how can healthy individuals decide in advance in specific terms the kind of treatments they would like to have or not, if they do not know in which situation they will be placed? In contrast, continuing powers of attorney have the great advantage of allowing the doctor to enter into a dialogue with a person (the attorney, or proxy), rather than being merely confronted with a piece of paper, which necessarily has to be interpreted. The proxy can directly discuss with the health care professional about the various available options, about the benefits and risks of each one, and this taking into account the concrete circumstances in which the patient is placed.

The proper role of the proxy in the decision making-process can differ depending upon which modality of surrogate decision is adopted. There are basically two different models:

a. *Substituted judgement*, where proxies, based on their knowledge of the patients' preferences, make a judgement intended to reflect, as closely as possible, the judgement the patients would make if they were competent. This approach attempts to simulate an incompetent patient's autonomous decision by considering the personal values and preferences held by the patient and is therefore justified by the *principle of respect for autonomy*.

b. *Best interests,* where the proxy makes an assessment of the patient's best interests and decides based on that assessment. In this approach, the proxy must consider, from an objective point of view, what course of action would result in the greatest benefit and least harm to the patient. Here the proxy does not need to imagine the situation from the incompetent patient's perspective, but rather makes a decision *on behalf* of the patient. This approach is justified by the *principles of beneficence and non-maleficence.* [11]

These two models of surrogate decision-making can be combined, but in such cases it is advisable to make it clear which approach has the priority and which one is only subsidiary to the other. For instance, when proxies have insufficient knowledge to make a judgment about the patient's preferences, it is reasonable to

---

(11)   J.E. SNYDER and C. GAUTHIER, *Evidence-Based Medical Ethics. Cases for Practice-Based Learning,* Charlotte, North Carolina, Humana Press, 2008, p. 19.

encourage them to consider the best interests of the patient. On the contrary, the attempt to simultaneously combine both approaches risks creating confusion about the proper role of the proxies and about the criteria they should use in making a decision. [12] It may happen that both criteria appear to be in conflict. What if the proxy considers that a particular treatment is in the best interest of the patient, but it seems to be contrary to the patient's wishes?

In this regard, the Recommendation (2009)11 is not sufficiently clear. On the one hand, proxies are required to make their decisions in accordance with the continuing power of attorney and in the (best) interests of the patient (Principle 10.1). On the other hand, they must also take into account, "as far as possible", "the wishes and feelings" of the patient and give them "due respect" (Principle 10.2). How can both requirements be harmonized? A possible way out of this dilemma is to consider that the best interest of the patient, which is mentioned in the first paragraph and without any particular condition, is a general principle that should always guide the proxy's decision. This standard embodies the basic guiding value for surrogate decision-making, and offers the conceptual framework for the proxy's decisions. On the contrary, the "wishes and feelings" of the patient are an element among others that the proxy must take into account, "as far as possible", to determine what is in the best interest of the patient.

It should be acknowledged, however, that the concept of "best interest of the patient" is highly abstract and can be interpreted in different ways when confronted with the need to make a concrete decision. For instance, can decisions leading to the withholding or withdrawal of a treatment because it regarded as futile or unduly burdensome be in the best interests of the patient? The most common answer to this question seems to be yes, even if it is foreseen that such a decision may also hasten that person's death. [13] However, in practice things are not always that clear-cut. In this regard, the UK Mental Capacity Act, passed in 2005, offers a very detailed and helpful guidance for identifying what might be, or not, in the best interests of the patient (Section 4). Especially important

---

(12) See A. WRIGLEY, "Proxy consent: moral authority misconceived", *Journal of Medical Ethics,* 2007, vol. 33, n° 9, pp. 527-531.

(13) This statement does not include the withdrawal of artificial nutrition and hydration of patients in persistent vegetative state, which remains controversial, as was shown by the cases of Terri Schiavo in the US and of Eluana Englaro in Italy.

is Section 4.5, which provides, in relation to life-sustaining treatments, that the individual making the decision "must not, in considering whether the treatment is in the best interests of the person concerned, be motivated by a desire to bring about his death". This means that the notion of "best interests" relates to the benefits and burdens of the treatment itself (and may eventually justify the withholding or withdrawal of life-sustaining measures), but such decisions should not reflect a judgement that the patient's life is not worth living. Thus, in the effort to determine what is in the best interests of the patient, a very delicate balance is needed to prevent, on the one hand, futile or too burdensome treatments and, on the other hand, a slippery slope towards intentional killing of incapacitated patients by omission.

The definition of "continuing power of attorney" given by the Recommendation (2009)11 is somehow confusing, and needs a clarification. According to Principle 2.1, it is "a mandate given by a capable adult with the purpose that it shall remain in force, or enter into force, in the event of the granter's incapacity". The use of two different expressions ("remain in force" and "enter into force") obeys to the fact that the definition includes the point of time in which the power of attorney will become operative, and this varies depending on the purpose of the document: those for economic and financial matters may become effective immediately, and remain valid after the granter's incapacity; those for health, welfare and personal matters only will be in effect in the event of the granter's incapacity.

Under the Recommendation, any competent individual, and not necessarily a family member, can be appointed as attorney (Principle 4.1). Granters can appoint more than one person, but in such cases they should indicate how the attorneys are to act (jointly, separately, jointly in relation to some matters and separately in relation to others, as substitutes, etc.) (Principle 4.2).

Regarding the formalities to be complied with, the Recommendation requires that the power of attorney "shall be in writing" (Principle 5.1), and that the document shall explicitly state that it will become effective in the event of the granter's incapacity (Principle 5.2). Although the Recommendation does not mention that the document must be signed, this seems to be an obvious requirement, especially considering that the attorney will have the power to make decisions on matters of life and death pertaining to the granter. The Recommendation leaves to the States to determine other formal requirements for the validity of the power of attorney (for instance, notarization, presence of witnesses, registration with a public office, etc.) (Principles 5.3 and 8).

C. – *Advance directives*

Principle 2.3 defines advance directives (living wills) as "instructions given or wishes made by a capable adult concerning issues that may arise in the event of his or her incapacity". The use of two terms ("instructions" and "wishes") does not serve a merely rhetorical function: the word "instructions" is employed to refer to advance directives that are legally binding, while "wishes" is used to indicate that such documents have a merely advisory value. [14] This double terminology, which also appears in Principle 15, shows well the deep disagreement between European countries concerning the legal effect to be given to advance directives.

The new Recommendation does not bring to an end this lack of consensus. States are still left to decide whether advances directives should be legally binding or not. This does not mean that no progress has been made in this field since the Biomedicine Convention. Today there is a growing awareness of the importance of enhancing patients' self-determination and avoiding futile or disproportionate treatments. Precisely in an attempt to promote patients' autonomous decisions, a number of European countries have in recent years passed specific laws on advance directives, or are on the way of enacting legislation in this area. The Biomedicine Convention has played a role in this process, and there is no doubt that it has even had an impact on those countries that did not ratify it yet. But the fact is that disagreements still persist about the norms that should govern advance directives.

Interestingly, the terminology used in Principle 15 to refer to previously expressed wishes is slightly different from the one found in Article 9 of the Biomedicine Convention. While this latter provides that such wishes "shall be taken into account", the Recommendation stipulates that they should be given "due respect". This latter wording sounds stronger than the one of the

---

(14) Explanatory Memorandum to the Recommendation, n° 178.

Biomedicine Convention. In this regard, it is interesting to note that some countries employ the verb 'to respect' in their domestic laws precisely in order to make advance directives binding.[15] Was this difference in the wording deliberate or simply an oversight? The latter is more likely since it only appears in the English version of the Recommendation, while the French text employs the same verb that is used in Article 9 of the Biomedicine Convention ("prendre en compte", that is, "take into account").

Regarding the formalities to be observed, in general, advance directives do not necessarily have to be in writing. A person can communicate orally his or her preferences to family members, friends, medical staff, etc. However it is clear that a written decision is to be preferred over a verbal one. In any case, if the advance directive is intended to have binding effect, it should be in writing, or at least recorded in some way (Principle 16). States are also asked to address the issue of substantial changes in circumstances in order to determine how that will affect the validity of advance directives (Principle 15.2).

In an additional effort to promote domestic legislation in this area, the Parliamentary Assembly of the Council of Europe issued in 2012 a Resolution recommending Member States to "sign, ratify and fully implement the Oviedo Convention, if they have not already done so" (para 6.1); to "apply Committee of Ministers Recommendation CM/Rec(2009)11 on principles concerning continuing powers of attorney and advance directives for incapacity" (para. 6.2); and to "review, if need be, their relevant legislation with a view to possibly improving it" (para. 6.3).[16]

---

(15) For instance, the new Article 372.2 of the Swiss Civil Code provides that advance directives must be "respected" by the doctor and this is commonly interpreted as a recognition that they are *prima facie* binding. Such binding effect is not absolute as the doctors is not obliged to follow the patient's preferences if he or she considers that there are serious reasons to believe that they do not reflect anymore the patient's wishes in the current circumstances. The French version of Article 372.2 reads: "Le médecin respecte les directives anticipées du patient, sauf si elles violent des dispositions légales, ou si des doutes sérieux laissent supposer qu'elles ne sont pas l'expression de sa libre volonté ou qu'elles ne correspondent pas à sa volonté présumée dans la situation donnée".

(16) Resolution 1859 (2012), Protecting human rights and dignity by taking into account previously expressed wishes of patients, 25 January 2012.

CONCLUSION

Respect for patient's self-determination, which is crucial in modern medical ethics and law, provides the grounds for the requirement of informed consent for any medical intervention. This fundamental principle has been enshrined in Article 5 of the European Biomedicine Convention. Today it is widely accepted that the right to informed consent also includes the possibility for patients to refuse treatment, especially when they regard it as disproportionate, excessive or futile. The role of advance directives is precisely to provide patients with a means to continue exercising this right also when they lose decision-making capacity.

The Council of Europe has achieved two important milestones in the promotion of patients' self-determination regarding medical care to be implemented in the event of future decisional incapacity: the Biomedicine Convention and the Recommendation (2009)11. The former represents the first European binding instrument recognizing that living wills should have, at least, an advisory value and that therefore they must be "taken into account" by health care professionals. The latter is an attempt to further develop that recognition by means of a soft law instrument, and especially, to draw the attention of European States to an alternative tool for planning health care in advance: the continuing power of attorney.

CONCLUSION

The overall message conveyed in this book is that we are witnessing the development of a set of global legal principles that aim to guide biomedical activities. The emerging normative system, which can be regarded as the first step towards an international biomedical law, has three main features: the central role assigned to human dignity, the use of a human rights framework, and the adoption of a set of broad, general principles instead of detailed prescriptive rules. The ultimate goals of international biolaw are to ensure that biomedical research and clinical practice are in conformity with human dignity and human rights, and to contribute in this way to the wellbeing of present and future generations.

Certainly, most intergovernmental instruments relating to biomedical issues have soft law status and are therefore not immediately binding for States. The most salient example of this is the Universal Declaration on Bioethics and Human Rights. However, despite their lack of binding force in principle, soft law agreements are not legally irrelevant; rather they represent a new and different form of normativity –a gradual normativity– for addressing especially sensitive issues. [1] In this regard, it is significant that the principles contained in the three UNESCO declarations on bioethics have been formally and unanimously agreed by the community of States, which considers them as appropriate basic standards for responding to biomedical challenges. The hope is that these principles will gain ever greater acceptance over time and be incorporated into domestic laws, be increasingly applied by national and international courts, and, in the future, become customary law or be formally enshrined in treaties (i.e. binding instruments). This was precisely the process by which the broad principles of the Universal Declaration of Human Rights of 1948 –a non-binding instrument– were ultimately converted into binding norms in the International Covenants on Civil and

---

(1)   J. PAUWELYN, "Is it international law or not, and does it even matter?", in J. PAUWELYN, R. VESSEL, and J. WOUTERS (eds.), *Informal International Lawmaking,* Oxford, Oxford University Press, 2012, pp. 125-160.

Political Rights and on Economic, Social and Cultural Rights of 1966. Given the importance of the issues at stake in the field of bioethics, not only for individuals, but also for humankind as a whole, it is not hard to predict that the development of treaties in this area will occur sooner or later. [2]

A decisive step towards a consolidation of biolegal principles will be their gradual recognition and application by national and international courts. Judges have indeed a decisive role to play in this process, because it is up to them to interpret and apply the legal norms to particular cases. The new biolegal instruments, by offering a number of general principles that have been accepted by the international community, provide courts with an invaluable tool in deciding cases which are presented to them. Principles would be particularly useful in the case when there is no national legislation on a particular bioethical issue, or when national laws are not sufficiently specific.

An important claim made in this book is that the emerging international biolaw is not a sort of strange, and indeed impossible, hybrid of ethics and law, but simply an *extension of international human rights law into the field of biomedicine*. It is not the scope of biolegal instruments to subsume bioethics because bioethics will continue to exist as a specific field of moral reflection and academic debate, even if a number of its principles have been recognized by and incorporated into legal frameworks. The scope of biolegal instruments is rather to reinforce the normative value of certain bioethical principles, whose importance for society is too great to be simply left to the conscience of individual researchers or to be merely enshrined in professional codes of ethics for healthcare providers.

In other words, human rights norms and biolegal principles are not two separate bodies of law, but are inextricably related to each other. Both are informed by the same logic; both aim to protect human beings from harm simply because they are humans, and regardless of nationality, ethnicity, sex, socio-economic status, religion, health condition, age, or any other particular feature. It is

---

(2)   M. KIRBY, "UNESCO and Universal Principles on Bioethics: What's next?", in UNESCO International Bioethics Committee, *Twelfth Session of the International Bioethics Committee (IBC). December 2005. Proceedings*, Paris, UNESCO, 2006, p. 135.

therefore natural that biolegal instruments have openly opted for a human rights approach to address biomedical issues.

Another recurrent idea in this volume is that the universality of human rights is an invaluable asset for dealing with bioethical dilemmas on a global level. Human rights standards assume that there are some moral truths that transcend boundaries between countries and cultures. This assumption is also valid for basic bioethical principles. Contrary to how it may seem, the fact that bioethical issues are closely linked to the deepest socio-cultural and religious values of every society is not an obstacle to the formulation of universal principles in this field. Quite the contrary. Precisely because bioethics is close to the most cherished aspirations of people, and since human needs are basically the same everywhere, it is not that difficult to identify some minimal standards with worldwide acceptance. Human rights and its foundational concept –human dignity– play a unifying role in this regard by reminding us that there are certain things that should not be done to anybody, anywhere (negative requirement) and that all human beings are entitled to some basic goods (positive requirement). [3]

On the other hand, it must be acknowledged that bioethical dilemmas are increasingly complex and ambivalent, and certain technologies tend to create totally new situations where it is not always easy to identify the basic goods that deserve to be protected. Examples of such issues, which will need to be tackled sooner or later by international law, include the use of various technologies for enhancement purposes, and neuroscientific developments.

Regarding the first challenge, a significant body of work in bioethics has developed in recent years in favor of enhancing the intellectual and physical abilities of human beings by using a combination of technologies such as genetic engineering, nanotechnologies, brain interventions, and psychopharmacology. [4] The prospect of moving towards the design of *posthuman* beings generates unprecedented ethical and legal dilemmas and obliges society to face fundamental questions that have been largely abandoned in modern philosophy

---

(3) R. ANDORNO, "International Policy and a Universal Conception of Human Dignity", in S. DILLEY and N. PALPANT (eds.), *Human Dignity in Bioethics. From Worldviews to the Public Square,* New York, Routledge, 2013, p. 141.

(4) See J. SAVULESCU and N. BOSTROM (eds.), *Human enhancement,* New York, Oxford University Press, 2011; J. HARRIS, *Enhancing Evolution. The Ethical Case for Making Better People,* Princeton N.J., Princeton University Press, 2010; J. GLOVER, *Choosing Children: Genes, Disability and Design,* New York, Oxford University Press, 2008.

and legal reflection, such as: What does it mean to be human? What is a meaningful life? What is good for a human society? It also raises totally new questions, such as the value that contingency (i.e. chance) may have in preserving future people's freedom, and the importance of preserving the identity of the human species.[5]

While such questions are never irrelevant, they have rarely been more important than they are now. The new biotechnologies are unique in that the object upon which they operate is not something external to us, but *ourselves*. In addition, the changes that some of them may introduce are *irreversible*, as they cannot be removed and could even be passed on to future generations. In this context, the main issue for many people is that, at a certain point, technological interventions on our bodies and minds could be counterproductive and degrade our sense of self, i.e. our status of *subjects* and not of mere *objects* designed by others. The assumption behind this concern is that our humanity is not something that we can shape into a design of our choice, but there are limits to the alteration of human capacities that need to be clearly identified by the international community. In this context, the central question is how to make biotechnological developments compatible with the preservation of our common humanity.

Another domain which is increasingly capturing the attention of legal scholars is neuroscience. Developments in this field are offering a better understanding of the brain processes that affect human behavior. As the law is concerned with regulating human behavior, it inevitably intersects with neuroscience on several respects. In this regard it has been said that both disciplines are "natural partners."[6] The crucial issue here is whether, or to what extent, neuroscience could, or should inform the law. Or to put it more bluntly, the question is whether brain research and its tendency towards a deterministic understanding of human behavior will lead the law to radically modify, or even abandon, its central concepts regarding responsibility and retribution, as some suggest.[7]

---

(5) See J. HABERMAS, *The Future of Human Nature,* Cambridge, Polity, 2003.

(6) O. GOODENOUGH and M. TUCKER, "Law and Cognitive Neuroscience", *Annual Review of Law and Social Science,* 2010, vol. 6, p. 62.

(7) J. GREENE and J. COHEN, "For the law, neuroscience changes nothing and everything", in J. ILLES and B. SAHAKIAN (eds.), *The Oxford Handbook of Neuroethics,* New York, Oxford University Press, 2011, pp. 655-674.

The most likely answer to this question is that new discoveries about the brain will not fundamentally alter the legal system. This is because the law does not make any assumption regarding how the brain works or how it influences human behavior. The important question for the law is whether people have a general capacity for rational behavior to make them responsible for their actions.[8] Unless evidence showing that an individual does not have such rational capacity, or has a diminished rationality (for instance, due to serious psychiatric problems), or that he or she did not enjoy freedom at the time of the action due to some external factors (for instance, coercion), there is a priori no reason for excluding his or her full legal responsibility.

What is clear is that neuroscientific developments have a potential for contributing to more fair and more evidence-based decisions in criminal procedures (e.g. by improving the assessment of the risk of recidivism of offenders); they can also play a valuable role in civil law procedures (e.g. to assess an individual's capacity to contract, or the severity of the plaintiff's pain in compensation claims). Neuroscience holds the promise of answering legal questions that have been difficult to resolve based on traditional models of academic psychology.

On the other hand, the risk of misuse of the new neuroscientific knowledge should not be ignored. Brain scans only provide probabilistic data, which cannot be used, for instance, to definitively predict the behavior of a particular person, or to determine with certitude whether an individual is telling the truth or lying. As this discipline is still developing and many of its potential applications in the legal area are not sufficiently reliable, it is important to proceed cautiously when introducing them as evidence in courts.[9] Probably some basic human rights principles relating to this matter will need to be incorporated into international instruments in the years to come.[10]

As noted in the introduction to this book, human rights law has as an extraordinary expanding force and tends to cover all new areas in which human dignity, rights and liberties are being

---

(8) S. MORSE, "Lost in translation? An essay on law and neuroscience", in M. FREEMAN (ed.), *Law and Neuroscience,* Oxford, Oxford University Press, 2011, pp. 529-562.

(9) O. GOODENOUGH and M. TUCKER, *op. cit.,* pp. 61–92.

(10) See T. SPRANGER (ed.), *International Neurolaw. A Comparative Analysis,* Heidelberg, Springer, 2012.

challenged. Biomedicine is undoubtedly one of these areas. Human rights offer at present the best available institutional and legal framework within which we can pursue answers to the question of what we owe to one another in the field of biomedicine. In this regard, it is crucial that the emerging international biolaw remains alert to identifying new situations which demand a global response in the protection of present and future generations.

TABLE OF CONTENTS

Chapter 3
The precautionary principle: a new legal standard
for the technological age

Section II
THE DEVELOPMENT OF PRINCIPLES
BY INTERNATIONAL ORGANIZATIONS

Chapter 4
The UNESCO declaration on the Human Genome and Human
Rights: an innovative instrument

Section III
THE APPLICATION OF THE COMMON PRINCIPLES
TO SPECIFIC ISSUES

str**a**da lex

L'accès le plus direct à toute l'information juridique
www.stradalex.com

Je ne suis pas encore abonné à Strada lex et je désire connaître
les conditions qui me permettront de consulter en ligne
les monographies Bruylant que j'aurai acquises

☐ Je demande à recevoir le passage d'un délégué de votre maison d'édition
de préférence à l'une des dates suivantes :
_____
_____

✓ Lors de son passage, le délégué me fera une démonstration des
fonctionnalités de Strada lex
✓ Lors de son passage, le délégué me communiquera le prix et les
conditions générales de l'abonnement à Strada lex

Je, soussigné(e),
Nom _____ Prénom _____
Société _____
N° TVA _____
Profession _____
Rue _____ N° _____
CP _____ Localité _____
Adresse e-mail _____

Signature   Date

INTBIO-74776–CDU34903

Nous vous remercions de compléter le formulaire ci-dessus et de nous le
retourner par courrier, fax ou courriel à l'adresse ou au numéro ci-dessous :

Groupe Larcier s.a.
rue des Minimes, 39 • 1000 Bruxelles
Tél. +32 (0)2 548 07 20 • Fax +32 (0)2 548 07 22
info@stradalex.com
www.stradalex.com • www.bruylant.be